THE LAND
AND
THE BOOK
An Introduction to the World of the Bible

THE LAND
AND
THE BOOK

*An Introduction to the World
of the Bible*

*Charles R. Page II
&
Carl A. Volz*

ABINGDON PRESS
Nashville

THE LAND AND THE BOOK:
AN INTRODUCTION TO THE WORLD OF THE BIBLE

Copyright © 1993 by Abingdon Press

This book is printed on recycled, acid-free paper.

Library of Congress Cataloging-in-Publication Data

Page, Charles R.
    The Land & the Book : an introduction to the world of the
Bible / Charles R. Page II & Carl A. Volz.
        p.   cm.
    Includes bibliographical references and index.
    ISBN 0-687-46289-4 (alk. paper)
    1. Bible—Geography.   2. Bible—History of Biblical events.
3. Palestine—Description and travel.   I. Volz, Carl A.   II.
Title.   III. Title: Land and the Book.
BS630.P24   1993
220.9'1—dc20   92-43245
                                                                      CIP

*Cover photo background used by permission
of the Biblical Archaeology Society 1993*

Scripture quotations are from the New Revised Standard Version
Bible, copyright © 1989, by the Division of Christian Education of
the National Council of the Churches of Christ in the United States
of America.

99 00 01 02—11 10 9

To our wives, Judy Halfacre Page and Lydia Anna Volz,

and to the many students through whose eyes we continue to see the Holy Land in a new and exciting way.

CONTENTS

LIST OF ILLUSTRATIONS

9

PREFACE

This book is the result of many years of teaching the Scriptures and history by its authors, both in Israel and in the United States. It is a readily apparent and unchallenged axiom that one's understanding of history or of the Bible requires some knowledge of geography (The Land), and no less so with the study of biblical history. This book was produced in the conviction that one cannot adequately understand or interpret the Hebrew Scriptures or the New Testament without some knowledge of the land in which the events recorded in the Scriptures took place.

Our purpose is straightforward—to introduce students of the Bible to the land of the Bible, on the assumption that such knowledge will enhance the understanding of the biblical accounts. The intended audience is twofold. It will serve as a guide for students of the Jerusalem Center for Biblical Studies and for any other visitors to the biblical lands of Israel, Jordan, and Egypt; and we hope that it may be useful as supplemental reading for students of the Scriptures and history, especially if they do not have the opportunity of visiting these sites in person. The generous inclusion of pictures and diagrams will assist these readers in visualizing the sites under discussion.

The authors have attempted to avoid controversial issues presented by contemporary historical-critical studies of the biblical texts—issues such as the nature of the Exodus, parallel but conflicting accounts of an event, or the chronology of Jesus' ministry. At times the narrative refers to such questions that still engage biblical scholars, but the primary purpose of this volume is to introduce the reader to the land where such events took place, or are said to have occurred. A second disclaimer is to acknowledge the fact that biblical lands include more than Israel, Jordan, and Egypt. To be accurate, such a definition must include Turkey (Asia Minor), Greece, and Italy. As already indicated, we hope that this volume will serve the purposes of those who are primarily interested in visiting or studying the lands of the Hebrew Scriptures and of the New Testament Gospels.

The authors utilize the disciplines of geography, history, geology, and anthropology, with considerable attention given to the most recent archaeological discoveries in the Holy Land. The book is arranged in three sections. Part I is a historical overview that offers a brief and at times uncritical acceptance of the biblical narrative, albeit recognizing challenges to the text and problems relating to it. The historical section is to set the context for the sites and events in The Land. Part II offers a description of the various sites, primarily in Israel, with some attention given to significant locations in Jordan and Egypt. Part III provides appendixes, chronologies, and suggestions for further reading.

We wish to acknowledge the assistance of those who have been helpful in the production of this book. Foremost among these is Dr. Rex D. Matthews, Senior Editor of Academic Books at Abingdon Press, who offered valuable criticism and advice. Members of the staff at the Laskey Library of the Scarritt-Bennett Center were most accommodating, especially Mary Lou Moore, Director of Library Services. Arthur David, acting president of Lane College, Jackson, Tennessee, as well as the students of Lane provided much encouragement. Special thanks are due to the students of Luther Northwestern Theological Seminary in Saint Paul, Minnesota, and to those of Calvin Seminary, Grand Rapids, Michigan, for field-testing an early version of the manuscript. Their comments were helpful and resulted in significant improvements in the text. Judy Page has read, questioned, corrected, and supported this work from the beginning. We also are appreciative of Thomas Piehl, for preparing the index. Finally, thanks are due to the faculty and staff of the Jerusalem Center for their advice, motivation, insights, and assistance: Kamel, Salim, Savana, Abe, Don, Jim, Chris, Jimmy, Tony, and all others who have made this book possible.

Charles R. Page II
Jerusalem, Israel

Carl A. Volz
Saint Paul, Minnesota

PART 1:
BACKGROUND

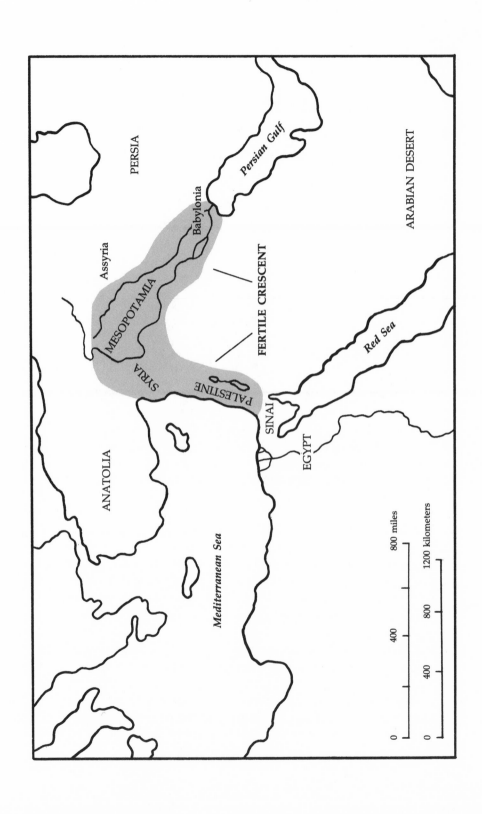

GEOGRAPHICAL OVERVIEW

Yohanan Aharoni begins his classic work *The Land of the Bible* with this statement:

> The history of any land and people is influenced to a considerable degree by their geographical environment. This includes not only the natural features such as climate, soil, topography, etc., but also the geopolitical relationships with neighboring areas. This is especially true for Palestine, a small and relatively poor country, which derives its main importance from its unique centralized location at a juncture of continents and a crossroads for the nations.[1]

The land of the Bible is unique not just because it is a crossroads for continents—Asia, Africa, and Europe—but also because it has so much diversity and variety. In Israel, and to a lesser extent Jordan, one finds an amazing variety of people, plants, animals, geology, and topography within a very small land area, measuring roughly 350 miles long (560 km) and 70 miles wide (112 km).[2]

Knowing something about the geography is very important for coming to understand the Bible more fully:

> Geography played a particularly important role in the biblical story. Both the location of Palestine and the physical features of the land itself were instrumental in shaping the history of the

people of Israel. Although a small country, Palestine was bordered for centuries by major players in the shaping of the modern world, while within its boundaries significant variations in climate and topography influenced the development of a surprisingly diverse culture.

These external and internal geographic influences produced two results: On the one hand, Palestine was a land bound by the common experience of people exposed to the same international influences and pressures; on the other, it was a land divided by localizing geographic features that often separated its inhabitants into highly individual cultural enclaves. The result of these diverse influences was a land more often divided than united, more often ruled by others than ruled by itself, and more often confessing its beliefs in diverse accents than with a unified voice.[3]

In this diverse land a few miles can make a great difference in the life-styles, commerce, and religious faith of those who dwell there. A good example of this diversity can be found by looking at two Judean cities: Jerusalem and Jericho. Jerusalem is located in the Judean hills, at an elevation of approximately 2,400 feet above sea level. Due to this height, there is usually a refreshing breeze in Jerusalem; even in the hottest part of summer, Jerusalem's average high temperature is in the upper 70s or 80s F. Jericho is located in the Jordan Rift Valley some 820 feet below sea level. Even though this is not the lowest point in the Jordan Valley, the temperatures in the summer can reach the 120s F. Jerusalem is located about 16 miles (25-26 km) west of Jericho. In this short distance there is a difference of some 3,000 feet and over 40 degrees F. This diversity in elevation and climate resulted in two very different life-styles in these cities and their surrounding areas.

The land of the Bible can be divided into four major geographic regions. Moving from west to east, these are (1) the Coastal Plain, (2) the Central Highlands, (3) the Rift Valley, and (4) the Highlands of Transjordan.

The first of these major geographic regions, the **Coastal Plain,** is a narrow strip of land adjoining the Mediterranean Sea on the west. The Coastal Plain extends some 70 miles (110 km) in length and 24 miles (40 km) in width at its widest point. This region is Israel's wettest, due to the abundance of high ground-level springs and the significant rain that falls here, and it contains Israel's most fertile farmland. Consequently it has always been the most populous throughout the land's history. The Coastal Plain comprises three sub-regions known as the Plain of Acco, the Plain of Sharon, and the Philistine Plain.

The *Plain of Acco* is found between Israel's northernmost border and the Carmel Range, near modern Haifa. This is the most narrow section of the Coastal Plain. On the extreme northeastern border of the Plain of Acco are steep cliffs overlooking the Mediterranean Sea. Farther south the Plain broadens into fertile farmland. This section of the Coastal Plain is named after the city of Acco, one of the more important ancient port cities during the biblical period. During the Old and New Testament periods Israel was never able to dominate this region, which was important for its maritime and agricultural activity. The Plain of Acco was, for the most part, controlled by the Phoenicians and their culture.

From Mount Carmel to ancient Joppa (Jaffa), at modern-day Tel Aviv, we find the *Plain of Sharon*. Sharon was the least fertile of the three plains along the coast due to the poor quality of its soil, which contains a high percentage of red sand, making it poor for farming but good for growing trees (Isaiah 35:2). Except for Joppa in the south and Dor in the north, there were no natural coves that could be used for harbors. Since this area had no ports and was not good for farming, few foreign powers had interest in the Plain of Sharon; consequently this is the only one of the three plains that was controlled by Israel for much of its ancient history. This was the land between the Philistines and the Phoenicians. Finally, during the reign of Herod the Great, a port city was built at Strato's Tower and the name was changed to Caesarea. This was to become one of the most important ports during the New Testament period.

Finally, in the south we find the *Philistine Plain*, so named for the people who dominated this region throughout most of the Old Testament period, beginning roughly in the thirteenth-

21

twelfth century BCE. The Philistines built five major cities here: Ashdod, Ashkelon, and Gaza on the coast; Ekron and Gath more inland but near the coast. Fertile farmland was also found here, making this valuable land for growing crops. The Philistines were commercially successful in both maritime trade and agriculture.

The *Via Maris* ("road along the sea") ran through the Coastal Plain. The Via Maris was the most influential and valuable trade route in this part of the ancient Fertile Crescent, the great arch of fertile lands extending from Egypt, north through Israel and Syria, east to the Tigris-Euphrates valley, and then south to the Persian Gulf. This trade route provided a vital commercial connection for the three continents of Europe, Asia, and Africa, which meet here. Foreign powers, therefore, struggled to control this ancient road; control of the Via Maris meant more wealth, which meant a stronger army, which meant more military and political power.

The second major geographic region, the **Central Highlands,** is actually a north-south mountain ridge running through the heart of Israel. The Jezreel Valley marks the only break in this mountain ridge. There are four principal subregions found in the Central Highlands: Galilee, Samaria, Judea, and the Negev.

Galilee can be divided into two sections: Upper and Lower Galilee. The mountains of Upper Galilee are the tallest in Israel; many of them exceed heights of 3,000 feet (900 meters). These mountains tended, in biblical times, to separate and to isolate the people who settled here, leading to the development among these peoples of a strong sense of independence. This is one reason why occupation under the Romans was so despised by the Galileans during the New Testament period. Lower Galilee is more hilly than mountainous. Trade routes and ancient highways through Lower Galilee allowed the people who lived here to be less isolated than their neighbors in Upper Galilee. The small villages known to Jesus were located in Lower Galilee.

South of the Jezreel Valley are the Mountains of *Samaria,* sometimes known as the Mountains of Ephraim. Like Lower Galilee, this area is more hilly than mountainous. During the

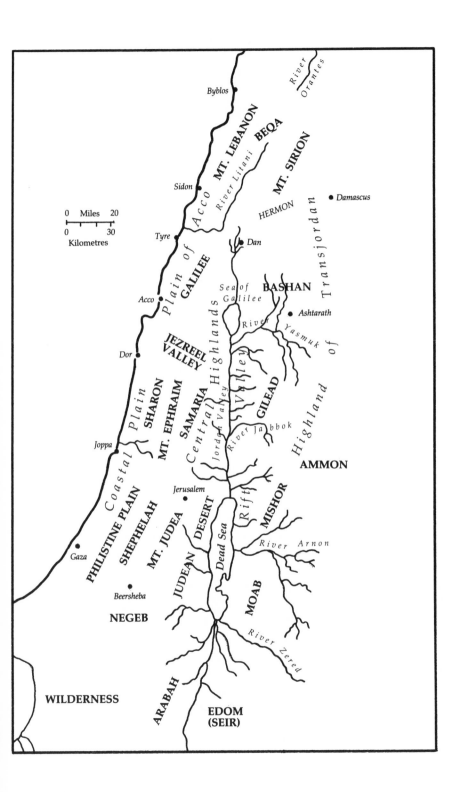

Byblos

River Orantes

MT. LEBANON

BEQA

MT. SIRION

Sidon

Acco

HERMON

● Damascus

River Litani

Tyre

Plain of GALILEE

● Dan

Sea of Galilee

BASHAN

Acco

River

● Ashtarath

River Yasmuk

JEZREEL VALLEY

Dor

SHARON

MT. EPHRAIM

SAMARIA

Central Highlands

Valley

GILEAD

Highland of Transjordan

Joppa

Coastal Plain

Jordan Valley

River Jabbok

AMMON

PHILISTINE PLAIN

SHEPHELAH

Jerusalem

MT. JUDEA

JUDEAN DESERT

Rift

MISHOR

Gaza

Dead Sea

River Arnon

Beersheba

NEGEB

MOAB

River Zered

WILDERNESS

ARABAH

EDOM (SEIR)

0 Miles 20

0   30

Kilometres

biblical periods this region was fertile for agriculture and was very populous.

Judea is located between Samaria and the Negev. Here one finds fertile hill country to the west and barren wilderness to the east. The area south of Jerusalem is generally more barren as well. The more fertile Judean Hill Country receives moderate annual rainfall. By contrast, the more barren Judean Wilderness receives minimal rainfall; the only fertile area found here is around the springs of En Gedi.

Finally, to the far south are the mountains of the *Negev,* Israel's barren desert. Beersheva, known as the "capital of the Negev," receives only 6-8 inches of rainfall annually (150-200 mm); the land to the south of Beersheva receives even less. Because of the lack of water, this has historically been the least populated area in Israel, usually inhabited by nomads.

Within the Central Highlands we also find the *Jezreel Valley,* a wide valley bisecting the regions of Galilee and Samaria. It is one of the most fertile growing areas in Israel because it receives abundant rainfall and because its alluvial soil is good for agriculture. The Jezreel Valley connects the Coastal Plain with the Central Highlands; through it ran an important ancient trade route that connected Megiddo with Beth Shean and other cities, such as Damascus, to the east and north. Many battles have been fought in the Jezreel Valley, dating at least to the time of the Canaanites. The author of the book of Revelation holds that the final battle between the forces of goodness and evil will be fought here near Har Megiddo ("Mountain" or "Hill of Megiddo," hence Armageddon). Some of the important biblical sites that surround the Jezreel Valley are Mount Carmel, Megiddo, Mount Gilboa, Mount Moreh, Mount Tabor, Nain, Shunem, and Nazareth.

The *Shephelah,* which means "lowlands," is a hilly subregion to the west southwest of Jerusalem, separating the Philistine Plain from the Judean Hills. In biblical times some of the villages of the Shephelah were famous as wine and olive oil centers. Israel/Judah also placed a series of fortified cities here to protect against a possible Philistine attack. One of the more famous areas in the Shephelah is the Valley of Elah (or Wadi Elah), the setting for David's victory over Goliath. Other well-known biblical towns and villages of the Shephelah are Gezer, Beth Shemesh, Lachish, and Azekah. The "Bell Caves" are also found in the Shephelah; these are actually mines dug in antiquity to obtain chalk, an important ingredient in the production of the plaster used to waterproof cisterns and water reservoirs.

The **Rift Valley** is the third of the major geographical regions of the Bible lands. The Rift Valley is the deepest depression or fault in the earth's surface. It extends from Syria in the north completely through the length of Israel/Jordan, under the Red Sea and into Africa. Like the other major geographical regions of the Holy Land, the Rift Valley can also be subdivided into four distinct subregions.

The *Huleh Valley* is the northernmost subregion of the Rift Valley. It is located between the Sea of Galilee and Israel's northern border. Until recently, much of this area was a swamp; there was also a small lake here, known as Lake Huleh. Through irrigation, this area has been transformed from swampland into productive agricultural land. Many new settlements have been established here as a result of Israel's population growth.

The *Jordan Valley* is located between the Sea of Galilee and the Dead Sea, covering a distance of approximately 70 miles (112 km). The Jordan River winds through this valley, and along its banks one finds some vegetation; away from the river one finds only barren wilderness. Jericho is located in the southern portion of the Jordan Valley. There is fertile farmland around Jericho due to the presence of the powerful Elisha Springs.

South of Jericho is the *Dead Sea*, the lowest point on earth, roughly 1,300 feet below sea level. Water from the Jordan River flows into the northern end of the Dead Sea, but there is no southern outlet to allow water to pass beyond this point.

South of the Dead Sea, the fourth subregion of the Rift Valley is the *Arabah*. The Arabah extends from the Dead Sea to the Red Sea at Eilat. The Arabah passes through the extreme southern portion of the Judean Wilderness and through the Negev Desert.

The **Highlands of Transjordan,** the fourth major geographical region, are located on the eastern side of the Jordan River in the present Hashemite Kingdom of Jordan. Four major rivers are found in this region: the Yarmuk and Jabbok Rivers, which flow into the Jordan River, and the Arnon and the Zered, which in biblical times flowed into the Dead Sea. Due to these many rivers and their tributary streams, this area has usually been more fertile than the land across the Jordan River in Israel. The biblical kingdoms and/or regions of Bashan, Gilead, Ammon, Moab, Edom, and Nabatea were all located here.

HISTORICAL OVERVIEW

The Patriarchs

Dating the Patriarchs is difficult, and there are several theories concerning their chronology. Some (for example, Leon Wood and Merrill F. Unger) relying on a strict interpretation of biblical chronology, which in turn assumes the historical accuracy and reliability of the biblical texts, date the Patriarchal period to the twenty-first century BCE.[1] Others (for example, James K. West) argue for the Middle Bronze (MB) II Period, roughly eighteenth/seventeenth century BCE.[2] Recently the work of Max Miller and John Hayes has illustrated the difficulty of dating the Patriarchal period with precision.[3] Still, as West suggests:

> Proponents of the MBII dating offered a large collection of cultural parallels to the patriarchal accounts drawn from contemporaneous extrabiblical texts. These parallels concern such matters as personal, ethnographic, and geographic names; socioeconomic patterns; and a broad array of customs, laws, and religious forms. Typically, these common elements have been used to support two claims: (1) that the patriarchal accounts are compatible with the culture of the MB age, but not with other periods, thus establishing the time of the patriarchs as the MB age; and (2) that such harmonization enhances the historical reliability of the patriarchal stories.[4]

According to the biblical account, upon which the following reconstruction of the patriarchal period is based, Abraham's father, Terah, along with Abraham, Lot, and their families, left Ur (an ancient and wealthy city on the Euphrates River in southern Mesopotamia[5]) to migrate to Canaan (Genesis 11:31ff.). When they reached Haran they stopped and settled there; only after Terah's death did Abraham move on to Canaan. While living there he fathered two sons, Ishmael and Isaac. Later Ishmael and his mother were sent away (Genesis 21:10-14), and Isaac became Abraham's sole heir.

Abraham arranged for Isaac to marry Rebekah, a woman from Haran (Genesis 24). After dwelling in several temporary campsites, Isaac and Rebekah settled in Beersheva (Genesis 26:23ff.); there they had two sons, Esau and Jacob. Jacob used trickery and deceit to gain his brother's birthright and inheritance, thus becoming the vehicle through which God would fulfill the promise made to Abraham to make of his family a great nation (Genesis 12:1-3; 17:4-8).

Jacob eventually fathered twelve sons whose descendants, according to biblical tradition, became the twelve tribes of Israel. One of these sons, Joseph, was sold into slavery by his older brothers. He was taken to Egypt, where after some initial difficulties, he rose to a position of power and prominence in the Egyptian government (Genesis 41).[6] After a famine created a severe food shortage in Canaan, Jacob sent his sons to Egypt to buy grain. This journey led to the reconciliation of Joseph and his brothers, after which Jacob moved with the rest of his family to Egypt. The Patriarchal stories end with the death of Joseph in Egypt.

The Hebrews in Egypt

The Hebrew[7] settlement in Egypt corresponds to the period of the Hyksos rule there (roughly 1720–1550 BCE). The Hyksos, like the Hebrews, were a mixed ethnic group. Some, perhaps many, were Semitic peoples. For this reason it seems plausible that they were, according to the biblical account, willing to offer a position of power to Joseph (also a Semite) and to give assistance to Joseph's family and other Semites who came to Egypt in search of food during periods of famine. This positive relationship with the Hyksos allowed the Hebrews to prosper in Egypt during this period.

Eventually the Hyksos domination in Egypt weakened, and they were driven from the land by Ahmose I in about 1552 BCE. Ahmose reestablished Egyptian domination, power, and culture. Following the expulsion of the Hyksos, according to the biblical account, "A new king arose over Egypt, who did not know Joseph. He said to his people, 'Look, the Israelite people are more numerous and more powerful than we. Come, let us deal shrewdly with them, or they will increase and, in the event of war, join our enemies and fight against us' " (Exodus 1:8-10). The Egyptians feared the return of the Hyksos and the Hebrews' support of and loyalty to them, and the Hebrews were enslaved and were forced to work in a massive new building program in Egypt. For the Hebrews this was a time of severe oppression. It is generally accepted that Seti I (1305–1290 BCE) was the "pharaoh of the oppression," and that the pharaoh of the exodus was Ramses II (1290–1224 BCE). Seti I initiated a major building program in the north, relocating the Egyptian capital from Thebes to Avaris and constructing the new cities of Pitham and Ramses (Exodus 1:11). An inexpensive labor force was necessary for such a massive building campaign, and Egyptian records report that the 'Apiru (among them the Hebrews) were used for this purpose. It seems likely that this is the time of the Hebrew enslavement recorded in the Bible.

The Exodus

According to the biblical record, the only source of information about him, Moses was born during this period of slavery and oppression. His parents were Hebrew slaves named Amram and Jochebed. Although there are no historical records from Egyptian sources to support the accusation, the Bible reports that the male children of the Hebrews were slaughtered by the order of the pharaoh (Exodus 1:22). Moses' parents were able to hide him, thus saving his life; he was discovered by the daughter of the Egyptian king (Exodus 2) and reared in the royal family. Later, he killed an Egyptian in anger for abusing a Hebrew slave, and in fear of punishment for his crime he fled to the Sinai Peninsula to seek refuge. There he met a Midianite priest, Jethro, and married his daughter Zipporah, settling into a new life as a shepherd.

According to the biblical story, it was while living as a shepherd with the Midianites that Moses encountered the voice of God (Yahweh) in a burning bush on Mount Sinai. Yahweh instructed Moses to return to Egypt and to lead the Hebrew slaves to freedom in the land promised to this people in Yahweh's covenant with Abraham (Exodus 3). Eventually the slaves were allowed to leave, and the exodus began.[8]

The Bible reports that the Hebrews were forced to wander in the Sinai Desert for forty years for failing to obey God and for not trusting in God's providence. It was during this period of wandering that the mixed people who came out of Egypt were able to form a national identity united by their commitment to Yahweh and the Mosaic Law (covenant). Moses remained the leader of this group until his death near the northern end of the Dead Sea. Upon his death, Joshua became the leader of the Hebrews and led them into the land of Canaan (Joshua 1:1ff.).[9]

The Conquest and Settlement

The biblical account provides two separate and distinct versions of the settlement of Canaan. The first version, found in the book of Joshua, reports that the Hebrews, under the leadership of Joshua, conquered the land through three separate military campaigns against the peoples and cities of Canaan. The second version, found in the book of Judges, suggests that the twelve tribes operated independently in the land without a unified army. Here there is no mention of a specific leader for the twelve tribes; God was the king for all the people, and from time to time raised up a judge to deliver the people from foreign powers who were oppressing a specific tribe.

Regardless of which version is of more value for historical reconstruction, the conquest and settlement of the "promised land" was most likely a lengthy process of assimilation rather than the immediate result of a unified military effort. The Bible reports that the Hebrews were not able to conquer all of the cities of Canaan; Jerusalem, for example, did not come under Israelite control until the time of David. Furthermore, the coastal regions later occupied by the Philistines and the Phoenicians were never conquered by the Israelites. In the end, the land was not fully conquered or controlled until the reign of David.

The Judges

The period of the judges was, in actuality, a continuation of the settlement of the land. Each of the twelve tribes tried to consolidate its power and assert control over the lands it had seized. During this period individual tribes were forced to defend their territory not only from outside invaders, such as the Midianites, Moabites, Ammonites, and Philistines, but also from the Canaanites who attacked them from within the territories they were trying to subdue.

The book of Judges tells the story of what later generations came to call Israel's "sin cycle." This cycle has four parts:

1. Israel (that is, one or more of the tribes) sins, or commits apostasy, against God.
2. God allows one of Israel's enemies to oppress the tribe or people.
3. The people repent and ask God for a deliverer or judge.
4. The people are redeemed or delivered, and then fall back into sin and apostasy to begin the cycle anew.

This cycle is found in several places in the book of Judges (e.g., Judges 3:7-31, 4:1ff.). The final result of this cycle was the yearning of the people for a king who could protect them from their enemies. God answered Israel by having the prophet Samuel anoint Saul as king.

Saul

The Bible presents two versions of Saul's ascent to the throne of Israel. The first, 1 Samuel 9:1–10:16, reports that while Saul was searching for his father's asses he met the prophet Samuel. On the day before this meeting, God had revealed to Samuel that he would meet Saul and that he was to anoint him as king, and this is what Samuel did. Here God is depicted as selecting Saul to be the king of Israel, and both God and Samuel seem to approve of Saul.

The second version of Saul's ascent is found in 1 Samuel 10:17-27. Here the Bible reports that Saul was selected as king by the casting of lots. Unlike the earlier version, Samuel seems to reject Israel's demand for a king, and he is portrayed as being angry about the situation:

> "Thus says the LORD, the God of Israel, 'I brought up Israel out of Egypt, and I rescued you from the hand of the Egyptians and from the hand of all the kingdoms that were oppressing you.' But today you have rejected your God, who saves you from all your calamities and your distresses; and you have said, 'No! but set a king over us.' Now therefore present yourselves before the LORD by your tribes and by your clans (1 Samuel 10:17*b*-19)."

Saul became king in approximately 1020 BCE and ruled for twenty years, until 1000 BCE. The biblical account does not present him as a regal or opulent monarch, as were David and Solomon. Instead, Saul is depicted more as a rustic warlord, somewhat barbaric and primitive. Even though he was called king, he did not function as did later kings; unlike David or Solomon, Saul had no standing army, he did not conduct foreign affairs, and he did not impose taxes on the people. He did lead Israel's army in a few battles or military campaigns, and he was, at times, a successful military leader (1 Samuel 15). When he was not functioning as the king or war leader, Saul is portrayed as a farmer (1 Samuel 11:5ff.).

How do we explain the apparent bias against Saul in the Old Testament? The consensus of modern scholarship is that David was glorified at the expense of Saul. As James K. West has put it:[10]

> Saul has probably not received his due in Israelite tradition as a result of the antimonarchical bias of some of his biographers, on the one hand, and the strong pro-David sentiment of others. So endeared to the later tradition was the figure of David, that it was inevitable that his strengths should be compared to Saul's weaknesses. One can hardly fail to note that once David appears in the accounts Saul's personality deterioration begins. (1 Samuel 16)[11]

In the end, Saul and three of his sons, including Jonathan, David's close friend, were killed in battle with the Philistines near Mount Gilboa (1 Samuel 31). Their bodies were taken to Beth Shean, where they were displayed on the city walls. The men of Jabesh-gilead came to Beth Shean, recovered the bodies of Saul and his sons, and took them back to Jabesh-gilead, where they were buried.

The United Monarchy

The ascension of David to the throne marked the beginning of Israel's "Golden Age," that period in Jewish history known as the United Monarchy.[12] The rules of David (c. 1000–961 BCE) and his son Solomon (961–922 BCE) have generally been regarded as Israel's most glorious historical era because it was a time of Israel's greatest accomplishments in religion, politics, and domestic and foreign affairs (both commercial and military).

David

There are at least two biblical accounts of David's rise to power. The first account (1 Samuel 16:1-13) reports that the prophet Samuel was directed to the home of Jesse, David's father, in Bethlehem. There Samuel was to anoint David as the king, or future king, of Israel. This followed God's rejection of Saul after his disobedience with respect to the Amalekites (1 Samuel 15:1-28). The second account (1 Samuel 16:14-23) reports that David was brought to Saul's court because David was a talented musician whose music might help to ease the king's troubled spirit. Saul was so pleased with David and his talent that he kept David in his service as the king's armor bearer.

There is a possible third account of David's rise to prominence in 1 Samuel 17, where David is depicted as becoming Israel's champion after he defeated the Philistine warrior, Goliath, in battle. This passage suggests that David and Saul had not known each other prior to this battle. However, it is possible that David's defeat of Goliath followed Samuel's anointing (1 Samuel 16:13). In the final analysis, we do not know which, if any, of these accounts is historically reliable.

The biblical account indicates that David served in Saul's court for a period of time. However, after God had rejected Saul (1 Samuel 15), his spirit became more troubled. As David became more and more popular with the people, Saul became more and more jealous and felt more threatened. The result of this jealousy was that David had to flee from Saul and live as a fugitive. While living as a fugitive, David was able to assemble a small guerilla army of some 400 soldiers, who took refuge in the Judean Wilderness. After Saul continued to try to capture him, David finally withdrew from the country, entering into a treaty with Achish, the Philistine king of Gath (1 Samuel 27:2ff.). David agreed to serve as a mercenary for Achish in return for the king's giving David and his army a place of refuge from Saul. Achish gave David and his followers the city of Ziklag (1 Samuel 27:6), which David used as a base from which he attacked the enemies of Israel; this made him even more popular with the people of Judah. Achish was led to believe that David was attacking and destroying the villages of Judah, when in fact David was defending these villages: "When David came to Ziklag, he sent part of the spoil to his friends, the elders of Judah, saying, 'Here is a present for you from the spoil of the enemies of the LORD' " (1 Samuel 30:26). This demonstrates David's political as well as his military genius.

Following the deaths of Saul and Jonathan, Ish-bosheth Saul's only surviving son,[13] became the king of the northern tribes. David became the king of Judah, establishing his headquarters in Hebron (2 Samuel 2:1-4). While David ruled in Hebron, there were sporadic minor hostilities between his army and that of Ish-bosheth. These encounters were usually won by David's army, gradually increasing his strength and reducing that of Ish-bosheth. "There was a long war between the house of Saul and the house of David; David grew stronger and stronger, while the house of Saul became weaker and weaker" (2 Samuel 3:1). Eventually, through secret negotiations between Joab and Abner, military leaders for both sides, and after the death of Ish-bosheth (2 Samuel 4:7-8), David was able to secure the support of the northern tribes and become the king of the United Monarchy.

To consolidate his support, David relocated the capital of the United Monarchy to Jerusalem, an independent city not located within the territorial boundaries of any of the tribes. This proved to be a strategic choice for the location of the capital because it was a neutral site—no tribe could bring the charge of favoritism. David also made Jerusalem the center of Israelite worship by bringing the Ark of the Covenant here (2 Samuel 6:16ff.) and by purchasing property upon which would be built the Temple of Yahweh (2 Samuel 24). This marks the beginning of Jerusalem's importance as a center of governmental and religious affairs.

During the reign of David, Israel became a prosperous and powerful nation. Under his leadership the Israelite army defeated Moab, Ammon, and Edom, all of which became vassal states paying tribute to David. He also made treaties with other nations, which further contributed to Israel's peace and prosperity. However, even though David was successful in foreign affairs, he proved to be a failure in handling domestic issues, especially within his own family. The two greatest crises of his reign, according to the biblical record, were both domestic problems: his affair with Bathsheba and the revolt of Absalom.

The report of David's affair with Bathsheba is found in 2 Samuel 11:2–12:24. One afternoon David was walking on the roof of his palace when he saw a beautiful woman bathing at a dwelling below the palace. David had her brought to the palace, where they committed adultery, and as a result Bathsheba became pregnant. Upon hearing the news of her pregnancy, David ordered that her husband, Uriah, be returned home so that he could sleep with his wife, and everyone would then think that the child was Uriah's. However, Uriah refused to sleep with his wife because he had been consecrated to the war against the Ammonites (2 Samuel 11:1), and sexual activity was prohibited during this war. David tried to use persuasion on Uriah, but to no avail. As a result of this failure, David ordered Uriah back into battle with the following instructions, " 'Set Uriah in the forefront of the hardest fighting, and then draw back from him, so that he may be struck down and die' " (2 Samuel 11:15). Uriah was killed in the battle, and Bathsheba became David's wife. This produced a moral crisis in the kingdom, according to the biblical account, and led to David's confrontation with the prophet Nathan, described in 2 Samuel 12.

The revolt of Absalom was related to the rape of his sister, Tamar, by their half-brother Amnon (2 Samuel 13:1ff.). To avenge this crime, Absalom had Amnon killed (2 Samuel 13:28-29). After Amnon's murder, Absalom went into hiding for a number of years. Then, capitalizing on growing discontent with David's rule (2 Samuel 15), he had himself proclaimed king in Hebron and launched a short-lived rebellion against his father. Although the rebellion was quickly defused by Absalom's death, it marked the first significant challenge to David's kingship.

Solomon

David made no provision for the succession to his throne. For this reason there was general confusion about which of his sons would follow him as king. Adonijah assumed the title (1 Kings 1:5) and was supported by some of his brothers and (more important) by Joab, who had served as David's military chief-of-staff. Adonijah brought his supporters to En-Rogel, a sacred site to the southeast of Jerusalem, to offer a sacrifice and to legitimize his claim to the throne.

The Bible reports that when Bathsheba heard of Adonijah's plan, she, along with the prophet Nathan, reminded David of an earlier promise that Solomon would follow David on the throne. After David had been informed of Adonijah's sacrifice at En-Rogel he called Bathsheba and said, "'As the LORD lives, who has saved my life from every adversity, as I swore to you by the LORD, the God of Israel, 'Your son Solomon shall succeed me as king, and he shall sit on my throne in my place,' so will I do this day" (1 Kings 1:29-30). David consequently ordered the prophet Nathan and the priest Zadok to anoint Solomon at the Gihon Springs.

So Solomon became the king of the United Monarchy in a controversial manner. After Adonijah and his followers had heard that Solomon had been anointed king, they fled from En-Rogel. Later, Adonijah and Joab were executed by the order of Solomon, who also executed others who were potential threats to his authority, thereby consolidating his power.

The Bible reports that Solomon's reign was characterized by both successes and failures. He carried out a monumental building program that required tremendous sums of money and a large labor force. Furthermore, even though his reign was generally a period of peace, Solomon maintained a large standing army. Taken together, these commitments placed a heavy strain on the national treasury. To ease the financial burden, Solomon initiated a system of taxation, which the people of his kingdom soon found to be oppressive.

To facilitate this taxation, Solomon created a new system of administrative districts (1 Kings 4:7ff.). These districts did not conform to the older tribal boundaries, and so created new internal tensions and divisions. Over each district Solomon appointed an administrator or governor who was responsible for keeping order and collecting taxes. He seems to have had two goals for this new system; first, he wanted to raise money to support both his building campaign and the army, and second, he hoped that the new districts would help to erase any tribal loyalties that might have remained. Instead the people became embittered because of the heavy taxation, and the new districts created a nostaglic sentiment for tribal identification.

To support his ambitious building program, Solomon initiated a system of forced labor; many citizens were required to give three months each year for this purpose (1 Kings 5:13-18; 9:15-23; 12:4). This added to the resentments already spawned by his new adminisrative districts and his policies of increased taxation, and it contributed to a growing dissatisfaction with his rule. This dissatisfaction was increased by Solomon's many political marriages, which led to the building of temples to pagan gods.

The long-term effect of these problems was that the United Monarchy fell into disarray following the death of Solomon (922 BCE), resulting in the creation of two separate states: Israel, in the north, and Judah, in the south. Under David and Solomon the United Monarchy had been relatively strong and independent (due at least in part to the preoccupations of the regional superpowers—Egypt, Assyria, and Babylon—with other matters). By contrast, the two new kingdoms were smaller and weaker, and were usually dominated by the regional superpower of the time, though Israel (the Northern Kingdom) was clearly the stronger of the two in both military and economic terms. This situation remained unchanged from the time of Solomon's death to the fall of the Northern Kingdom (Israel) in 722/721 BCE.

The Divided Kingdom

The period of the Divided Kingdom began when Solomon's son Rehoboam became the king after Solomon's death in 922 BCE (1 Kings 12:1ff.). According to the biblical account,

Rehoboam gathered the people of the kingdom at Shechem. Jeroboam, who had opposed some of Solomon's more oppressive policies,[14] returned from his exile in Egypt to challenge Rehoboam. On behalf of the ten northern tribes, Jeroboam asked Rehoboam to lighten the heavy taxation and forced labor practices initiated by his father. Rehoboam asked the people for three days in which to consult his advisors and to formulate an answer. After consulting with older advisors of his father and his own younger advisors, Rehoboam informed the people that he would be even harsher than Solomon: "My father made your yoke heavy, but I will add to your yoke; my father disciplined you with whips, but I will discipline you with scorpions" (1 Kings 12:14). Following Rehoboam's statement, Jeroboam led the ten northern tribes out of the union, establishing his rule over the Northern Kingdom of Israel. He formed a new government and created a new religious system. Rehoboam remained the king of the Southern Kingdom of Judah.

Israel (The Northern Kingdom)

Within the Northern Kingdom, Jeroboam I (922–901 BCE) built new worship centers at Dan and Beth-el, and he created a new priestly order and a new sacrificial system. Jeroboam seems to have discouraged his subjects from returning to Jerusalem because he did not want them to yearn for a return to the glorious days of the United Monarchy nor to develop any loyalty to the Southern Kingdom, which they might do if they went to the Temple in Jerusalem.

The biblical accounts indicate that following the death of Jeroboam I (901 BCE), Israel went through a period when the reigns of her kings were characterized by instability and assassination. Eventually Omri, a former military general, assumed the throne and brought much needed stability to Israel. His reign was short (876–869 BCE), but he established a dynasty that provided the kingdom with considerable peace and prosperity. Omri's skill in foreign affairs resulted in peace with his neighbors; as is evident in the political marriage he arranged for his son Ahab to Jezebel, the daughter of the Sidonian king Ethbaal (1 Kings 16:31).

Ahab (869–850 BCE) continued the policies of his father. He also proved to be shrewd in foreign affairs, as he formed a coalition with the kings of Damascus and Hamath to repel the attempted invasion of Shalmaneser II, the king of Assyria (859–825 BCE). Ahab also completed the construction of a new capital city, Samaria, which had been begun by Omri.

The Bible sets the ministry of the prophet Elijah during the reign of Ahab. Jezebel had brought with her to Israel the worship of her national god, Baal.[15] She had a temple for Baal built in Samaria, and it is quite possible that she planned to make Baal the national god of Israel; in fact, the Bible suggests that Jezebel initiated a systematic campaign against the prophets of Yahweh (1 Kings 18:4). Against this background, according to the biblical account, Elijah appeared on the scene to expose Baal as a false god and his prophets as false prophets. After Elijah defeated and killed the prophets of Baal in a contest on Mount Carmel, he fled to Sinai believing he alone was faithful to Yahweh. The Baal cult remained formidable (1 Kings 18:20ff.).

Two primary factors led to the destruction of the Northern Kingdom: the rise of the Assyrian king Tiglath-pileser III (745–727 BCE), and the chaos and political turmoil in Israel during the nation's final years.

Tiglath-pileser III came to power in 745 BCE, bringing about a revival of Assyrian power and prominence. As part of his expansionist policy, he began military campaigns against Syria and other nations to the west in about 743 BCE. His goal was not only to receive payment of tribute from other nations, but to conquer new territory and incorporate it into the Assyrian Empire. To this end, he initiated a new program of deportation and immigration; when he conquered a country, he would deport the most prominent citizens of that country to another conquered nation and replace them with deportees from other lands. This happened in Israel after it was conquered in 722/21 BCE.

During the period leading up to the Assyrian invasion of the Northern Kingdom, Israel found itself in political chaos. There was no strong or charismatic leader who could gain the confidence of the people sufficiently to provide for the nation's defense. However, even a strong king would not have been able to withstand the power and might of Assyria. Between 745–722/21 BCE there were six kings in Israel, most of them dying violent deaths. In desperation, the last king of Israel, Hoshea, made a treaty with Egypt and withheld Israel's payment of tribute to Shalmaneser V, who had succeeded his father as king of Assyria in 727 BCE. This led to the total occupation of Israel and the destruction of Samaria in 722/21 BCE. Many of the people of Israel were deported and new people were brought in, creating a new ethnic make-up in the population of the nation.

Judah (The Southern Kingdom)

Judah, the southern kingdom of the former United Monarchy, was the weaker of the two new states. With the one exception of Athaliah (the daughter of Ahab and Jezebel and Judah's only reigning queen, who ruled for about seven years) there was no disruption of the Davidic dynasty in Judah. Under Rehoboam and Abijah (915–913), Judah continued to experience some of the oppressive policies that had flourished during the time of Solomon, and periodically non-Yahwistic cults became strong. However, when Asa (913–873 BCE) became king, he began a system of reforms that brought internal peace and stability to Judah. Asa's policies were continued by his son Jehoshaphat (873–849 BCE).

Following the reign of Jehoshaphat, Judah experienced a period of general weakness, which lasted until the reign of Hezekiah (715–687 BCE). Hezekiah's father, Ahaz (735–715 BCE), had chosen to be a vassal of Assyria in order to secure Assyrian help against Syria. This policy had been rejected by the prophet Isaiah. After the death of Ahaz, Hezekiah initiated reforms that, according to the biblical account, were welcomed by his people:

He removed the high places, broke down the pillars, and cut down the sacred pole. . . . He trusted in the LORD the God of Israel; so that there was no one like him among all the kings of Judah after him, or among those who were before him. For he held fast to the LORD; he did not depart from following him but kept the commandments that the LORD commanded Moses. The LORD was with him; wherever he went, he prospered. He rebelled against the king of Assyria and would not serve him. (2 Kings 18:4-7)

The result of Hezekiah's rebellion against Assyria was an Assyrian attack on Judah. Jerusalem was besieged, but never fell. Sennacherib (704–681 BCE), who had followed his father, Sargon, as the Assyrian king, destroyed most of the other cities of Judah, including Lachish, but did not conquer Jersusalem (possibly because in the end Hezekiah did pay tribute, as reported in 2 Kings 18:13ff.). Hezekiah died one year after the siege of Sennacherib in 687 BCE. Manasseh, Hezekiah's son, returned to the practice of paying tribute to Assyria, thus ending the period of rebellion and reform.

The reign of Josiah (640–609 BCE) coincided with a period of Assyrian weakness, during which Judah realized some independence. It was during this period that Josiah launched the most dramatic reform in the country's history. Parallel accounts of this reform are found in 2 Kings 22:3–23:25 and 2 Chronicles 34:1–35:19. According to the account in 2 Kings, it began while the Temple was being repaired; by accident the book of the Law was discovered and read, and upon hearing the Law, Josiah immediately began his reform in 622/21 BCE. The account in 2 Chronicles has Josiah beginning his reform about six years before the rediscovery of the Law. In either case, a key element of the reform was the removal of pagan temples and high places and of all Israelite worship centers that did not conform to the Law.

The biblical account records almost nothing else of Josiah's reign, other than that he was killed in a disastrous battle with Pharaoh Neco of Egypt at Megiddo in 609 BCE. With his death began the slow disintegration of Judah. Egypt gained military control of much of the kingdom after Josiah's death, and maintained that control until approximately 605 BCE, when Judah was conquered by the Babylonians. Judah's last two kings, Jehoiachin (who ruled for three months in 598 BCE) and Zedekiah (597–587/86 BCE), refused to pay tribute to the Babylonians. Zedekiah joined with Egypt in a revolt against Babylon, provoking the military campaign of Nebuchadnezzer in which Jerusalem was destroyed and many of the people of Judah were taken into exile in Babylon.

The Babylonian Exile and Return

In antiquity, the rationale behind the deportation of conquered people was to separate the religious and political leaders from the rest of the people. By taking the citizens with higher education and greater promise to the land of the conquerors, the remaining population was left without competent leadership and was thus no longer a threat. The exiles were not treated as slaves in Babylon, but lived in their own territory and enjoyed a measure of self-rule according to their tribes. Not only were the Judean nobility transported to Babylon, but it appears that there were tradesmen (carpenters, locksmiths) and farmers as well (2 Kings 24:14). Ezekiel writes they were "placed in fertile soil" and planted "by abundant waters" and "set . . . like a willow twig" (17:5).

The Jews in Babylon enjoyed virtual religious freedom, with the possible exception of the reigns of Nebuchadnezzar and Belshazzar. They continued to observe the Sabbath under the leadership of the priests and Levites, but at first they had no place to worship. Psalm 137 reflects such earlier times:

> By the rivers of Babylon—
> there we sat down and there we wept
> when we remembered Zion.

Out of this need for communal worship developed the synagogue (the term means literally "coming together"), which was a house of prayer, a place for studying the Scriptures, and a school for the young. Unlike the customs of worship in the Jerusalem Temple, there were no sacrifices. It was during this period that the focus of activity was placed on the study of the Torah, and as a result the office of the scribe increased in dignity.

Babylon itself was one of the most splendid of ancient cities; it covered an area of 260 square miles with a circumference of 40 miles. Within its walls were beautiful fountains, marbled porticoes, parks with zoos, and paved streets, and as the magnificent centerpiece, Nebuchadnezzar had constructed the fabled hanging gardens. The culture was equal to the material splendor, as Babylon was noted for its literary productions in law, medicine, grammar, and natural history. But above all else, it was famous for astronomy and mathematics. The attractions of living in Babylon may account for the fact that large numbers of Jewish exiles chose not to return to Judah when that became possible.

Of enduring interest both to historians and to theologians are the prophetic writings that come from the time of the exile. The prophet Jeremiah was active in Judah at the time of the conquest by Nebuchadnezzar, but he did not go into exile. He remained in Jerusalem for a number of years where he incurred the enmity of those who remained in political power, and according to tradition he finally was killed in Egypt. The prophet Ezekiel was taken to exile and was the first to receive his prophetic call outside of Israel. The occasion for his prophesying was the fact that "having received generous treatment from their Chaldean conquerors, the displaced Judahites soon became Babylonians as enthusiastically as once they had been Canaanites, thus confronting themselves with new dangers to their faith while preserving in fact for the most part the vices they had brought with them from their homeland."[16] Ezekiel laid the foundations for the reverence for the Law, which characterized post-exilic Judaism. He opposed the acculturation of the Jews in exile to the ways of Babylon, speaking of them as those who have eyes but are blind, who have ears but are deaf, and who have hearts of stone (Ezekiel 2:26).

The author of Second Isaiah (Isaiah 40–55) was also active

during the exile, preaching that deliverance from bondage was imminent. He predicted that Cyrus, the king of Persia, whom he called the Messiah ("anointed one") of the Lord, would bring release to Israel (Isaiah 45:1). The book breathes the spirit of Israel's new vocation as a light to the nations and reveals Yahweh as a God of all the peoples. The work also contains canticles of the Servant of the Lord (Isaiah 42:1-4; 49:1-6; 50:4-9). In all probability Psalms 79 and 137 were also written during the exile. Psalm 79 is a penitential prayer, asking God to be mindful of the suffering of God's people, and Psalm 137 begins with the lament, "By the rivers of Babylon—there we sat down and there we wept."

The Babylonian exile had a significant influence on shaping Israel's identity and religious tradition. It may be due to the association with a great world empire that Second Isaiah and his contemporaries began to see Yahweh as a universal god and not just Israel's national or tribal deity. Before the captivity, Israel was primarily concerned with agriculture, and it appears likely that this interest shifted to commerce as a result of being "set in a city of merchants" and into "a land of trade" (Ezekiel 17:4). Before the captivity the people had been called Hebrews or Israelites; after the exile they were called Jews because of Judah, their homeland.[17] It was also in Babylon that the Israelites learned Aramaic, which became their common language after the exile and was the language of Jesus and his disciples. The destruction of Solomon's Temple in 586 BCE and the ensuing exile was the occasion for the creation of a new focus in worship: the preaching of the Law in the synagogue. Most scholars agree that the synagogue began in Babylon, accompanied by the increasing prominence of the scribes as exponents of the Law.

The Babylonian Empire rose meteorlike with the conquest of Nebuchadnezzar, but within seventy years of its ascension it fell just as quickly. The successors of Nebuchadnezzar were unable to preserve or extend what he had built, and they fell into political and religious strife. Meanwhile a young nation was growing to maturity east of the Zagros Mountains, where Cyrus the

Great had united the Medes and the Persians into one kingdom. In October 539 BCE, the Persians captured the city of Babylon, and with its fall they assumed control of a vast empire, stretching from the Dardenelles to the Persian Gulf, from the Hindu Kush to Egypt.

Soon after taking Babylon, Cyrus permitted the exiles from Jerusalem and Judah to return to their homeland. His decree is given twice in the Bible:

> "Thus says Cyrus, King of Persia: The LORD, the God of heaven, has given me all the kingdoms of the earth, and he has charged me to build him a house at Jerusalem in Judah. Any of those among you who are of his people—may their God be with them!—are now permitted to go up to Jerusalem in Judah, and rebuild the house of the LORD." (Ezra 1:2-4; cf. 2 Chronicles 36:22)

This decree was in keeping with similar decrees by Cyrus that offered repatriation to other nationalities that had been deported by the Babylonians.

Josephus (*Antiquities* 11:8) writes that "when Cyrus had said this to the Israelites, the rulers of the two tribes of Judah and Benjamin, with the Levites and the priests, went in haste to Jerusalem. Yet did many of them stay in Babylon, not willing to leave their possessions." Those who returned were given vessels of silver and gold as well as animals, and the vessels from the Temple, which had been confiscated by Nebuchadnezzar seventy years earlier, were returned to the Israelites (Ezra 1:6-8).

The return from Babylon was made in three expeditions. The first was under the leadership of Zerubbabel in 536 BCE, as recorded in Ezra 2, which indicates that about 50,000 made the trip. With the conquest of Babylon, Judah had also come under the jurisdiction of Cyrus, which naturally facilitated the resettling of the returning exiles. They did not receive all of their former homeland; the territory over which Zerubbabel was governor amounted to an area of about 20 square miles in and around the city of Jerusalem. Their first task was to build homes and find a livelihood, but they also built a new altar at the same place where the Solomonic altar had stood; also they resumed the morning and evening sacrifices, which had been neglected for two generations. They also reintroduced the observance of national festivals and religious traditions, which had been neglected. The Samaritans, who lived north of Judah, offered to help in the project of rebuilding the Temple, but Zerubbabel and Joshua, the high priest, refused the offer (Ezra 4:2-4). The Samaritans were angered by this rebuff, and they succeeded in delaying the building program for sixteen years, in part by calling into question the loyalty of the Jews to the Babylonian Empire by sending letters to the successors of Cyrus (Ezra 4:21). It was only with the accession of Darius to the throne of Babylon (ruled 522–485 BCE) that work could be resumed.

The Jews in Judah had lost interest in the Temple building program, but a Persian governor sent by Darius to Judah verified the fact that Cyrus had decreed that the Temple should be rebuilt, and Darius ordered that work should be resumed. It was at this time that the prophets Haggai and Zechariah appeared to encourage the work of rebuilding. "And the LORD stirred up the spirit of Zerubbabel . . . and the spirit of all the remnant of the people; and they came and worked on the house of the LORD" (Haggai 1:14-15). Finally the Temple was completed in 516 BCE, exactly seventy years after its destruction. A great dedication service was held (Haggai 6:16), and the observance of Passover was restored. Although the new Temple was somewhat larger than that of Solomon, and a court of the Gentiles was added, it lacked the Ark of the Covenant, which had been lost.

Meanwhile, Darius attempted to extend his empire over the Greeks in Europe. When some Greek cities in Asia Minor arose in revolt against the Persians, Athens came to their aid. Using this as a pretext, Darius resolved to invade Greece and punish the Athenians. After an abortive start in which a storm almost demolished their navy, the Persian forces invaded Macedon and northern Greece. They were met by the Athenian army under the leadership of Miltiades on the plains of Marathon. Though greatly outnumbered, the Greeks inflicted a crushing defeat on the invading enemy in 490 BCE.

Darius was succeeded by his son Xerxes, who is generally associated with the biblical Ahasuerus (485–464 BCE). Some scholars associate the king with Queen Esther, but others place her much later, between 150 and 100 BCE. Xerxes continued his father's attempts to conquer the Greeks. He was stopped at the celebrated battle of Thermopylae (480 BCE), was defeated at the naval battle at Salamis which followed, and was nearly annihilated at Plataea. Little is heard of the Jews either in Persia or Judah during the reign of Xerxes.

Xerxes was succeeded by his son Artaxerxes, who was favorably disposed toward the Jews. He believed that Egypt had designs on Palestine; and to strengthen his forces to resist Egypt and at the same time populate Palestine with those loyal to him, he issued a decree similar to that of Cyrus eighty years before. In this edict he encouraged Jews living in Persia to resettle in Judah. Artaxerxes even made contributions of silver and gold for the Temple at Jerusalem. The story is told in Ezra 7:11-26. This occurred in 458 BCE, and it was the second large migration of returning exiles, the first being under Zerubbabel in 536 BCE.[18] The leader of this contingent was Ezra, who was commissioned for this task by Artaxerxes and enjoyed his support. Indeed, Artaxerxes gave Ezra a long letter outlining his duties and program of reform in Judah, which is found in Ezra 7:11-26.

Ezra's object in going to Jerusalem was to instruct the people in the Law of Moses and to bring about some necessary reforms in their social and religious life. He was discouraged at what he found. The Israelites had grown indifferent to their religious traditions, intermarried with the people around them, and neglected the Temple sacrifices; and the walls of Jerusalem had not yet been rebuilt. Ezra began his reform program by leading the people in a general confession of sin and by reading to them from the Law of Moses (Ezra 9). The people responded by acknowledging their sin and by promising to reform.

Ezra installed judges, as he was ordered to do by Artaxerxes: "Appoint magistrates and judges who may judge all the people in the province Beyond the River [Judah] who know the laws of your God; and you shall teach those who do not know them. All who will not obey the law of your God and the law of the king, let judgment be strictly executed on them" (Ezra 7:25-26). Of great significance for the history of Judaism is that it was Ezra, the first great scribe, who made the principle of following the Torah a sign of difference between Jews and non-Jews. "In his time Judaism became a book religion. . . . In the end it was the strict adherence to the Torah that guaranteed the continued life of Judaism."[19] This is to say that, from the time of Ezra, Jewishness was not defined only by one's nation, language, or ethnic group; fidelity to the Law came to play an increasingly significant role in Jewish self-understanding.

Nehemiah was a younger contemporary of Ezra. During the reign of Artaxerxes, Nehemiah rose to the position of cupbearer of the king (his story is told in Nehemiah 7 and parts of 11, 12, and 13). The high position he attained indicates that he had considerable gifts. He received word from his brother that the walls of Jerusalem were still broken down, and this news caused him distress. The king noticed his sorrow, and after learning the cause he commissioned Nehemiah to direct the rebuilding of the walls (Nehemiah 2:1). He was given letters of commendation to the governors of Palestine, who were under the control of Persia. So Nehemiah was given leave to return to Jerusalem and supervise the rebuilding of the walls, for which he was given a leave of twelve years.

He set out with a bodyguard in 444 BCE, and this constituted the third wave of returning exiles, though the number with Nehemiah was much smaller than those under Zerubbabel in 536 and Ezra in 458. After his assessment of what had to be done, Nehemiah gathered the people to explain his program. Their response was, " 'Let us start building!' So they committed themselves to the common good" (Nehemiah 2:18). The entire project was divided into forty-four separate units, each of which was assigned to certain groups or families. But the Samaritans, led by Sanballat, the governor, and Tobiah, opposed the project and tried by various stratagems to frustrate the work. The builders were required to wear their swords while they worked on the walls (Nehemiah 4:18). The biblical account (Nehemiah 6:15) says that in spite of this opposition, the walls were rebuilt in fifty-two days, although Josephus (*Antiquities* 11:104ff.) reports that the construction took seven years to complete. Of this monumental undertaking, Josephus (*Antiquities* 11:183) wrote over four centuries later: "When Nehemiah had done many other excellent things, and things worthy of commendation, in a glorious manner, he came to a great age, and then he died. He was a man of a good and righteous disposition, and very ambitious to make his own nation happy; and he hath left the walls of Jerusalem as an eternal monument for himself."

Other problems presented themselves once the walls had been rebuilt. One was a serious exploitation of the poor by the rich. In order to meet the levy required for the walls, some people had been forced into debt and even to the bondage of their children. Nehemiah angrily confronted those who were guilty of such exploitation, and they promised to make restitution (Nehemiah 5). Another problem was the depopulation of Jerusalem. Only a few more than 3,000 adult citizens resided in the city, far too few to offer a credible defense. Lots were cast among the Israelites, and every tenth man was required to take up residence in the city. At the end of twelve years, Nehemiah returned to Persia.

But now, according to the biblical account, a third problem revealed itself in the low spiritual level of the people, and Nehemiah found it necessary to return to Jerusalem to attend to it. It seems that during Nehemiah's early years in Judah, Ezra had returned to Persia, but now he returned to Jerusalem to assist Nehemiah in the work of spiritual reform. The study of the Law had been neglected, part of the Temple precinct was being used for unscrupulous purposes, and intermarriage had again become common. Ezra called for a great assembly of the people, where he expounded the Law for seven consecutive days, and the Temple was cleansed of its abuses. Nehemiah was also engaged in this reform by using physical force: "I contended with them and cursed them and beat some of them and pulled out their hair. . . . Thus I cleansed them from everything foreign, and I established the duties of the priests and Levites, each in his work" (Nehemiah 13:25, 30).

Ezra and Nehemiah were contemporaries, and they worked together on the reforms necessary among the returning exiles and the rebuilding of Jerusalem. "The achievements of the two men complement each other and the work of both was necessary if Judaism, at its center, was to preserve its identity. . . . Both were men of deep faith, without which their reforms would have been emptied of any lasting significance."[20] Politically Judah remained a Persian province, and resettlement proceeded slowly. It was not until the third century that the country had a population comparable to what it had supported before the exile.

Alexander the Great and Hellenization[21]

Palestine remained subject to Persia for almost a century after the death of Artaxerxes (423 BCE), the king at the time of Nehemiah. Since the time of Cyrus the Great (539 BCE) both Egypt and Palestine had been governed by rulers sent by the king in Susa and were directly responsible to him. The land was divided into territorial units called satrapies, with Palestine coming under the jurisdiction of the satrap of Damascus. At the turn of the fourth century, the zenith of Persian power had passed, as rival claimants for the throne fought and intrigued against each other. In one of these civil wars more than ten thousand Greek mercenaries sided with Cyrus the Younger, and after his defeat and death (401 BCE) the Greeks had to struggle to return to their homeland. This is the famous story told by Xenophon in the *Anabasis*.

Meanwhile a new star was rising toward the northwest. In the year 336 BCE Alexander the Great became king of Macedonia at the age of twenty-one. A war against Persia had been planned by his father, Philip, who died before he could realize his goal. The ostensible reason for the war was to free the

Greeks who lived in Asia Minor from Persian domination, but given the political weakness of Persia the prospect of expanding the goal was tempting. Alexander crossed the Dardanelles with an army of 40,000 men, and after two decisive battles the Persian forces were routed at Issus in 333 BCE. The next objective was to secure naval bases along the Mediterranean. Tyre refused to surrender, and after a seven-month siege the city was destroyed. Messengers were sent by Alexander to order Jerusalem to surrender, but the High Priest, Jeddua, who held both civil and religious authority, refused. Alexander proceeded down the coast and destroyed Gaza before he turned his attention back to Jerusalem.

Josephus (*Antiquities* 11:329ff.) informs us that upon Alexander's arrival, the High Priest went out to meet him with a large procession of dignitaries and offered his submission, together with a petition that the city be spared. Not only was the request granted, but Alexander also permitted the Jews to follow their traditional religious practices, both in Palestine and in Persia. Josephus also indicates that Alexander was shown prophecies that were interpreted to refer to his conquest, which caused him to show favor to the Jews. From Jerusalem, Alexander marched south to Egypt, where he was welcomed as a liberator from Persian oppression. He also established the foundations of a new city at the Nile Delta and called it Alexandria, which became one of the great commercial and cultural centers of the Hellenistic world as well as a significant center of Jewish and (later) Christian thought.

Alexander and his army next marched north and east to encounter the remnant of the Persian forces at Arbela, near Nineveh, where they crushed the remaining Persian resistance. There followed his famous march over the Kyber Pass and beyond the Indus River, where his generals refused to go further. He sent a garrison to Egypt while he led the army back to Babylon, which he made his capital. His empire was now the largest the world had ever known, stretching from the Nile to the Indus, from the Black Sea to the Adriatic Ocean. In order to bring about a closer union between East and West, Alexander married the daughter of the last Persian king and obliged 10,000 of his troops to marry Persian women. But in Babylon, Alexander succumbed to malaria and died in 323 BCE, at the age of thirty-two.

At his death the empire fell into the hands of a group known to history as the Diadochi, or Successors. The primary divisions of land were:

1. Egypt, under the Ptolomies
2. Syria and the East, under the Seleucids
3. Macedonia, under Antigonus and Cassander
4. Phrygia and Thrace, under Lysimachus.

Of these, the two kingdoms most directly related to the lands of the Bible are those of Egypt and Syria. Palestine came under the jurisdiction of the Ptolomies in Egypt from 320–198 BCE. Predictably, there were numerous wars between Egypt and Syria, with Palestine serving as the unhappy battleground between these forces.

Ptolomy I Soter, the first of the Ptolomies, was especially interested in extending Greek culture in Egypt. He made Alexandria his capital and spent lavishly on its beautification. He built the famous museum dedicated to the cultivation of fine arts, which also housed the library of Alexandria. The foundation was laid for the university, which produced such scholars as Euclid, the mathematician; Ptolomy, the astronomer; and Eratosthenes, the geographer. He also had the famous Lighthouse of Pharos constructed. In addition to the attention Ptolomy I gave to Egypt, he Hellenized several cities in Palestine: Rabbah became Philadelphia, Geraza became Pella, Beth Shean became Scythopolis, and many more were either changed into Hellenistic cities or new Greek cities were founded.

During this period many Jews migrated to Egypt, settling primarily in Alexandria. They lived in their own communities, having a high degree of autonomy and freedom of worship. In later years fully 20 percent of this city's population would be Jewish, producing some of the most important Jewish thinkers and literature, including a translation of the Hebrew Scriptures into Greek (the Septuagint). This was the Bible used by the early Christian church. The new translation was needed because Greek had become the common language of the Jews in the Hellenistic diaspora, as well as of the supporters of Hellenism inside Israel. Other Jews settled at Heliopolis, where they built a temple to rival that in Jerusalem.

In 198 BCE, Palestine came under the rule of the Selucids of Syria, whose ruler, Antiochus III, the Great, decisively defeated the Ptolomies in a battle near Banyas, or Caesarea Philippi. Egypt was never to regain control of Palestine. Antiochus occupied Jerusalem and befriended its inhabitants by paying for the Temple sacrifices, keeping the Temple in repair, giving the residents a three-year rebate of taxes and the right to the free exercise of religion. However, this goodwill was short-lived. In 190 BCE Antiochus was defeated by a Roman army at Magnesia, and he was forced to make exorbitant payments, which he secured by robbing temples, including that in Jerusalem. His successor, Seleucus IV, continued to take Temple monies, which aroused the hostility of the Jews.

He was followed by Antiochus IV (175–164 BCE) who chose to be called Epiphanes ("The Manifest One") but whom the common people called Epimanes ("the madman"). He secured revenues by selling the Jerusalem high priesthood to the highest bidder, which resulted in a rapid succession of unusually unsuitable and incompetent holders of that high office. Under Antiochus the pro-Greek factions tried to make Jerusalem into a thoroughly Greek city. They built a Greek gymnasium directly below the citadel and introduced Greek fashion into dress. During a struggle between two contenders for the high priestly office, one of the contestants helped himself to Temple money in order to bribe Antiochus, and so he was appointed to the office. Meanwhile Egypt was intermittently fighting with Syria to regain Palestine. So Jewish factions favored one side over the other, the pro-Egyptian naturally opposed to Antiochus. After being humiliated by Egypt, Antiochus took his revenge on Jerusalem. In a savage massacre, he put to the sword 40,000 men, women, and children and sold many survivors into slavery. Then he plundered the Temple: "He arrogantly entered the sanctuary and took the golden altar, the lampstand for the light, and all its utensils. . . . He took the silver and the gold and the costly vessels; he took also the hidden treasures that he found" (1 Maccabees 1:21-23).

The goal of the king apparently was to stamp out the Jewish religion and to make Jerusalem the capital of a thoroughly Greek state. The climax of his ruthless campaign occurred in 167 BCE when Antiochus forbade all worship of Yahweh, had idols erected in all the places of Jewish worship for the sacrifice of swine, and ordered the people to stop the practice of circumcision. Indeed, women who had their sons circumcised were put to death. Inspectors were appointed to carry out the king's decree that in every city of Palestine the sacred books were burned. The ultimate insult was the erection of an altar to Zeus in the Temple itself on which swine were sacrificed. Yet many resisted. "Many in Israel stood firm and were resolved in their hearts not to eat unclean food," or to profane the holy covenant, and "very great wrath came upon Israel" (1 Maccabees 1:62-64).

The Maccabean Revolt and the Hasmoneans

Twenty miles northwest of Jerusalem lived an elderly priest, Mattathias, who had retreated to a small town with his five sons while Jerusalem was being ravaged. When an official arrived in the village demanding that everyone offer pagan sacrifices, Mattathias not only refused, but he attacked the official and killed him. As a result of this act, the father and the sons fled to the Judean hills where they gathered together like-minded guerilla fighters. Under cover of darkness they threw down pagan temples in several towns, circumcised baby boys, and reestablished synagogues. After a few months of fighting, Mattathias died, and he was succeeded by his third son, Judas. The five sons—John, Simon, Judas, Eleazar, and Jonathan—are known as the Maccabees from the nickname given to Judas: "The Hammer." Their small band defeated two forces sent against them by the governors of Judah. Antiochus became alarmed and sent an army of 40,000 infantry and 7,000 cavalry, which the rebels defeated near Emmaus. Another battle the next year also went to the Maccabees, and Antiochus abandoned his plan to establish a Hellenistic state. Thereupon Judas and his men occupied Jerusalem and cleansed the Temple area, building an altar of new stones to Yahweh. So it was that in 164 BCE the cleansed altar was rededicated, three years to the day after it had been desecrated. The Feast of Hanukkah, also known as the Feast of Dedication or the Feast of Lights, recalls this event.

While Jerusalem seemed secure, Judas and his followers now attempted to bring assistance to the many devout Jews who were under oppression by the Hellenists in the towns and villages of Judah. The governor of Judah, Lysias, countered this by bringing an overwhelming force against the Maccabees; the rebels fought valiantly but were unsuccessful, and Eleazer was killed when he was crushed by a falling elephant. Meanwhile, Antiochus died and was succeeded by his eight-year-old son, Antiochus V, for whom Lysias was regent. Lysias was unwilling or unable to continue the struggle, and a treaty was signed granting the Jews the right to live according to their own laws and to worship God according to the precepts of their own religion. Politically the Jews remained subject to Syria, but no further attempts were made to Hellenize them. Religious freedom had been achieved. But the Syrians broke the treaty, and Judas was forced back into the field with troops, at the same time appealing to the Roman government for assistance. The Roman Senate ratified the independence of Judah and declared a form of protectorate over it in return for the promise of mutual aid in case of an attack by a third power. This treaty is recorded in 1 Maccabees 8. But while the ambassadors were away in Rome, Judas died in battle with the Syrians.

Judah was again torn into factions: the Hellenists, who reemerged after having gone into hiding; the Hasidim,[22] who were interested primarily in religious freedom and not politics; and the followers of the Maccabees. The Hellenists once again gained power, and the Maccabees under the leadership of Jonathan (161–143 BCE) waged guerilla warfare against them in the countryside for seven years. But in 153 BCE a revolution broke out in Syria, and in reward for his support, Alexander, the new king of Syria, appointed Jonathan both high priest and governor. He enjoyed this dignity for ten years, but he was treacherously murdered by the Syrians when he accepted their safe conduct on a mission of diplomacy.

The only living son of Mattathias who remained was Simon, who succeeded Jonathan (143–135 BCE). Whereas his brother Judas had excelled in military achievements, and Jonathan combined diplomacy with martial prowess, it was Simon's legacy that he consolidated the Hasidim, the Hellenists, and the Maccabees into a unified nation. First he removed the Syrians from their last strongholds, Gezer, Hebron, and the citadel in Jerusalem. He also made safe the way to Joppa, the only seaport for Judah, and he rescued as many prisoners of war as he could locate. The writer of 1 Maccabbees describes the time of Simon in idyllic terms:

> The land had rest all the days of Simon.
>   He sought the good of his nation;
> his rule was pleasing to them,
>   as was the honor shown him,
>   all his days.
> . . . .
> He established peace in the land,
>   and Israel rejoiced with great joy.
> All the people sat under their
>   own vines and fig trees,
>   and there was none to make them afraid.
>   (1 Maccabees 14:4, 11-12)

Simon renewed the mutual defense treaty with Rome, and the Roman Senate sent letters to all of Israel's neighbors warning them against disturbing Judah. As a sign of his newfound position, Simon also coined money, which was a sign of sovereignty as well.[23] In 140 BCE, decrees were read in the Temple, granting Simon the hereditary titles of high priest, commander-in-chief, and ethnarch of the Jews; this marks the beginning of the Hasmonean dynasty (from the family name). However, Simon met a tragic end when his own son-in-law had him killed, hoping to succeed to the throne. In this he was not successful, as John Hyrcanus, Simon's son, now became high priest in place of his father.

Hyrcanus (135–105 BCE) was, in all but name, king. He had his own name stamped on the coins. In a campaign to the north he avenged a small Jewish town by destroying the city of Samaria and capturing Scythopolis. He also captured Shechem and destroyed the temple on Mt. Gerizim. These campaigns brought all of the territory of Samaria under his control. He then turned his attention southward to Idumea (Edom), the land between the Dead Sea and the Gulf of Aqabah, and forced the inhabitants to accept Judaism. All males were circumcised, and Josephus (*Antiquities* 13:9:1) writes, "From this time on they too were Jews." In this way Herod, the Idumean, became a Jew, though not through belief or blood but through compulsory ritual.

It was during Hyrcanus's time that we first hear of the Pharisees, a group with origins among the Hasidim. Although they were "separate ones" and strict followers of the Torah, demanding a school in every town in Judea, they were also influenced by the Hellenistic ideal: "By accepting the principle of the Hellenic paideia but using it for specifically Jewish spiritual content the Pharisees found a synthesis between universal Hellenistic culture and traditional Jewish life."[24] The Pharisees also believed in oral tradition alongside the written Law. They gradually secured a following among the common people, who admired their austerity and hatred of pagan rulers. John Hyrcanus had a dispute with the Pharisees over the role of politics and religion, with the result that he supported the cause of the Sadducees.

We first hear of the Sadducees (the name means "righteous ones") under the Hasmoneans about this time; they stood for the interests of the priestly aristocracy and the rich and were in opposition to the Pharisees. To maintain their power and position they favored Hellenizing tendencies and opposed what they perceived to be unnecessary strictness in observing the

Law. They rejected the idea of life after death as well as the authority of the oral tradition and the existence of angels. They disappear from history after the fall of Jerusalem (70 CE).

John Hyrcanus was the first member of the second generation of the Maccabees, now known as the Hasmoneans, and he was the last to earn the respect and admiration of his people. He extended the land of Israel from Mount Carmel in the north to the Gulf of Aqabah in the south, and to the west he secured the coastland. His boundary on the east was the Jordan River. He died in 104 BCE and was succeeded by his son Aristobulus, who ruled for only one year. In that time he displayed unbridled ferocity against those whom he suspected of treason, killing his own mother by starvation.

Next came Alexander Jannaeus (104–78 BCE). Aristobulus had designated his wife, Alexandra, to succeed him. Instead, she married her husband's brother, Alexander, who then became high priest. He was ambitious and without scruple, and as a Hellenist he favored the Sadducees. He ruthlessly killed 6,000 of his political opponents, including many Pharisees. He was successful in extending the kingdom almost to the limits of that in David's time, but his ruthlessness resulted in determined opposition, which erupted in a rebellion and a civil war that raged for six years (94–89 BCE). Alexander died while attempting to bring Ragaba, a Transjordan fortress, under his control.

Alexandra, his wife and the former wife of Aristobulus, now ruled in her own right for nine years (78–69 BCE), with her son John Hyrcanus II serving as high priest. Alexandra followed a remarkable domestic policy of conciliation toward her husband's enemies and of enlightened reform toward religion. All exiled Pharisees were recalled, and some were given high positions. Prisoners were released. Neglected religious ceremonies were restored, such as drawing water from the pool of Siloam during the Feast of Tabernacles. A poll-tax of a half-shekel was required of every Israelite and was used to support the Temple and its worship. This enabled the Sanhedrin[25] to become independent of control by the Sadducees. Finally, compulsory education for all Jewish children was introduced. It was during

Alexandra's time that the Jerusalem council enjoyed more authority than before, and a new office developed, that of the scribe (learned interpreter of the Jewish law). Although Ezra is generally credited with being the archetype of the Scribes, it was under Alexandra that the Scribes and their supporters, the Pharisees, became the religious leaders of Israel.

Despite her moderation, Alexandra was opposed by the friends of Jannaeus who had been the exploiters and oppressors of the people—that is, the warlords and nobility who shared in the outrages of Alexandra's former husbands. They found a willing ally in Hyrcanus II, son of Alexandra, who was high priest. He was weak minded, unscrupulous, and thoroughly incompetent. When Alexandra died from illness, John Hyrcanus saw his opportunity.

But there was a rival for the throne in John's brother, Aristobulus II, who allied with the Sadducees in a civil war in which John Hyrcanus was defeated and Aristobulus II assumed the leadership. Now the story becomes a bit more complicated. Idumea had come under the jurisdiction of Israel during the reign of John Hyrcanus I, and at this time it was governed by the wily Antipater. When Antipater saw that Aristobulus II had defeated John Hyrcanus II, his brother, he persuaded Hyrcanus to flee to Petra and its king, Aretas. There an agreement was made that in return for Aretas's assistance against Aristobulus II, Hyrcanus would restore twelve cities that had been taken from him by John Hyrcanus I. In the battle that resulted, Aristobulus was soundly defeated by the Arabians under Aretas, and the way seemed open for John Hyrcanus II to be restored as the leader of Israel.

While these intrigues were proceeding, a new power appeared on the horizon, one that would forever change the destiny and role of Judea. That power was Rome. Since 88 BCE the Roman legions had been in Asia Minor attempting to crush Rome's archenemy, Mithradates of Pontus. This feat was finally accomplished by Pompey the Great in 65 BCE, when the greater part of Asia Minor became subject to Rome. But Pompey had far greater visions of conquest in which Rome would extend its boundaries all the way to the Euphrates, which of necessity included Syria and Palestine. It was at this moment that John Hyrcanus II, with the help of Aretas, defeated his brother, Aristobulus. But shortly thereafter, Pompey's general Scaurus arrived and took the side of Aristobulus, whom he reinstated as governor of Judea until Pompey could come in person. Not until two years later did Pompey make his appearance, and after considerable intrigue, warfare, and bloodshed, in which 12,000 lost their lives, Hyrcanus found himself reinstated by the Romans as the high priest and ruler of Judea. This was in the year 63 BCE, which marks the end of the independent Jewish state until modern times.

Pompey confined the jurisdiction of Hyrcanus to Judea proper with the title of ethnarch; he was responsible to the Roman governor of Syria. The outlying cities, the seacoast, Samaria, and Galilee were under various forms of subjugation to Rome. Aristobulus, his two sons, a daughter, and 362 other captives were carried to Rome to be displayed as trophies in the grandest triumphal procession Rome had ever seen. In an uncharacteristic gesture of generosity Pompey set the captives free, and they formed the nucleus for the Jewish quarter on the right bank of the Tiber in Rome, which would play a prominent role in later Christian history. With the conquest of Palestine by Rome there was finally peace in the land. It was Rome's policy not to interfere in local politics, but to permit local native rulers a considerable amount of authority in domestic affairs. Rome controlled foreign policy and the army, and usually maintained a garrison to ensure the peace. With the incorporation of Judea into the Roman Empire, the Hasmoneans (Maccabees) passed from the scene.

Herod the Great

The Idumeans (Edomites) were, according to tradition, the descendants of Esau; they settled south of the Dead Sea with their capital in Petra, which today is in Jordan. In 300 BCE they were driven out by the Nabateans, and so they moved westward to southern Palestine, where Hebron became their capital. When Alexander Janneus made Antipas the governor of Idumea, a family was brought into prominence that would play a decisive role in Palestine during the time of the birth of Christianity. Antipas was succeeded in office by his son Antipater, whose intrigues gained for him the friendship of Pompey. When Pompey was defeated by Julius Caesar at the battle of Pharsalus (48 BCE), Antipater and Hyrcanus submitted to Caesar. As a reward, Antipater became the procurator of Judea and Hyrcanus received the high priesthood. But Julius Caesar was murdered on March 15, 44 BCE, and Antipater was poisoned the following year, leaving four sons.

One of his sons, Herod, had already been governor of Galilee, and at the death of his father was made ruler ("tetrarch") of Judea. But one of the remaining Maccabees rallied his forces, overunning Judea and forcing Herod to make a quick trip to Rome. There he succeeded in convincing the joint Roman rulers, Octavian and Anthony, as well as the Senate, to make him king of Judea. He returned with an army and with some difficulty took over two years to defeat his opposition. Having finally claimed victory, he was crowned king of Judea in 37 BCE. His jurisdiction included Samaria and Galilee as well as Judea, and he was directly responsible to the princeps (emperor) in Rome. Josephus (*Antiquities* 14:490) writes: "Thus did the government of the Asmoneans cease, a hundred and twenty-six years after it was first set up. This family was a splendid and illustrious one . . . but they lost their government by their dissensions one with another, and it came to Herod."

Herod was a skilled diplomat and an accomplished military tactician, and despite his deserved reputation for ruthlessness, he displayed on many occasions a generosity of spirit and philanthropy. He was a lover of Greek culture, and although nominally Jewish, he also built shrines for the Greek gods. He is best remembered for his monumental building activities throughout Palestine. But overshadowing his admirable traits were those of paranoia, autocratic personality, and a murderous ferocity against any who was perceived as opposing his designs.

Herod displayed his adroit political sense when in 31 BCE his patron, Anthony, was defeated by Octavian (Caesar Augustus) at the Battle of Actium. He quickly gave his loyalty to Augustus, and during his entire reign he never wavered in that loyalty. Such loyalty did not extend to his family and friends, however, and during the early years of his rule he removed any who could threaten his authority. He had the remaining members of the Hasmonean family killed, including Aristobulus III, the high priest, who was drowned in Herod's swimming pool at Jericho. Alexandra, the mother of the slain high priest, brought charges to Augustus, and Herod was forced to go to Laodicea to defend himself. Augustus accepted his claims of innocence. Salome, Herod's sister, accused Mariamne, his wife, of infidelity, whereupon Herod had his wife killed. Alexandra, the mother of Aristobulus III and of Mariamne, was next to be killed, together with many others including some of Herod's closest friends. Having momentarily secured his position, he gave his attention to matters of governance.

As noted above, the abiding legacy of Herod lay in his building activity, the remains of which can be seen by modern pilgrims to Israel on every side. He erected a theater in Jerusalem and an amphitheater outside the walls where Greek dramas were produced and such Greco-Roman activities as horse and chariot races were held. He rebuilt the city of Samaria in central Palestine and renamed it Sebaste in honor of the emperor (Sebaste is the Greek equivalent of Augustus). Herodian remains are still visible there today. Fortresses were built in various parts of the kingdom, in Galilee, Perea, Judea, and Jerusalem. One of the more interesting fortresses is the Herodium, just south of Bethlehem. Herod built this as a retreat and as one of a string of southern fortresses. What makes it unique is that in order to raise the height of the hill on which it sits, the top half of the hill next to it was removed, and the dirt was transferred to the Herodium hill. Today one can easily see the hill from which the top was removed. Josephus reports that Herod was buried here (*Jewish War* 1:673), but his remains have never been found.

One of Herod's most prodigious feats was the construction of a new port at Caesarea, named after Caesar Augustus. A sea wall 200 feet wide was constructed of stones measuring 50 x 10 x 9 feet. There was an inner and an outer harbor, and along the shoreline there remains evidence of up to seventy warehouses. The city was constructed with a grid pattern, much like a modern American city arranged according to "blocks." A drainage system ran under the streets, which the rising and falling tide would wash out each day. Caesarea was intended to be a thoroughly Greek city, and it was provided with a theater (restored today), an amphitheater, a hippodrome, and a temple to Augustus (now being restored). In later years it was the capital of Palestine, where Pontius Pilate had his residence. Philip the evangelist brought the gospel to Caesarea (Acts 8:40) and entertained Paul (Acts 9:30). Peter preached to the Gentiles in the home of Cornelius (Acts 10:34). Paul was in Caesarea several times, including his two-year imprisonment (Acts 24:27). The early church father Origen (d. 252 CE) lived here for twenty years, and the father of church history, Eusebius (d. c. 340 CE), was its bishop. Today Caesarea is being actively excavated and is worth a visit.

Another notable structure of Herod was the fortress at Masada, at the southwestern end of the Dead Sea. It was built as a defense along the southern perimeter of the kingdom and as a winter home. Masada is especially famous for its role in the Jewish uprising of 70 CE as the place where over 900 defenders chose death rather than slavery. At the northern end of the Dead Sea, Herod constructed a summer palace at Jericho, the ruins of which remain impressive. It was here that he drowned one high priest and where he died himself. In Jerusalem, Herod built his palace, which occupied the citadel area on the western wall of the city, covering about fifteen acres. Part of the remains of Herod's palace are the lower walls of the citadel just inside the Jaffa Gate.

Of all his enormous building feats, none can compare with Herod's restoration of the Temple in Jerusalem. The main part of the Temple, begun in 19 BCE, was completed in eighteen months, but the entire project was not completed until 64 CE, long after his death and only six years before it was completely destroyed. It was built of white marble with an overlay of gold and precious stones, resplendent in the sunshine on the summit of Zion. Josephus (*Antiquities* 15:396) wrote, "No one else had so greatly adorned the temple as he had done."[26]

Herod's reign was marked by a combination of ruthless cruelty and enlightened diplomacy. He secured for Jerusalem an adequate water supply, and his string of fortresses guaranteed the longest period of security from external attack that the land had known for many years. In times of famine he relieved the distress. Twice he made drastic reduction in taxes of 33 percent and 25 percent. His building program provided employment for thousands of artisans and workers. Trade flourished with the new harbor at Caesarea. Despite all of this, Herod was viewed with suspicion by his subjects. He lived in isolation from his people and was seen as a foreigner, "brutish and a stranger to all humanity" (*Antiquities* 16:151). When he died he was not mourned, although he was determined that mourning would take place at his death. He imprisoned a number of prominent citizens with instructions to his sister, Salome, that they be murdered at his death to make certain there would be sadness in the land. However, Josephus reports that when he died, Salome released the prisoners, and there was great rejoicing in the land (*Jewish War* 1:666).

After Herod's death, the emperor divided Palestine among several successors. Herod's son Herod Antipas (4 BCE–39 CE) ruled over the northern province of Galilee and the area across the Jordan called Perea. He lived with Herodias, his brother's wife, and it was this relationship that aroused the anger of John the Baptist and caused his beheading (Matt. 14:1-3). During Jesus' trial in Jerusalem, he was sent by Pontius Pilate to Herod Antipas because he had come from Galilee (Luke 23:6-12).

Herod Archelaus, another son of Herod, was given Judea and Samaria to rule, but because of his oppressive tyranny he was removed after ten years and, after standing trial in Rome, was banished to Gaul by the emperor (6 CE). It is of this ruler that we read that Joseph, when he heard that Archelaus was ruling in his father's place, did not return to Judea but went back to Nazareth to live.

The banishment of Herod Archelaus gave Rome the opportunity to incorporate Judea, along with Samaria and Idumea, into the empire with a governor whose title was procurator, with his capital at Caesarea, the great port city that Herod the Great had built. The procurator was responsible for public order and taxation, but as was often the case in other Roman provinces, internal administration was left up to the local population. Taxes were collected by Roman agents, but customs duties were farmed out to collectors, who were called publicans. Pontius Pilate was the governor of this province during Jesus' ministry and at the time of his trial and crucifixion (26–36 CE). Jesus' ministry falls into the period of the procuratorship of Pontius Pilate and the reign of Herod Antipas, tetrarch of Galilee.

Meanwhile Herod Antipas, who had married Herodias and had killed John the Baptist, had tried to make himself a king in Galilee and was banished by the Romans to Gaul for his insubordination. His place was taken by Herod Agrippa, who received the governance of Galilee, and after 41 CE the entire realm—Judea, Samaria, and Galilee—became a Roman province with the name of Judea. Herod Agrippa II was to become ruler of this expanded territory, but because he was only seventeen, the Romans appointed governors to serve in his place. One such governor (procurator) was Felix (52–60 CE) before whom Paul was tried at Caesarea, where he had been sent for protection after the riots in Jerusalem (Acts 21:38). Although Paul made a good impression upon him, Felix kept him under guard for two years. Festus succeeded Felix, and it was before him that Paul appealed for a trial before Caesar himself. This hearing was also attended by the nominal king, Herod Aggripa II (Acts 26).

The Fall of Jerusalem

During this time, at least since Herod Aggripa I, there was turmoil in the land. Robbers and bandits increased in numbers and power. Josephus (*Antiquities* 20:185) reports that "Judea was afflicted by robbers and all the villages were set afire and plundered by them." Added to this was a continuous strife between the high priest and the lower priests. There were armed factions in Judea and Jerusalem. Albinus, the governor who succeeded Festus, is described by Josephus as one who did not fail to practice every kind of wickedness, and his successor, Gessius Florus, as even more rapacious and cruel: "And [he] did almost publicly proclaim it all the country over, that they had liberty given them to turn robbers, upon this condition, that he might go shares with them in the spoils . . . and a great many of the people left their own country, and fled into foreign provinces" (*Jewish War* 2:278-79).

It was in this overcharged atmosphere that a nationalistic movement developed; it was led by the Zealots, founded by Judas the Galilean. Their mistaken idea was that peace would be restored if the Romans could be expelled and if the purity of religious practices were restored. The spark that ignited the rebellion occurred in Caesarea where the governor, Gessius Florus, deceived and robbed the small Jewish colony who had requested more land around their synagogue. When the governor robbed the Temple in Jerusalem of seventeen talents and imprisoned a delegation of Jews who pleaded with him, a riot broke out in Jerusalem in which 3,600 were killed. At the same time more than 25,000 Jews were killed at Caesarea.

Now the uprising spread throughout Judea, accompanied by plunder and bloodshed. When the high priest, Eleazer, refused further sacrifices to support the warfare of the emperor, it was tantamount to treason and an act of war against Rome. The emperor, Nero, sent Vespasian to restore order in Judea. To reinforce his troops, Vespasian sent Titus, his son, to gather Roman forces from Egypt. Vespasian himself began the campaign with an attack on Galilee, in which the fortress city of Gamla played a dramatic role. The architect of its defenses was the general Josephus, who managed to escape the inevitable Roman conquest through some duplicity. The residents of Gamla chose to commit suicide by jumping off the cliff near the city rather than face slavery. Although Josephus recounts this episode (*Jewish War* 4:70ff.), some scholars have questioned it, since very few skeletons have ever been found at the base of the cliff. Because of this story Gamla has become known as the "Masada of the North," and in modern times some officers of the Israeli military forces have taken their oath of service at this site. Josephus was captured at the last stronghold in Galilee, Jotapata, and received a friendly reception by Vespasian, probably because Josephus predicted that his host would become the next emperor, which in fact happened. After the war was over Josephus enjoyed a comfortable retirement in Rome, which was fortunate for him since the Jews in Judea understandably viewed him as a traitor. He is perhaps best remembered for his two valuable works, *The Jewish War* and the *The Antiquities of the Jews.*

Vespasian was not in a hurry to attack Jerusalem itself, as a fierce civil war was being waged within its walls between the fanatical Sicarii[27] and their allies the Zealots, against the more moderate citizens who sought peace. Josephus (*Jewish War* 5:33) writes that "no regard for the living was any longer paid by their relations; no thought was taken for the burial of the dead; those who took no part in the sedition lost interest in everything." Famine followed, and after that a fearful pestilence, which Josephus describes in gruesome detail. While besieging the city, Vespasian was declared emperor in Rome (70 CE) and the leadership of the campaign was given to his son Titus. In July of 70 CE Titus managed to enter the city, and a mass carnage of the residents ensued. Titus tried to preserve the Temple, but some soldiers threw brands of fire into it and soon the magnificent structure was destroyed in the flames. The city itself was destroyed as far as was possible. Thousands of its inhabitants were killed or sold into slavery.

Some evidence of this destruction has remained for archaeologists to view: charred stones and layers of ashes at the lower levels of the walls. The modern tourist can see pavement stones in near perfect condition just outside the southern end of the western wall, at the corner. These look as though they were placed there only yesterday. The reason is that the Temple mount was not completed until four years before its destruction, and these stones had not known much traffic before the great conflagration.

The end of this tragic episode was the capture of Masada, Herod's fortress on the western shore of the Dead Sea. From Jerusalem the Roman army pursued the fleeing Zealots toward Jericho and on toward the Dead Sea, where Qumran, the home of the Essenes, had been destroyed in 68/69 C.E. It was during this crisis, with the Roman army advancing toward their community, that the Essenes hid their sacred writings in jars scattered in the caves nearby; these writings were rediscovered only in modern times and are known today as the Dead Sea Scrolls. When the Romans reached Masada, they besieged the fortress, building around its base eight camps, which were connected by walls to prevent the defenders' escape (though small groups of the Jewish defenders were able to conduct sporadic raids through the Roman lines).

After a three-year siege, the defenders recognized that the end was near. The Romans had constructed a large ramp up to the walls on the western side to enable them to batter the walls and to give the troops easier access. The siege ramp can still be seen there today, as well as the outlines of the Roman camps. On the night before certain capture, Eleazer, the Zealot leader, gave a stirring speech (as recorded by Josephus, *Jewish War* 7:323ff.) in which he suggested that death was preferable to slavery. So the heads of the households agreed to kill their families, and the heads of tribes killed the householders, until Eleazer, the only one remaining, took his own life. Some older women hid in a well and lived to tell the story. Since that time Masada has stood as a symbol of bravery and the preference of freedom over slavery. Elements of the Israeli military forces today take their oath of office at Masada, as a stirring symbol of identification with the brave defenders of the Roman period, with the promise that "Never again!" will Israel be dominated by foreign powers.

The Life and Ministry of Jesus

The reconstruction of a history of Jesus' life and ministry is filled with difficulties. The primary sources—the Gospels of Matthew, Mark, Luke, and John—present the activities and teachings of Jesus from the point of view of Christian faith, and they do not always agree as to the sequence, chronology, or place of particular events. The following pages intend to offer a simple historical outline, based on a composite reading of all four Gospels, without delving into the numerous complex issues of historical evidence and critical biblical interpretation over which responsible scholars and theologians may disagree.

From earliest times the Christian tradition has located the birth of Jesus in Bethlehem (Luke 2), and the generally accepted dates are sometime between 7 and 4 BCE. The primary reason for this is the fact that Herod the Great was responsible for the slaughter of the innocent children when Jesus was born (Matthew 2), and Herod died in 4 BCE. The biblical stories say that Jesus was born in a manger; this may have been a cave, of which there are many in the Bethlehem area. The early church father Justin Martyr (d. 165 CE) writes that in his time a cave in Bethlehem was pointed out as the birthplace of Christ.[28] It was not unusual for houses to be built over or adjacent to caves, which could be used for stabling cattle, as is still done today. The Church of the Nativity in Bethlehem is built over such a cave, which Christian tradition has held to be the site of Jesus' birth at least since the mid-second century CE. The foundations of the present church date from the time of Constantine, who initiated construction of the church in 329 CE.

According to the biblical account, Joseph and Mary fled to Egypt with Jesus shortly after his birth; Joseph had been warned by God in a dream to do so, in order to escape Herod's designs on the child's life (Matthew 2:13-23). When they learned that Herod had died, they returned to Nazareth, where Joseph worked as a carpenter. The Bible says little about the early life of Jesus, with the exception of his journey to the Temple in Jerusalem with his parents when he was twelve years old (Luke 2:41ff.). Although several apocryphal gospels dating from later centuries attempt to fill this void with stories of miracles and childhood adventures, these accounts cannot be taken seriously. Only Matthew and Luke record birth/infancy narratives of Jesus, and that only briefly; the early church was much more interested in Jesus' ministry than in his birth. The celebration of Christmas ("Christ's Mass") was not introduced into the church calendar until around 340 CE, to counteract the Saturnalia (the pagan festival of the winter solstice, December 21) and to make a theological statement against those who denied the reality of his humanity by celebrating a Feast of the Incarnation.

Mark and John begin their accounts of Jesus with the story of John the Baptist, which Matthew and Luke each pick up beginning with chapter 3. As noted above, Judaism experienced considerable turmoil after the death of Herod the Great, which was intensified by the provocations of Pilate about 26 CE. There were factions of various religious persuasions as well as those who advocated Hellenism, all under the ever-present surveillance of Roman soldiers. It was in this context that John the Baptist appeared, with an urgent message: "Repent, for the kingdom of heaven has come near" (Matthew 3:2). His was the very image of some of the Old Testament prophets, crying out in the wilderness, wearing simple clothing, and sustained by a spartan diet. His message and challenge made a profound impression, and many people came out to see him. "Then the people of Jerusalem and all Judea were going out to him, and all the region along the Jordan, and they were baptized by him in the river Jordan, confessing their sins" (Matthew 3:5-6).

Ceremonial washings were not new in Judaism; indeed, the *miqveh,* or ritual bath, had long been a feature of religious life. Apparently those who were so baptized returned again to their homes and did not form a special sect led by John the Baptist, although he had a few disciples—such as Andrew and John. Jesus traveled from Nazareth to be baptized by John the Baptist, an event that probably occurred near Jericho. Through the story of the voice calling from heaven and of the dove resting upon him (Mark 1:9-13 and parallels), the Gospel writers confirmed that Jesus indeed was the chosen one of God. After his baptism,

Jesus is said to have secluded himself in the barren Judean hills for forty days, no doubt to meditate and pray and so prepare himself for the work to come. The Gospel account says that during this time he was continually tempted by Satan (Matthew 4:1-11); today this is commemorated by a Byzantine monastery that stands on "the Mount of Temptation," near the ancient tell of Jericho.

Shortly after Jesus' baptism, John the Baptist was apprehended by Herod Antipas. Mark writes that "after John was arrested, Jesus came to Galilee, proclaiming the good news of God" (Mark 1:14). It was during this time that Jesus selected his group of disciples, the first two being those former disciples of John the Baptist, Andrew and John. He seems to have traveled first to his hometown of Nazareth, where he was rejected by his own people; thereupon he made Capernaum the center of his ministry (Matthew 4:13; 9:1).

Many of Jesus' activities took place near Capernaum around the northern end of the Sea of Galilee. Capernaum was the home of Matthew (Levi) the tax collector, as well as the army officer whose servant Jesus healed, who was also responsible for building the first synagogue here. Today the foundations of the first-century CE synagogue can still be seen under the remains of a later Byzantine synagogue built over it. This structure is near the remains of a complex known today as St. Peter's House, which, according to later Christian tradition, was the place where Jesus lived with his followers and where he healed Peter's mother-in-law. Despite Jesus' presence, the people of Capernaum did not believe his message, and Jesus warned them of the judgment to come (Mark 1:21-34; 2:1-17; Luke 7:1-10; 10:13-16).

Although a chronology of Jesus' Galilean ministry is difficult to reconstruct, three major journeys can be found in outline from Mark's Gospel, all starting and ending in Capernaum. The first journey (Mark 4:35–5:21) finds Jesus crossing over to the pagan territory of the Decapolis—that is, the region of a federation of ten Hellenistic cities that were not on good terms with the Jews. Sometimes this territory is simply referred to as "the other side." This included the region of the Gadarenes and Gerasenes. It was when making this crossing of the Sea of Galilee that Jesus is said to have calmed the sea (Mark 4:35-41). Once on the other side, he is said to have liberated the man possessed by a demon; the demons entered a herd of swine, which then rushed headlong into the sea (Mark 5:1-13). The man who was thus delivered spread the news to the nearby city of Hippus and throughout the Decapolis. Today this event is commemorated at the fifth-century Byzantine church at Kursi along the eastern shore of the Sea of Galilee.

When he returned to Capernaum, Jesus is reported to have healed the daughter of Jairus, a ruler of the synagogue, and the woman with an issue of blood (Mark 5:21-43). Then he traveled to Nazareth, "to his own country," where he preached on the sabbath and was rejected by his own people. After this rejection, Jesus made Capernaum the center of his Galilean ministry. He sent out his disciples in pairs in order to preach "that all should repent." Meanwhile, news of Jesus' ministry had attracted Herod's attention. Herod Antipas had been responsible for the beheading of John the Baptist, and he feared now that "John, whom I beheaded, has been raised" (Mark 6:16). After the disciples returned from their missionary journeys, Jesus invited them to come apart and rest, and so began the second Galilean journey (Mark 6:30–8:10).

The Gospels report that after leaving Capernaum for a quiet place, the small group was besieged by a large crowd; this became the occasion for Jesus' feeding of the five thousand. Later Christian tradition locates this event at Tabgha, where it is commemorated today by the presence of a Byzantine church. It was also near Tabgha that Jesus may have delivered the Sermon on the Mount, an event remembered at the beautiful Chapel of the Beatitudes. Another event that is commemorated by a nearby church, although it did not occur on the second Galilean journey, is the appearance of Jesus to Peter following the Resurrection, when Jesus gave the disciple the command to feed his lambs and sheep. Hence the church is known as the Primacy of Peter.

After the feeding of the five thousand, according to the Gospels, the disciples set sail for Bethsaida, and during the night a strong wind arose so fierce that they feared for their lives. In the midst of the storm they saw Jesus walking on the water. He calmed the storm and went with them the remainder of the way (Mark 6:45-52). They were met by a large group of people, including some Pharisees with whom Jesus engaged in a dispute about the Law (Torah). Jesus offered a radical critique of the prevailing interpretations of the Temple, the land, and the Law. His view of the Temple made it appear to be unnecessary for true religion, although he observed its rituals. His view of the Law was that its observance had lost the initial spirit and had become a mere observance of externals for their own sake. Codes of diet and of dress meant nothing unless one's heart was changed (Mark 7:20-23).

From Bethsaida, Jesus went to Tyre and Sidon, a considerable journey of about 120 miles, where he is said to have healed a Gentile woman's daughter. This is all we know about this lengthy trip to Phoenicia. He returned to the Decapolis, where the Gospels report that he healed a man who had a speech impediment, followed by the feeding of the four thousand. Then Jesus probably returned to Capernaum, which was nearby, but he also visited Magdala (Mark 8:10). Mark also records a number of miracles and further disputes with Pharisees.

The third Galilean journey found Jesus and the disciples traveling to Caesarea Philippi, near the source of the Jordan river, some fifty miles north of Capernaum. In ancient times this was the site of the worship of Pan, a god of nature, and so the place came to be called Panias (today Banyas or Banias). It was also the home of Philip, one of the disciples. It was here, according to Matthew, that Jesus inquired of his disciples concerning his identity—"Who do people say that the Son of Man is?" Peter responded with his bold confession, "You are the Messiah, the Son of the living God" (Matthew 16:13-16), and in return Jesus spoke the words that became the center of considerable dispute in the history of the church, "You are Peter, and on this rock I will build my church."

All three Synoptic Gospels agree in reporting that following the visit to Caesarea Philippi, there occurred an event known as the Transfiguration, when Moses and Elijah appeared to Jesus and three of the disciples, Peter, James, and John (Matthew 17:1-8 and parallels). Since Jesus was still in the north of Galilee, the most likely setting for this event was somewhere on or near Mt. Hermon, on the northern border with Syria. Another possible location is on Mt. Tabor, five miles east of Nazareth and twelve miles west of the Sea of Galilee. Today there is a Franciscan Church of the Transfiguration on top of Mt. Tabor.

After descending from the mountain, Jesus is said to have healed an epileptic boy; moving through the villages of Upper Galilee, he and the disciples returned again to Capernaum. There he taught the disciples for a short time, but "when Jesus had finished saying these things, he left Galilee and went to the region of Judea beyond the Jordan" (Matthew 19:1). The village of Batanea, situated east of the Jordan River, is identified by later tradition as the place where Jesus engaged the Pharisees in continued disputations and taught a number of parables (Matthew 19–20). These continued disputations with the religious aristocracy were ominous, and made any criticism of the status quo doubly dangerous.

According to the Gospels, Jesus now began his journey to Jerusalem, telling his disciples, "We are going up to Jerusalem, and the Son of Man will be handed over to the chief priests and the scribes, and they will condemn him to death . . . and after three days he will rise" (Mark 10:33-34). He is reported to have made his entry into Jerusalem riding on a donkey and accompanied by cheering crowds who spread palm branches and garments on his way; this is the event the Christian church has come to observe as Palm Sunday. He entered the Temple, driving out money-changers and causing something of a tumult. The chief priests were especially angered at the impudence of this "country rabbi," who had the temerity to refer to this magnificent Second Temple of Herod as "my father's house," and they asked him by what authority he was doing this. His response and instructions during this final week are found in

Mark 12–13 and Luke 20–21. The site of these instructions was undoubtedly the teaching or rabbinical steps that have been uncovered south of the Temple Mount, by the Hulda Gates, and can be seen today.

As with many events in Jesus' life and ministry, there is no consensus on the chronology of his final week. The Synoptic Gospels agree that the Last Supper took place on a Thursday night and that it was the Passover. John, on the other hand, states that Jesus was already dead "on the eve of the Passover" (19:31). Mary anointed Jesus with oil in Bethany two days before the Passover, or so the Synoptics insist, whereas John maintains it was six days before. What is clear is that the Gospels agree in depicting Jesus as increasingly conscious of being the Messiah, as shown by his entry into Jerusalem; this was seen as fulfilling the prophecies concerning such an event in Isaiah 62:11 and Zechariah 9:9 (Matthew 21:4-5). The New Testament passion narratives are filled with such Messianic allusions.

So Jesus ate the Passover with his disciples, although the room that today is shown to tourists as the Upper Room is undoubtedly not authentic. After the dinner, they crossed over the Kidron Valley to the Garden of Gethsemane, whose location today is the same as that of the first century. There Jesus prayed, as he often did, in solitude, after which he was betrayed by Judas to a "large crowd with swords and clubs, from the chief priests and the elders of the people" (Matthew 26:47). They led Jesus to Caiaphas, the high priest (although John's Gospel says he was first taken to the house of Annas, father-in-law of Caiaphas), where a preliminary inquiry was conducted in preparation for a later hearing before the Sanhedrin. Matthew reports that Peter, lounging in the courtyard, was recognized as being one of Jesus' disciples, and he denied it three times. Today the Church of St. Peter in Gallicantu (meaning "the rooster crowed") is said to be built on the site of Caiaphas's palace. After the hearing before Caiaphas, Jesus went before the entire Sanhedrin, although some members (such as Nicodemus) may have been absent. When he was asked directly if he was the Son of God, Jesus replied in the affirmative, and in so doing brought upon himself the charge of blasphemy (Matthew 26:64-65).

Since the Sanhedrin was not permitted to inflict capital punishment, it was necessary to bring Jesus before the chief Roman official. Pontius Pilate was then the governor of Judea; his official residence was in Caesarea, but he was in Jerusalem during the Passover in order to be as near as possible to flashpoints of trouble. Here Jesus' enemies portrayed him as a political rebel, as a charge of blasphemy would not have weighed heavily with the governor. After some questioning, Pilate discovered that Jesus was a Galilean, so Pilate sent him to Herod Antipas, who had heard much about this prophet and wanted to see him and he "was hoping to see him perform some sign" (Luke 23:8). But Jesus stood silent. And "Herod with his soldiers treated him with contempt and mocked him; then he put an elegant robe on him, and sent him back to Pilate" (Luke 23:11). It is highly probable that Herod's residence at this time was the Citadel, the ruins of which are found today just inside the Jaffa Gate.

So Jesus was returned to Pilate, who was most likely staying at the Antonia Fortress, adjacent to the Temple itself; the ruins of the Antonia are extant today. There Pilate interrogated Jesus further and made three declarations of his innocence. Jesus' accusers, when given the opportunity of freeing a prisoner, chose the condemned criminal Barabbas. Pilate's wife interceded on Jesus' behalf on the basis of a dream. Finally, Pilate gave the sentence of death, declaring himself "innocent of this man's blood" (Matthew 27:24).

After this, the soldiers mocked the regal claims of Jesus by placing on him a robe and a crown of thorns. Pilgrims to Israel today, when visiting the lower level of Antonia Fortress, which is now in the Convent of the Sisters of Zion, will be shown the traces of a game carved by Roman soldiers on the surface of some of the stones; this pavement is known as the Lithostratos.[29] The "King's Game" apparently helped to boost the morale of soldiers posted in Judea, which was considered to be the worst assignment in the Roman army. By throwing dice, the soldiers would choose a burlesque "king"; following additional throws of the dice, the "king" would be mocked and abused both verbally and physically. The resemblance between this game and the mockery of Jesus by the soldiers reported in the Gospels (Matthew 27:27-31; Mark 15:16-20) is striking.

So they took him to be crucified. The Via Dolorosa, or "Way of Sorrows," begins just outside the Antonia Fortress. This is the route that later Christian tradition believes Jesus to have followed from the judgment hall of Pilate to Calvary, the site of the crucifixion. It is marked by fourteen Stations of the Cross where various events, biblical and traditional, are remembered, until the final Stations are observed with the Church of the Holy Sepulchre itself. Every Friday afternoon throughout the year Franciscan friars lead any pilgrims who care to join in a procession of devotion down the Via Dolorosa.

The Gospel accounts agree that Jesus was crucified at Golgotha, or Calvary, along with a thief on either side. The traditional site of the crucifixion is today remembered within the Church of the Holy Sepulchre. As early as the second century there are indications of Christians who honored this as the site of Jesus' death, and since Hadrian (117–138 CE) built a pagan temple to Venus Aphrodite at the site to desecrate the memory of anything associated with Judaism (as he viewed Christianity) it seems possible that it may be the actual place. The Church of the Holy Sepulchre has gone through many changes over the centuries, and what may be authentically first-century no doubt lies some distance below the present structure.

The resurrection of Jesus and his appearance to many eyewitnesses are affirmed by all four Gospels. This belief remains central to the Christian message. Ordinary people risked their lives by witnesssing to this belief, and Christian traditions say that all of Jesus' disciples except John (and Judas, of course) died a martyr's death. In spite of the search or desire for evidence to support it, the conviction that Jesus in fact rose from among the dead requires faith, and it is from this faith that the remainder of the New Testament was written.

From the Fall of Jerusalem to the Arab Conflict

After he had crushed the Jewish Rebellion of 70 CE, the victorious general Titus returned to Rome in triumph. The Senate erected an arch of triumph in his honor, which still stands in the Forum today, with carvings of Romans carrying away the seven-branched candlestick and Temple vessels. A new coin was issued showing sorrowing women sitting with fettered hands, and on the coin was the caption *Judaea Capta* ("Captive Judea"). With Jerusalem destroyed, and with it the Temple, the nation's visible heart and center ceased to exist. Yet the Jewish religious leaders regrouped at Jamnia, thirteen miles south of Jaffa, and its elders continued to provide authoritative interpretation and application of the Law; it also made decisions on internal matters, which the Romans gave it freedom to do. Jamnia continued to be an important center of Jewish learning until the end of the second century CE.

Judea was now constituted as a separate province with a governor of senatorial rank, and the presence of a full Roman legion served to maintain the peace. The Flavian emperors (69–96 CE) and Trajan (98–117 CE) established a number of city-states within Palestine, some with considerable autonomy, including the right of coinage. The territory of Flavia Neapolis (modern Nablus) covered the entire area of ancient Samaria. Together with urbanization went the spread of Greco-Roman culture, which effectively discouraged any revivals of Jewish religious ardor. Trajan also annexed the Nabatean Kingdom east of the Jordan and constituted a new province of Arabia.

A final Jewish uprising occurred from 132 to 135 CE under the leadership of Bar Kochba; five Roman legions were required to put it down. Unlike the earlier revolt of 70 CE, we have no Josephus or other historian to rely upon, and details of the revolt are unclear. It may be that it was sparked by an order forbidding circumcision, although this is disputed. Certainly the decision of Emperor Hadrian (117–138 CE) to build a Roman colony in Jerusalem was a contributing factor. It was an uneven contest, and the rebels were defeated, a large number being killed and far more sold into slavery.

The remnant of the Israelite population was reduced to the point that the land was now truly a Roman province, and Hadrian carried out his plan to make Jerusalem into a Greco-Roman city. He renamed it Aelia Capitolina, and forbade entry to it by any Jews under pain of death. Judea was renamed Syria Palestina. Jerusalem was renovated on a much smaller scale than before, and it appears that it became a city of soldiers, primarily that of the Tenth Roman Legion. Meir Ben-Dov, one of the principal archaeologists of Jerusalem, writes that "emperors came and went, some hostile to the Jews, others developing friendly relations with the Jewish leadership of the day; but none allowed the Jews to return to Jerusalem and restore the city so central to Jewish life."[30]

During the early third century the urbanization of Palestine continued with a flourishing Greco-Roman culture. A map from around 250 CE indicates that all the city-states had by now been given Greco-Roman names. From 70 CE the capital of Palestine had shifted from Jerusalem to Caesarea, but in the fourth century under Diocletian (285–305 CE) the land was subdivided into two, and then three, provinces. The Jews were given freedom of worship and of religious expression, including the construction of synagogues, but not the right of entry into Jerusalem. The city of Tiberias on the Sea of Galilee became a notable center of Jewish scholarship, but the Jewish community remained a minority group and culture.

After the time of Jesus, Christianity began its slow growth in Palestine, as recorded in the book of the Acts of the Apostles. The Christians in general did not share in the calamaties of 70 CE and 132–135 CE. However, as the Roman government sporadically persecuted the new religion, Christians in Palestine were not exempt. Justin Martyr was a Palestinian Christian from Nablus who was executed in Rome in 165 CE. In the first centuries after Christ a growing number of pilgrims made their way to sites that they believed had been made holy by Christ's presence—notably Bethlehem, Jerusalem, and Nazareth. In 1982, archaeologists discovered on a stone wall within the lowest level of the Church of the Holy Sepulchre a carving of a ship with the words *Dominus nimus* ("Lord, we have come"); the carving dates from between the first and third centuries CE, and indicates that this site was already a magnet for pilgrims.

Since there were a number of bishops of Jerusalem during these centuries, Christians apparently were not included in the ban on Jewish residents of the city. Origen, the most prolific and profound Christian theologian of the third century, made two trips to Palestine, and on the second he was ordained priest by the bishops of Caesarea and Aelia Capitolina. Shortly thereafter he took up residence in Caesarea, where he lived the last two decades of his life, which ended in 254 CE as a result of wounds suffered in persecution. His story indicates that Christians could usually move about freely, write and copy books, convene councils, and in general go about their business unmolested. It seems from the writings of Justin and Origen that relations between Jews and Christians in Palestine were not uniformly cordial.

One of the most dramatic events in the early church's history occurred in 312 CE: the conversion to Christianity of Emperor Constantine. Although he subsequently took a benign attitude toward non-Christians, permitting freedom of worship to all, the fact that Constantine favored the church and brought persecution to an end prompted large numbers to prepare for Christian baptism. After 324 CE he became sole ruler of the empire, which included the provinces of Palestine.

Constantine is especially significant for pilgrims to Israel because of his building activity there. In 326 CE he sent his mother, Helena, to locate the holy places. With the help of long-standing tradition (and a few miracles) she located what she believed to be the place of Christ's birth in Bethlehem, his burial and resurrection in Jerusalem, and his ascension on the Mount of Olives. Constantine ordered Macarius, the bishop of Jerusalem, to oversee the construction of churches at these places at imperial expense, and in 331 CE the emperor himself made a pilgrimage to the Holy Land to dedicate these churches. The Church of the Ascension is today a mosque, but the remains of Constantinian foundations can still be seen in the

Church of the Holy Sepulchre, and at the Church of the Holy
Nativity one can view fourth-century mosaics through open-
ings in the present flooring.

Soon after, in 333 CE, a pilgrim from Bordeaux (in southwest
France) visited the holy sites in Palestine and wrote an account
of his visit.[31] His vivid descriptions and fervent piety made it a
best-seller, and soon thousands of others were flocking to the
sacred shrines. "Within a few decades, the desire to pray at the
sacred places in the Holy Land became the ruling passion of
multiplied thousands who classified themselves as followers of
the Christ of Calvary."[32] Most came and left; some came and
stayed. According to tradition, Jerome, one of the foremost theologians of the fourth century, lived in the caves under the
church in Bethlehem for the last thirty-four years of his life.
Among his many writings was a Latin version of the Bible, the
Vulgate, which endured in some forms of Western Christianity
as the authoritative version until the twentieth century.

Numerous monks and nuns settled in various places around
Palestine. Eusebius, the father of church history, succeeded Origen at Caesarea. In addition to the anonymous pilgrim from
Bordeaux, we have a diary written by Egeria, a nun from Spain,
who made the long journey to the Holy Land toward the end of
the fourth century.[33] It is a work of considerable intelligence and
powers of observation. She describes in detail her journey
across North Africa, Egypt, and Mt. Sinai. She spent several
months in Palestine, including Holy Week and Easter. Her
account is filled with the details of worship, the vestments, pro-
cessions, and routes, as well as descriptions of the holy places.
Egeria is a goldmine of information for those today who desire
to do serious work on Christian sites in Israel, and her work is
recommended reading for any who aspire to be guides.

With the large number of pilgrims flocking to Palestine,
bringing with them money to spend, there was a revival in economic health and numerical growth. Jerusalem was now controlled by Christians; it occupied a place of honor among the
chief cities of the church, with its bishop numbered among the
ruling patriarchs. The first ecumenical council, held at Nicea in

325 CE, acknowledged this honor (Canon 7). Among the earliest Christians to settle in Jerusalem were the Armenians, the first nation officially to accept Christianity (in about 300 CE). Since that time they have maintained a strong presence in the city, centered on the Cathedral of St. James in the Armenian quarter.

Constantine built a new city along the Bosporus, the strait connecting the Sea of Marmora with the Black Sea. After his death it was named Constantinople (modern Istanbul), and it became the capital of the Eastern Roman Empire. Because it was at the site of an earlier town called Byzantium, the civilization and culture ushered in by the new Christian emperor came to be called Byzantine. It maintained a continuous existence until 1453 CE, when Constantinople fell to the Turks. Although the empire was considered to be a continuation of the Roman Empire, its language was Greek and its religion was Christianity. There existed a close relationship between the church and civil government, usually with the state dominating the church. The period following Constantine, therefore, is referred to as Byzantine for the territory from Greece eastward to Persia.

Along with pilgrims, a large number of monks came to Palestine and established religious houses. A number of these monasteries of Byzantine foundation still remain, including St. George's in the Wadi Qelt, between Jerusalem and Jericho; Latrun, a short distance west of Jerusalem; and Mar Saba, near Bethlehem.

Almost from the beginning the Byzantine Empire was under threat by external forces. In the seventh century the menace was Persia, which under Chosroes II was expanding its borders. In 614 CE he advanced into Syria and from there marched unchallenged into Jerusalem. The city was sacked and the monuments to the faith were burned, including the Church of the Holy Sepulchre. It was said that over 90,000 perished in this onslought in which the Persians were partly assisted by the fighting between the Christians and the Jews. The shock of this event roused the indolent Byzantine emperor, Heraclius, who collected an army and recovered the Holy Land, restoring the Church of the Holy Sepulchre with contributions that poured in from all of Christendom. Pilgrims once again arrived in the Holy Land while Heraclius and his forces pursued the Persians.

The Islamic Conquest

Meanwhile a new religious and military force was gathering strength in the Arabian peninsula. The rise of Islam dates from the Hegira, Muhammad's visit to Medina, in 622 CE. After the prophet's death in 632 CE, his followers quickly subdued Arabia, Syria, and Egypt, and by 638 CE the victorious Caliph Omar turned his army toward Jerusalem. After a four-month siege the city capitulated, and Omar agreed to terms that were generous, permitting both Christians and Jews the freedom to practice their religion in return for the payment of taxes. Within fifty years of the conquest the Mosque of Omar (the Dome of the Rock) was constructed on the Temple Mount, the site (according to Muslim tradition) of Muhammad's ascension to heaven and (according to Jewish tradition) of Abraham's demonstration of faith through his willingness to sacrifice his son Isaac. About the same time the Al Aksa mosque was also constructed on the Temple Mount, on the site of the Christian church that had been built by Justinian in 536 CE and dedicated to the Virgin Mary.

Omar's successor as caliph, Othman, was assasinated in 656 CE. His successor was Ali, the cousin of Muhammad and the husband of his daughter Fatima. But Ali was opposed by Muawyia, an Arab general and a member of the powerful Ummayad family of Mecca. This division led to the breach between the two major branches of Islam, which continues to this day. The Sunni (those who follow the *sunnah,* which means "the path" or "the way") were faithful to the Ummayads, or the line of Muawiya, and today they constitute a large majority of Muslims. The Shia, or Shiites, who comprise about 10 percent of Islam today, are followers of the line of Ali and Fatima.

Under Umayyad leadership, the center of the Arab world shifted from Mecca to Damascus, where Muawiya had been the governor of Syria. After a century of control, the Umayyads were challenged and defeated by a revolutionary group from eastern Persia, known as the Abbasids. In 750 CE the Abbasids moved the capital of Islam to Baghdad, inaugurating the golden age of Arabic culture in the Middle East.

Arabic culture and the religion of Islam usually, but not necessarily, went together. The Arabic language gradually supplanted the local tongues in North Africa, Egypt, and Mesopotamia (modern Iraq). In Palestine, where Greek had been the most commonly spoken tongue, Arabic became the official language. Persia (modern Iran) adopted the Shiite form of Islam but retained its own culture and language, using Arabic script. Turkey was never conquered by the Arabs and is not considered an Arab country; however, the Turks did adopt the Sunni form of Islam as their national religion, but retained the Turkish language, using Arabic script. The Kurds never had their own nation, and although they embraced the Sunni form of Islam, they retained their own language and cultural identity; today they are dispersed in lands from northwestern Iran to eastern Turkey.

The Armenians were the people of Asia Minor who most fiercely resisted Islamic influence. They had formed their own nation in the sixth century BCE in what is today eastern Turkey, and they became the first nation officially to embrace Christianity with the baptism of their king in about 300 CE. In 390 CE, the Armenian nation was divided between the Byzantine and Persian empires, and by 430 CE Armenian independence was lost to a succession of Persian, Arabic, and Turkish conquerors; yet a strong sense of cultural identity survived.

The Arab/Islamic expansion was rapid following Muhammad's death in 632 CE. All of North Africa quickly succumbed, and in 711 CE the Arab forces crossed the Straits of Gibralter into Spain. Only twenty years later they had advanced as far north as Tours, in modern France, where in 732 CE Charles Martel defeated them in battle. Thereafter their retreat was slow, and through most of the medieval period the Arab/Islamic presence in Spain was powerful.

During the ninth century Turkish mercenary troops

(Mamelukes) set up military dictatorships in various Eastern lands. In 867 CE a Turk named Ibn Tulun seized power in Egypt, and he quickly extended his rule to Syria, which then included Palestine. In 969 CE the Turkish power was broken by a new Egyptian dynasty, the Fatimids, who took their name from Fatima, the daughter of Muhammad and the wife of Ali. About 1000 CE they founded Cairo as a rival caliphate to Baghdad. Now Palestine became a battleground between competing Arab empires, one centered in the Tigris-Euphrates valley and the other along the Nile. Meanwhile Byzantium experienced something of a revival, and Byzantine armies invaded Syria thirty-eight times between 962 and 1000 CE.

During the eleventh century CE a new force came upon the scene from central Asia—the Seljuk Turks. In 1050 CE they captured Baghdad and made its caliph their vassal. In 1071 they captured Syria and Palestine from the Egyptian Fatimids. Then they turned north to the Byzantine Empire, and in the same year (1071) they defeated a large Byzantine army and captured the Byzantine emperor at the battle of Manzikert in eastern Turkey. For centuries Jews and Christians had been permitted to continue their worship life, and pilgrims had continued to visit the holy places. The Seljuk Turks ended this, harassing and in some cases killing religious pilgrims, and effectively ending the possibilities of pilgrimage. Now all of Asia Minor was open to the invaders, and Constantinople itself was in danger. The Eastern emperor, Michael VII (1071–1078), appealed for assistance to Pope Gregory VII (1073–1085), but the pope was preoccupied with a major church-state controversy in Europe. It was left for his successor, Urban II (1085–1099), to respond by calling for the First Crusade. Thus the initial impulse of the Crusades was not to rescue the Holy Land from "the infidel" but to come to the assistance of the Byzantine emperor in Constantinople.

The Crusades

Visitors to Israel today cannot help seeing evidence at every hand of the presence of the Crusaders and their building activities nearly nine hundred years ago. Such reminders include the Crusader city at Caesarea, the majestic ruins at Belvoir or Nimrod, the present walls surrounding the Old City and its several gates, and the structures of the Church of the Holy Sepulchre and the Church of the Holy Nativity. A brief outline of the Crusades, therefore, may enhance the visitor's understanding of this remarkable phenomenon of the Middle Ages.

In Western Europe the eleventh century was a time of increasing religious zeal, together with the growth of cities and a general improvement of life. The pilgrimage was popular, as were religious relics that one might find at a holy site. In addition to this, the new dynamism of emerging urban areas and of capitalism found itself at war with fading feudalism, with the result that there was considerable civil strife. Pope Urban II called for a Crusade at the Council of Clermont in France in 1095 CE. In his call he included enticements for everyone—material advantages, ending civil strife by joining together against the "infidel," doing a noble and God-pleasing task—and he also issued the first plenary indulgence whereby those who fell in the struggle were declared to gain immediate admission to heaven.

A true crusade was thus a military expedition summoned by the pope, preached by the clergy, against the unbelievers, in order to recover the Holy Land, with the promise of indulgence. Each Crusader took a vow to fulfill these objectives and wore a cross on his garments as a sign of his intention. Most historians count seven Crusades in all, but only the first three have any direct significance for the Holy Land. The Fourth Crusade was diverted to the sack of Constantinople, the fifth was the abortive Children's Crusade, the sixth found Louis IX of France a prisoner of war, and he died on the Seventh Crusade.

The call of Pope Urban II for the First Crusade was met with enthusiasm; the crowds shouted *Deus vult*, "God wills it!" After a premature and abortive false start by Peter the Hermit and Walter the Penniless, the main group set out. It was composed of four sizable armies: one from lower Lorraine, commanded by Godfrey of Bouillon and his brother, Baldwin of Flanders; a second from northern France, led by Robert of Flanders and by

Robert, Duke of Normandy; a third from southern France, led by Raymond of Toulouse; and a fourth from southern Italy, led by Bohemond and Tancred. There was no single general, but the coordinator was the pope's legate, Bishop Adhemar of Le Puy, who advised all parties to converge at Constantinople. Taking various routes, they met there by the spring of 1097, but Emperor Alexius was displeased by the disorder the westerners caused and by their rude behavior. In May 1097, they besieged Nicea, which surrendered, and by October they had reached Antioch. It was only after a seven-month siege that the city capitulated in June 1098, and Jerusalem was not reached until a year later. The carnage that followed the capture of Jerusalem is one of the darkest blemishes on medieval Christendom, as over 70,000 innocent Jews and Muslims were put to the sword. The booty was immense and brought great reward in return for the hardships and dangers of the two-year journey. Next came the task of governing the newly conquered territory. It was divided into four territories: to the far north was the County of Edessa, under King Baldwin; south of that was the Principality of Antioch, under Bohemund and Tancred; south of that was the County of Tripoli, under Raymond of Toulouse; and the Kingdom of Jerusalem was from Beirut south to the Negev desert. Godfrey of Bouillon ruled this territory with the title "Protector of the Holy Sepulchre" as he insisted that no one should assume the title of king where his Lord had been king. Each state was practically autonomous and was organized according to the feudal customs of Western Europe. Maintaining the four kingdoms offered a challenge, as the Crusaders suffered considerable attrition. Some had been killed in battle, and many more had returned to their homes. Those who remained in Palestine seemed to lose their aggressive spirit as they intermarried with the native population and adopted a life-style more suited to a warm and languid climate.[34]

The defense of the new Latin states was strengthened by the rise of two orders of military monks: the Knights of St. John, or the Hospitallers, and the Knights Templar. The Hospitallers were founded in 1070 in order to care for the sick pilgrims at the hospice named after John the Baptist, but in 1140 they assumed military duties as well. The Templars were founded specifically to defend the Holy Land and to protect pilgrims. Bernard of Clairvaux (d. 1154), theologian and counselor of popes, himself wrote the Rule for the Templars, patterning it after that of the Cistercian Order. Both military orders required their members to take monastic vows as well as those involving military obligations. A third order, that of the Teutonic Knights, was founded in 1190, and did not realize its full potential as shock troups for Christianity until the end of the Crusades, with their energies utilized in Prussia.

G. Frederick Owen comments that:

> The idea of combining the chivalrous with the charitable vows presented an extremely popular combination for that age. Nobles and princes from all over Europe came to Jerusalem to join the new orders. They grew so popular they were given the control of all hospices and hospitals in Palestine and were granted over twenty-eight thousand farms and manors in different parts of Europe.[35]

Those who, because of age or other reasons, could not go personally to Palestine could share in the mission by contributing money or land to the Military Orders, and it was not long before the Templars especially became a powerful and wealthy order in Europe.

The first serious setback for the Crusaders came with the capture of the Principality of Edessa by Zenghi, Sultan of Mosul, on Christmas Day 1144. When the news reached Europe, Pope Eugenius III called for a Second Crusade, which was preached by the indomitable Bernard of Clairvaux. This Crusade was led by Louis VII, king of France, and Conrad III, German emperor. The Germans went first, but they encountered numerous difficuties on the way, and at the last were betrayed by a guide who led the army into a narrow defile near Iconium, where they were slaughtered. Conrad traveled to Jerusalem as a pilgrim. There he met Louis VII of France, who had encountered similar misfortunes en route to the Holy Land. After a short stay, both returned to their homelands, and the Second Crusade ended as a disastrous failure.

The Crusade had been called to avenge the fall of Edessa, but after its failure the other three kingdoms continued to prosper. There was no intention by the Arabs to attack the other states. Indeed, the Kingdom of Jerusalem entered into an alliance with the Fatimite Muslims of Egypt to defeat the allied forces of Arabs from Damascus and Baghdad. But in 1169 a Kurdish general, Saladin (1137–1193), became master of Egypt, and within five years he succeeded in uniting all the Muslim powers that had been feuding among themselves. Saladin then confronted and defeated the entire Latin Crusader army at the Horns of Hattin (or Hittim) near Nazareth in July 1187; as a result Jerusalem was lost, along with most of the Holy Land, and "the flower of the crusader army" was "destroyed by a single blow at Hattin."[36] The length of time the Crusaders occupied the Holy Land was a mere eighty-eight years (1099–1187 CE). Saladin invested Jerusalem, but unlike the Crusaders who devastated the city in 1099, he permitted the Christians to leave with their lives and possessions.

When news of this disaster reached Europe, Pope Innocent II called for a Third Crusade, which was promptly endorsed by three monarchs—Emperor Frederick Barbarossa of Germany (1152–1190), King Philip Augustus of France (1180–1223), and King Richard "The Lionhearted" of England (1189–1199). Much of Europe appeared enthusiastic for this enterprise, and a "Saladin Tithe" was collected from the Christian faithful to support the cause. The German emperor led his army of 100,000 men overland through Turkey into Syria, but in June 1190, while crossing a stream in Celicia, he drowned, and his troups scattered. It was an inauspicious beginning for so great an undertaking.

King Richard of England joined forces with King Philip of France in the summer of 1190. The two armies spent the winter at Messina in southern Italy, but a personal difficulty arose between the kings. Richard was engaged to marry Philip's sister, Adelia, but he now decided he was no longer interested in her. Philip and his army proceeded by ship to Acre, where they joined the other Crusaders in a siege of that city. Richard was shipwrecked at Cyprus, where he captured the ruler and levied taxes on the people. He also was married there to Berengaria of Navarre. He and his army finally arrived at Acre, and on July 12, 1191, the fortress fell to the Crusaders. Saladin had agreed to pay a ransom for five thousand prisoners, but when the money was not immediately forthcoming, Richard had them all beheaded. Saladin retaliated by killing the Christian prisoners he had in his keeping.

From Acre the English army marched south and recaptured Jaffa, but there was dissension among the leaders, and they decided not to recapture Jerusalem. A truce was signed with Saladin, giving the Christians Tyre, Acre, and Jaffa, with free access for pilgrims to visit the holy places. On his way home, Richard was captured by the Duke of Austria, whom he had slighted at Acre, and was held for ransom for fifteen months. In 1227 CE the German emperor Frederick II led a Crusade while he was under the ban of excommunication. He received no help from the Military Orders or the Christian clergy in Palestine, but so skillful was he in diplomacy and military tactics that he succeeded in arranging a treaty with the Sultan whereby the Christians once again had control of Jerusalem and other holy cities. It seems ironic that one of the most successful Crusades was led by an excommunicate with very little bloodshed, who regained considerable territory by diplomacy alone.

But the Christians in Palestine were slow to occupy the city, and Frederick returned home with his army, so that within a few years Jerusalem was back in Muslim hands. King Louis IX of France (1226–1270 CE, known as Saint Louis) made two attempts to regain Palestine, but with limited success. On the first he was captured, and he died in Tunis in 1270 CE on the second attempt. Within twenty years the Arab forces succeeded in gaining control of all of Palestine. With the fall of Acre in 1291, the period of the Crusades came to a close, having lasted about two hundred years.

Today historians generally agree that the Crusades produced

no positive results and many that were negative. They failed in their original purpose, they did not halt the advance of Islam, and instead of helping the Eastern Empire (the original request) they hastened its demise in the disastrous Fourth Crusade, thus hardening the schism between East and West. Preached as the fulfillment of spiritual ideals, the Crusades themselves were usually impelled by baser motives with conduct that disgraced the crusaders' religion. Some observers suggest, perhaps with a touch of cynicism, that Europe's civil strife was reduced by the exodus of a large number of quarrelsome landless nobility, many of whom failed to return.[37]

Two prominent Crusader castles often visited by pilgrims to the Holy Land are Belvoir and Nimrod's Fortress. Belvoir sits 1,500 feet above the plain in eastern lower Galilee. It was built by the Hospitallers in the twelfth century. It saw fierce fighting from 1180 to 1184, and it was again besieged by Saladin after his victory at the Horns of Hattin. Because of the valor of the defenders, Saladin permitted them to leave without harm after they capitulated. In 1968 a team of archaeologists led by Meir Ben-Dov restored the beautifully impressive fortress to be accessible to visitors.

Nimrod's Fortress, named for the mythical character of legendary strength, sits on Israel's northern border in the Golan Heights. It changed hands several times between Crusaders and Muslim, but after 1156 CE remained in Muslim hands.

The present walls of Jerusalem's Old City were built under Suleiman in the sixteenth century, four hundred years after the Crusades, but in places they rest upon Crusader foundations.

Historical Update from the Ottoman Period to Now

In 1517 the Ottoman Turks defeated the Mamelukes and gained control of Palestine, along with other areas of the Middle East. During this period a certain degree of religious toleration was present in the land and small communities of Jews and Christians thrived. In the middle and later parts of the nineteenth century Zionism was spreading throughout Europe and thousands of Jews were emigrating to Palestine with the goal of establishing a Jewish homeland here. At the same time the land witnessed the rise in Arab nationalist groups, not only in Palestine but throughout the Middle East.

When World War I began, Turkey aligned itself with Germany against the Western Allies. Palestine was being governed by a Turkish military general headquartered in Damascus. The British funded and supported the formation of an Arab army led by Prince Feisal of Saudia Arabia with the assistance of T. E. Lawrence, an officer in the British army. They, along with General Edmund Allenby, commander of the British army in Egypt and Palestine, drove the Turks out of the country in 1918.

During the war a controversial proclamation was issued by the British Foreign Secretary, Arthur James Balfour. The goals of the Balfour Declaration were disputed by Arabs and Jews. Jewish people interpreted the declaration as supporting the establishment of a Jewish homeland in Palestine. Arabs refused to accept this interpretation. The British national interest in the Middle East was to have access to the Suez Canal. Therefore, they did not offer an interpretation of the Balfour Declaration in hopes of not alienating support for their interests from the Arabs or Jews. The end result of this confusion was the action taken by the League of Nations giving the British control over Palestine. The period known as the British Mandate rule began in 1922 and ended in the establishment of the Jewish state in 1948. Due to the confusion concerning which groups would have an independent homeland in Palestine, there was widespread unrest and acts of violence were committed by Arabs against Jews, Jews against Arabs, and both against the British. Frequently there was rioting in Palestine and acts of political terrorism by rival factions against one another.

Tensions in Palestine eased during World War II. The British, Jews, and Arabs were united in their opposition to Germany. However, after the end of World War II and the revelations of Nazi atrocities against the Jews of Europe, there was an even stronger movement among Jews and Western allies to establish a Jewish homeland in Palestine. Finally, the United Nations voted in 1947 to divide Palestine into separate Jewish and Arab states. This proposal, adopted by the UN on November 29, 1947, was accepted by Jews and rejected by Arabs. After an independent state of Israel was announced on May 14, 1948, five neighboring Arab states declared war on Israel on May 15, 1948. The Israelis defeated the invading Arab armies and took control of additional land which had been assigned to the Palestinian Arab state by the UN. The Israeli army also occupied the Western half of Jerusalem as a result of this war.

Even though their armies had been defeated by the Israelis, the invading Arabs nations refused to recognize Israel's right to exist. As a result of this non-recognition there were to be several other major wars between Jews and Arabs. In 1956 Israel was invaded by Egypt through the Gaza Strip. The Israelis captured the Gaza Strip on November, 1956. In 1967, in what is known as the Six-Day war between Israel and the Arab nations of Syria, Jordan, and Egypt, the Israelis were again successful in defeating the combined Arab army. As a result of this war Israel occupied the West Bank, Gaza Strip, the Golan Heights, and the Sinai Peninsula. The occupation of the West Bank gave Israel control of East Jerusalem for the first time since the Roman destruction of 135 CE; for the first time in almost two thousand years the Western Wall was under Jewish control. Finally, in 1973 Egypt and Syria again attacked Israel in what became known as the Yom Kippur War. As a result of this war the Israelis annexed the Golan Heights and established settlements in the Sinai. The Sinai was returned to Egypt as a part of the Camp David agreement brokered by President Carter of the United States.

PART 2:
BIBLICAL SITES

ISRAEL (Outside Jerusalem)

Abu Ghosh (Kiriath-jearim)

Biblical References: 1 Samuel 7:1; 1 Chronicles 13:5-8

Abu Ghosh is a small village about 8 miles (13 km) west-northwest of Jerusalem on the highway that connects Jerusalem with Tel Aviv.

The only significant biblical events connected with Abu Ghosh are associated with the capture of the Ark of the Covenant by the Philistines at the battle of Aphek.[1] According to 1 Samuel 5–6, the Ark was taken to Ashdod, where its presence among the Philistines caused problems, provoking its return to the Israelites. The Ark was first taken to Beth-shemesh and then to Kiriath-jearim, where it remained for twenty years. After David became king and relocated the nation's capital in Jerusalem, he had the Ark moved from Kiriath-jearim to Jerusalem (2 Samuel 6:12ff.; 1 Chronicles 13:5-8).

Acco (Acre)

Biblical References: Judges 1:31-32; Acts 21:7 (Ptolemais)

Acco is a beautiful coastal city on the Mediterranean Sea between Haifa and the modern border between Israel and

Lebanon. It is an ancient city with an interesting history, both before and after the biblical periods.

Acco was mentioned as early as the nineteenth century BCE in Egyptian texts. Judges 1:31-32 reports that during the period of conquest and settlement, members of the tribe of Asher were not able to drive the indigenous population from Acco; the city remained in the hands of people who were probably the forerunners of the Phoenicians, who later controlled the area. Later the city was taken by Alexander the Great, who established a mint here in 333 BCE. After the death of Alexander, the city was given to his general Ptolemy and was renamed Ptolemais. In 200 BCE the Seleucids gained control of the city, to be succeeded by the Romans when Pompey took the land in 63 BCE. It was this Roman city that Paul visited during his third missionary journey (Acts 21:7).

Some nonbiblical historical events associated with Acco include visits by both Marco Polo and St. Francis of Assisi. During the Crusades, Acco was refortified by the European armies, and it became an important trade center at this time. The city served as the capital of the Crusaders after Jerusalem was lost to the Moslems. The present walls of the Old City of Acco date to the Crusader occupation. In 1187 Saladin, the famous Arab leader, took the city, only to lose it again ten years later to the Crusaders under the leadership of Richard the Lionhearted. Finally, in 1291, the Mamelukes retook the city from the Crusaders after a forty-three day siege.

Ai

Biblical References: Genesis 12:8; 13:3; Joshua 7:2–8:29; Ezra 2:28; Nehemiah 7:32; Jeremiah 49:3.

Although there is some debate about the exact location of ancient Ai, it is now generally identified with the modern site of et-Tell. In Hebrew, Ai means "ruin," thus paralleling the modern Arabic name, which means "mound" or "heap." Et-Tell is about a mile east of Beitin, the site of biblical Bethel, just west and north of Jerusalem.

Ai is best known for two biblical events. First, Abraham is said to have camped between Bethel and Ai on his migration to Canaan and to have built an altar here (Genesis 12:8; 13:3). Second, Ai is reported to have been the second city conquered by Joshua and his army during the Israelite invasion of the land (Joshua 7:2–8:29). According to this account, Joshua's first attempt to conquer the city failed due to the sin of Achan; on the second attempt, after Achan had been punished for his disobedience, Joshua succeeded in taking the city. Excavations at the site have revealed the presence of a small, unwalled Iron Age village, but not of a large, fortified city, raising questions as to whether the biblical account of the Israelite conquest of Ai may have referred originally to the capture of nearby Bethel.

Aphek (Antipatris)

Biblical References: Joshua 12:18; 1 Samuel 4:1-11; 29:1; 31:1-7; 1 Kings 20:30; 2 Kings 13:17; Acts 23:31.

This site is located several miles to the east-northeast of Tel Aviv in the Plain of Sharon at modern Ras el-Ain. Aphek was mentioned in ancient Egyptian texts as early as the nineteenth century BCE, and as early as 3000 BCE there was a walled city here, indicating that it was already a place of some prominence.

In the twelfth century BCE, the Philistines launched a military campaign against the Israelites from Aphek. The Israelites brought the Ark of the Covenant to their camp, believing that it would guarantee them victory in battle (1 Samuel 4:1-11). However, during the battle the Israelites were defeated, and the Ark of the Covenant was lost to the Philistines. A second battle between these two armies is associated with Aphek. It was from Aphek that the Philistines launched the battle of Gilboa, in which Saul and Jonathan were killed (1 Samuel 29:1).

Under Herod the Great, Aphek was restored and renamed. Josephus (*Jewish War* 1:417) comments that "Herod was a lover of his father, if any other person was so; for he made a monument for his father, even that city which he had built in the finest plain that was in his kingdom, and which had rivers and trees in abundance, and named it Antipatris." This city, named for Herod's father, was built on the site of Old Testament Aphek. By the New Testament (Roman) Period, Antipatris had become a stopping point for people traveling between Jerusalem and Caesarea Maritima. Paul spent the night here when he was traveling to Caesarea to stand trial (Acts 23:31).

Arad

Biblical References: Numbers 21:1-3; 33:40; Joshua 12:14; Judges 1:16; 2 Kings 18:22; 22–23.

Although not mentioned often in the Bible, Arad is a very important Old Testament site. It is found on the northern fringe of the Negev Desert five miles (8 km) west of the modern Israeli city of the same name and approximately 20 miles (32 km) east of Beersheva. Due to the excellent preservation of its ruins and the important historical finds uncovered there, Arad is one of the most interesting sites in the land. However, its remote location has prevented all but a few visitors from seeing it.

The settlement of the site dates back to the late Chalcolithic Period (roughly 3400 BCE). Archaeologists have discovered that the evolution of the site took place in three stages. The first stage was the Chalcolithic settlement, involving a small population and covering a period of time between 3400 and 3200 BCE. An early Bronze Age city occupied the site from 3000–2900 BCE, when the Canaanites built a fortified city, which was to become an important commercial center. This settlement was destroyed by 2700 BCE and was not resettled until the Early Iron Age (1200 BCE).

The next important phase in the history of the site is from the reign of Solomon (c. 960–920 BCE), when Arad was a military outpost guarding Israel's southern border. At this time the settlement was smaller and located on a high hill overlooking the old Canaanite city. This area is known today as the Citadel. Habitation of this site continued into the Byzantine Period (324–640 CE).

The excavations of ancient Arad have yielded several important pieces of information. First, they have disclosed that the Canaanites were a sophisticated people who were capable of building well-planned cities. At first one might wonder why the Canaanites would build Arad below the hill upon which the Israelite Citadel would later be located. Yohanan Aharoni offers this explanation:

> At the lowest place in (the city ruins), there is an artificial depression, the remnant of a big water cistern in which water could be collected from the entire town area. . . . The Arad ridge is formed of Eocene limestone which holds water well even without coating or plastering. Evidently, the climate has not changed in any appreciable manner from that period to the present time. Furthermore, it is obvious from the geological structure of the area that near Arad there is no well or other water source. The water supply came, therefore, solely from the collection of rain. This is limited to a few winter days, and does not exceed an annual average of between 150 and 200 millimeters.[2]

The city was built in such a manner as to maximize its ability to catch and collect rainwater. Aharoni has estimated that the central water cistern or reservoir could collect and hold approximately two and a half million gallons of water a year.[3]

Second, Arad reveals much about Canaanite construction practices from the Early Bronze Period. Several houses have been uncovered and at least one has been partially restored, disclosing the fact that the typical Canaanite house found here was built below the surface. The houses were entered through a doorway with steps down to the floor of the house. Most of the houses were part of an insula complex,[4] but some were not. The houses contained one or two rooms; when there were two rooms present it is believed that the larger room served as a family room and the smaller was used for cooking and storage. Benches were placed around the walls of the larger family room.

1: Arad: Two-room House

Third, the excavations at Arad render problematic the role played by the city in the Exodus and conquest traditions of the Bible. Numbers 21:1ff. (and Numbers 33:40ff.) states that the king of Arad would not allow the Hebrews to enter Canaan through his country. The Hebrews had to choose an alternative route through the Moab Desert along the eastern side of the Dead Sea. Later, Joshua 12:14 lists the king of Arad as one of the kings defeated during the Conquest Period. No physical evidence has been found to confirm these events in the excavation and restoration of Arad.

Other major discoveries at Arad relate to the Iron Age city/fortress that occupied the Citadel. During excavations here archaeologists discovered the remains of an Iron Age Israelite temple with an inner sanctuary, or Holy of Holies, patterned after that of the Temple in Jerusalem. Since our knowledge of the Holy of Holies in Jerusalem has heretofore depended on its description in the Bible, this discovery is very important. It is possible that Solomon had this worship center built so that the

2: Arad: Holy of Holies

military garrison stationed in Arad would have a place for worship without making the long trip to Jerusalem.

Excavations also have uncovered two *mazzevot* (standing stone pillars) inside the Holy of Holies and two incense altars just outside it at the entrance to the sacred area. Yet, only one of each was required. Jack Campbell, one of the people involved in the excavation and restoration of the site and the manager of Arad for the Israel National Parks Authority, suggests that the extra *mazzevah* and incense altar might have been placed here because the original ones were defiled or contaminated by the Egyptians during their military campaign against the city under Pharaoh Shishak in 920 BCE. The original altars and *mazzevot* found here are now on display at the Israel Museum in Jerusalem.

Adjacent to the Holy of Holies site sits a sacrificial altar where burnt offerings were made. The altar is most interesting in that its dimensions conform to the requirements found in Exodus 27: "You shall make the altar . . . five cubits long and five cubits wide; the altar shall be square, and it shall be three cubits high" (27:1).[5] Furthermore, the altar is constructed of unhewn stones. This satisfies additional requirements from the book of Exodus: "But if you make for me an altar of stone, do not build it of hewn stones; for if you use a chisel upon it you profane it" (Exodus 20:25; see also 1 Kings 6:7).

3: Arad: Iron Age Altar

The reasons why this temple fell into disuse and ceased to function are unclear. The Bible suggests two possible explanations: the reforms of kings Hezekiah and Josiah. It is possible that Hezekiah was responsible for the ending of sacrificial worship at Arad. Second Kings 18 tells the story of Sennacherib's military campaign against Judah. One of Sennacherib's servants came to Jerusalem and said to Hezekiah and the citizens of the city, " 'But if you say to me, "We rely on the LORD our God," is it not he whose high places and altars Hezekiah has removed, saying to Judah and to Jerusalem, "You shall worship before this altar in Jerusalem"?' " (2 Kings 18:22). This passage indicates that Hezekiah had been destroying altars and high places outside Jerusalem. Josiah carried out a similar program of removing high places and altars outside Jerusalem. Second Kings 23:8 reports that Josiah "brought all the priests out of the towns of Judah, and defiled the high places where the priests had made offerings, from Geba to Beer-sheba." In the final analysis no one knows which, if either, of these kings is responsible for removing the high place from Arad, but it seems likely that one of them did do this during his acts of reform.

4: *Arad: Sketch of Citadel Ruins*

LEGEND
1 City Hall
2 Israelite Fortress
3 Water reservoir
4 The sacred compound
5 The palace
6 Restored dwelling

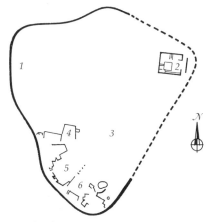

Ashdod

Biblical References: Joshua 13:1-3; 15:46-47; 1 Samuel 5:1-8; 6:17-18; Amos 1:8; 1 Maccabees 5:68; 10:84; 11:4 (as Azotus).[6]

Ashdod was one of the five principal cities of the Philistines. The ruins are found roughly halfway between Gaza and Tel Aviv, about 3 miles from the Mediterranean Sea. Ashdod is best remembered as being the place to which the Ark of the Covenant was brought after it was captured by the Philistines during the battle of Aphek (1 Samuel 5:1).[7]

King Uzziah of Judah destroyed the walls of the city during his war against the Philistines, along with those of Gath and Jabneh (2 Chronicles 26:6), and it was later captured by the Assyrians under Sargon. During the Hellenistic Period, Ashdod was known as Azotus. During the war between the Seleucids and the Maccabees many Greeks sought refuge in Azotus before the city was taken by Judas Maccabeus (1 Maccabees 5:68). Judas removed all the pagan religious symbols from the city. Later the city was burned by Judas's brother Jonathan (1 Maccabees 10:84-85).

Josephus (*Antiquities* 14:75, 88) reports that the Romans took control of the city after the successful invasion by Pompey in 63 BCE. Later, according to Josephus (*Antiquities* 17:188-189), Herod the Great "bequeathed Jamnia, and Ashdod, and Phasaelis, to Salome his sister."

Ashkelon

Biblical References: Judges 1:18; 14:19; 1 Samuel 6:17; 2 Samuel 1:20.

Ashkelon, one of the five principal cities of the Philistines, is located in Israel's southern Coastal Plain (in the Philistine Plain). Its history dates to 3,000 BCE. Biblically speaking, Ashkelon is best remembered for its association with Samson: "Then the spirit of the LORD rushed on him [Samson], and he went down to Ashkelon. He killed thirty men of the town, took their spoil, and gave the festal garments to those who had explained the riddle" (Judges 14:19). Samson killed these thirty men for their clothing, to pay a gambling debt.

The Assyrian king Tiglath-pileser III invaded the city in about 734 BCE, but it soon regained its independence; it joined Judah's revolt against Assyria during the reign of Hezekiah, until Sennacherib reconquered it for Assyria in 701 BCE. After the fall of Assyria, Egypt controlled Ashkelon briefly, before it was destroyed by Nebuchadnezzar in 609 BCE (see Jeremiah 47:5-7). It became a Ptolemaic possession during the Hellenistic Period.

Herod the Great may have been born in Ashkelon; his grandfather had been a community leader in the temple and cult of Apollo here. Herod spent more money remodeling this city than on any other of the former Philistine cities. Josephus (*Jewish War* 1:422b) writes that he "built baths and costly fountains, and also cloisters round a court, that were admirable both for their workmanship and largeness." With all this special attention given to Ashkelon it is clear that the city was favored by Herod. After his death, Augustus Caesar gave Herod's palace in Ashkelon to Salome, Herod's sister (Josephus, *Antiquities* 17:321).

During the first Jewish revolt (66–70 CE) the people of Ashkelon sided with the Romans against the Zealots, and they were rewarded by grants of many special privileges. Ashkelon became a city of great wealth, status, and power from 70 CE until it fell to Caliph Omar during the Islamic invasions of the seventh century.

Azekah

Biblical References: Joshua 15:35; 1 Samuel 17:1; Jeremiah 34:6-7.

Located in the Shephelah[8] near Tell Lachish, Azekah was for-
tifed under Rehoboam (2 Chronicles 11:9). It was one of the last
of the Judean cities to fall to Nebuchadnezzer during his campaign, beginning in 597 BCE (Jeremiah 34:7). Azekah is mentioned prominently in the Lachish letters,[9] one of which speaks
of Azekah as the people of Lachish await the advancing Babylonian army: "And let [my lord] know that we are watching for
the signals of Lachish, according to all the indications which my
lord hath given, for we cannot see Azekah."[10] This passage
implies that Azekah had been destroyed by this time.

Banyas (Caesarea Philippi)

Biblical Reference: Matthew 16:13-20

Banyas is a modern corruption of the ancient name Panyas
(or Panias). It is located at the southwestern foot of Mount Hermon and north of the Sea of Galilee, and it was known as Caesarea Philippi during the time of Jesus. During the Canaanite
Period, worship centers for the god Baal were located at this
site. Later, during the Hellenistic Period, the god Pan was worshiped here, hence the name.

In 198 BCE the Seleucids defeated the Ptolomies in the general
vicinity of Panyas in the final battle of their long war, gaining
control of Judea/Palestine. Later, the Romans took this area
through the conquests of Pompey. After the death of Herod the
Great this territory was given to Herod's son Philip. Herod
Philip built Caesarea Philippi as his capital, naming it after Caesar (Tiberias) and himself.

Josephus, speaking of the Cave of Pan, writes that "hard by
the foundations of Jordan . . . there is a top of a mountain that is
raised to an immense height, and at its side, beneath, or at its
bottom, a dark cave opens itself; within which is a horrible
precipice, that descends abruptly to a vast depth; it contains a

mighty quantity of water, which is immovable; and when any-body lets down anything to measure the depth of the earth beneath the water, no length of cord is sufficient to reach it" (*Jewish War* 1:404-406). Bargil Pixner, a scholar in residence at the Dormition Abbey in Jerusalem, suggests that pagans may have made sacrifices to the gods and demons of the underworld at this cave, which was thought of as the passageway to Hades during the Hellenistic and Roman periods.[11]

The Gospel of Matthew places Peter's confession of Jesus as the Christ in the area of Caesarea Philippi (Matthew 16:13-20). It is possible that Jesus and his disciples were somewhere in the

vicinity of the Cave of Pan when Jesus asked them, "Who do people say that the Son of Man is?" After Peter's confession, Jesus stated that the "gates of Hades" could not stand against the church (Matthew 16:13-18).

5: Banyas: The Cave of Pan

Beersheva (Beer-Sheba)

Biblical References: Genesis 21:14, 33; 26:23-33; 28:10; 46:1-7; Judges 20:1; 1 Samuel 3:20; 8:2; 15:2-9; 1 Kings 19:3; and others.

Tell Beersheva is located roughly 5 miles (8 km) east of the modern city of Beersheva. It is approximately 40 miles (64 km) south-southwest of Jerusalem and is known as the "Capital of the Negev." The name Beersheva (or Beer-sheba) has at least two possible meanings. First, it could mean the "Well of the Seven," since it was here that Abraham traded seven lambs for a well (Genesis 21:25-31). Second, it could mean the "Well of the Oath," in honor of either Abraham's oath with Abimelech (Genesis 21:31) or Isaac's oath with Abimelech (Genesis 26:28-33).

In the Old Testament, Beersheva came to be symbolic as the southernmost border of Israel. The phrase "from Dan to Beersheva" was used to define Israel's geographical limits (north and south), and it occurs many times in the Bible (Judges 20:1; 1 Samuel 3:20; 2 Samuel 3:10, etc.).

Beersheva is best known for its association with the Patriarchs. It was here that Abraham made a treaty with Abimelech and that Isaac built an altar in memory of Yahweh's promise to Isaac's father. Jacob left from here for Egypt during a time of famine (Genesis 46:1-7), leading to his reunion with his son Joseph.

Beersheva is also mentioned in the Bible as the place where the corrupt sons of Samuel—Joel and Abijah—served as judges (1 Samuel 8:2). Later, Saul launched his attack against the Amalekites from Beersheva (1 Samuel 15:2-9). It was during this campaign that Saul disobeyed God's command, which led to God's rejection of Saul as king. Later, Elijah visited Beersheva when he fled from Jezebel (1 Kings 19:3).

Beersheva, along with rest of the Negev, was taken from Judah by the Edomites in the seventh century BCE, and it was regained under Nehemiah in the sixth century BCE (Nehemiah 11:27).

Today, Beersheva is a center for Bedouin culture in southern Israel.

Bethany

Biblical References: Matthew 21:17; 26:6-13; Mark 11:11; 14:3-9; Luke 10:38-42; 19:29; 24:50-51; John 11:1-44; 12:1-11.

Bethany is a small village found on the eastern slope of the Mount of Olives, approximately 2 miles (3 km) east of Jerusalem. The name means "House of the Poor" or "House of the Afflicted." It could also mean "House of Ananiah."[12] Bethany was the home of Jesus' friends Mary, Martha, and Lazarus. Jesus was a frequent guest in their home, and during the week before his arrest and execution, he stayed here with these friends.

The Gospel traditions associate with Bethany four events related to the life and ministry of Jesus. First, Jesus had a discussion here with Mary and Martha in their home concerning priorities (Luke 10:38-42). Second, Jesus was anointed here by a woman in the home of Simon the leper (Matthew 26:6-13). Third, Jesus performed the miracle of raising Lazarus from his tomb here (John 11:1-44). Finally, Jesus shared a last meal here with his friends (John 12:1-11) before his entry into Jerusalem.

Excavations at Bethany have revealed the remains of a fourth-century church built over the traditional site of Lazarus's tomb; it was replaced by a fifth-century church, which was extensively renovated through the centuries. A new church, built in the 1950s over the older foundations, today preserves the traditional tomb of Lazarus.

Bethel

Biblical References: Genesis 12:7-8; 13:3-4; 28:10-22; Joshua 12:16; 16:2; 18:21; Judges 1:22-26; 4:5; 20:18-28; 1 Samuel 7:16; 10:3; 13:2; 1 Kings 12:25-33; 13:1; 2 Kings 2:2-3; 23-24; Amos 3:14; 4:4; 7:10-17.

Bethel, which means "House of God," is located about 12 miles (19 km) north of Jerusalem, at the site of modern Beitin, and was first settled as early as the third millennium BCE.

Many important biblical events took place in and around Bethel. The city is prominently identified with the Patriarchs. Abraham camped here and built an altar between Bethel and Ai (Genesis 12:7-8). Abraham and Lot separated here (Genesis 13:2-7). It was here that Jacob dreamed of a ladder (or a staircase) connecting heaven and earth (Genesis 28:10-22), and it was in Bethel that God renewed his covenant with Jacob (Genesis 35:1-15).

At the time of the Israelite invasion and conquest, Bethel was a Canaanite royal city (Joshua 12:16). Excavations have revealed that this city was destroyed in the late thirteenth century BCE, a date that corresponds to the Israelite invasion of the land. The Bible does not mention Bethel as being one of the cities conquered by the invading Israelites, but Ai, which was a much smaller, unfortified village at the time, is mentioned. Because Ai and Bethel are located so near to each other, it is possible that the biblical account of the destruction of Ai (Joshua 7:2–8:29) actually refers to the conquest of Bethel.

During the Period of the Judges, Bethel was also an important city. Deborah lived and judged in the general vicinity of Bethel (Judges 4:5). It was also visited by Samuel on his itinerant rounds while serving as a judge (1 Samuel 7:16; 10:3). The city served as an important worship center for the Israelites during this period (Judges 20:18), and the Ark of the Covenant was temporarily kept here before it was moved to Shiloh.

During the reign of Jeroboam I of the Northern Kingdom of Israel (during the Divided Monarchy), one of the nation's two worship centers was located here (1 Kings 12:26-33; 1 Chronicles 13:8-9). The other worship center was at Dan. In establishing these two centers of worship for the Northern Kingdom, Jeroboam may have hoped to keep his subjects from returning to Jerusalem for worship, and thus to remove any sentimental or nostalgic attachment to Judah, Jerusalem, and the Temple.

Bethlehem

*Biblical References: Ruth; 1 Samuel 16:1-4; 17:12, 15; 20:6, 28;
2 Samuel 23:13-18; Micah 5:2; Matthew 2:1, 6, 7-16; Luke 2:4-16;
John 7:42.*

Bethlehem, which means "House of Bread" in Hebrew (in Arabic it means "House of Meat"), is located approximately 6 miles (10 km) south of Jerusalem.

Several significant biblical events occurred in and around Bethlehem. The story of Ruth and Boaz is set here. Bethlehem was David's family home, and it was here that Samuel anointed him king (1 Samuel 16). Bethlehem was one of the Judean cities fortified by Rehoboam. Jesus was born in Bethlehem, and according to the Gospel of Matthew, Herod the Great had all of the male children under the age of two killed because he feared

111

that a new king had been born here. Today there is debate among some biblical scholars, both in Israel and abroad, about Mary and Joseph's presence here at the time of Jesus' birth. It has been suggested by some that Bethlehem, not Nazareth, was the home of Jesus' parents. There are at least three reasons why this is plausible. First, the Bible implies that this may be so. The Gospel of Luke seems unambiguous in claiming Nazareth as their home. However, according to the Gospel of Matthew, Mary and Joseph were still in Bethlehem after Jesus' birth when Joseph received a warning in a dream to flee to Egypt in order to avoid Herod's massacre of the infants (Matthew 2:13-15). It was in response to two other dreams that Mary and Joseph returned with Jesus to Nazareth and settled there (Matthew 2:19-23b).

Second, it is unlikely that a pregnant woman would have been allowed to make the long journey from Nazareth to Jerusalem without her husband to visit her relative Elizabeth (Luke 1:39ff.). Third, it is unlikely that Mary would have gone with Joseph to Bethlehem for the census. If she was in the latter stage of her pregnancy, it would have been irresponsible to have brought her along on such a long and difficult journey.

These three arguments seem to make a strong case for locating Joseph and Mary's home in Bethlehem rather than Nazareth. There is one other reason for supporting this claim that should be mentioned. The New Testament Apocrypha also locates Mary's home in the Jerusalem area.[13] If she lived in Bethlehem or even near Bethlehem, Mary would have been near to her own family as well as her cousin Elizabeth.

The focal point of Bethlehem today is the Church of the Nativity. The church dates to the reign of Constantine; its construction began in 329, and it was dedicated by Queen Helena on May 31, 339. Although the church has been renovated several times over the centuries, the beautiful mosaic floor of the original church has been preserved. The entrance to the church is through a doorway, which was reduced in height during the Crusades to keep people from riding into the church on horseback.

Badly damaged during a Samaritan revolt in 521–528 CE, the church was rebuilt during the later sixth century in very much its present form by Emperor Justinian. It is the one church in Israel that was not destroyed during the Persian invasion of 614 CE. Mosaics of the three magi in Persian costume helped to save the church, because they resembled the physical appearance of the invaders, who assumed that the place was sacred to earlier people from Arabia, and consequently they spared the church.

6: Bethlehem: The Church of the Nativity

Bethlehem is also remembered for its importance in early church history. Saint Jerome moved to Bethlehem in 384 CE. While he was here he wrote, among other works, the Vulgate, a translation of the Old and New Testaments into Latin. He lived here for some thirty-six years, dying in 420 CE. The cave where Jerome lived is adjacent to the Church of the Nativity and under the Latin (Roman Catholic) Church of St. Catherine.

Three fields around Bethlehem are known as the "Shepherd's Fields." These are traditionally associated with the shepherds to whom the birth of Jesus was announced. Two of the fields are owned by churches (Greek Orthodox and Roman Catholic); the third is privately owned. All three of these fields are still used for pasturing sheep and goats or for farming. No one knows which, if any, of these sites relates to the first Christmas, nor can one be certain that the story found in Luke 2 is historically reliable.

Bethphage

Biblical References: Zechariah 9:9; Matthew 21:1-11; Mark 11:1-11; Luke 19:29-40.

Bethphage is located on the eastern side of the Mount of Olives, between Bethany and Jerusalem. The name means "House of Unripe Figs." According to Christian tradition and the witness of the Synoptic Gospels, Jesus began his Palm Sunday processional into Jerusalem from here. Anyone entering Jerusalem from the east would have had to pass through Bethphage.

Bethsaida

Biblical References: Matthew 11:21; Mark 6:4-5; Luke 9:10; 10:13; John 1:44; 12:21.

Bethsaida is found on the northern shore of the Sea of Galilee, about 3 1/2 miles (6 km) east-northeast of Capernaum. Bethsaida means "House of the Fisher." It was the home of several of Jesus' disciples: Philip, Andrew, Peter, and perhaps James and John (John 1:44; 12:21). The city was cursed by Jesus for not repenting, even though the residents there witnessed many of Jesus' miracles and heard his teaching (Matthew 11:21; Luke 10:13).

Although Christian tradition locates the miracle of the multiplication of the fish and loaves near Tabgha, on the western shore of the Sea of Galilee, it may have taken place near Bethsaida. Luke mentions Bethsaida specifically in relation to the miracle, but no one can be certain where it took place.

Beth Shean (Scythopolis)

Biblical References: Joshua 17:11; Judges 1:27; 1 Samuel 31:10; 1 Kings 4:12.

Beth Shean is located on the Via Maris, an ancient trade or caravan route that runs through the Jezreel Valley. It is approximately 15 miles (24 km) south of the Sea of Galilee on the modern highway through the Rift Valley. The meaning of the name Beth Shean has been lost.

The habitation of Beth Shean dates to the Chalcolithic Period, about 3500 BCE, and continues through today. The city, which has known over 5,000 years of continuous habitation, was first mentioned in early Egyptian texts. The Israelite occupation began in the Late Bronze/Early Iron Period with the settlement of the land by Hebrew invaders. When the land was divided among the twelve tribes of Israel, the city was given to the tribe of Manasseh. However, the Israelites were not able completely to drive out the local inhabitants (Judges 1:27).

During the Iron Age, Beth Shean was occupied by the Philistines and later by the Israelites. The Philistines occupied the city during the reign of Saul. This occupation has been confirmed through excavations by the discovery of large quantities of Philistine jewelry, pottery, tools, and arms dating to this period. The Bible also affirms that Beth Shean was a Philistine city at this time (1 Samuel 31:10). After Saul's death during the battle of Mount Gilboa, his body was taken to Beth Shean and displayed on the city walls. By the reign of Solomon, the city had come under the control of Israel (1 Kings 4:12).

During the Hellenistic Period the city's name was changed to Scythopolis, meaning "The City of the Scythians." The Scythians had been mercenaries who served the Ptolomies. In 63 BCE, Pompey took the city for Rome. Scythopolis was made one of the ten cities of the Decapolis, the only one found on the western side of the Jordan River. Following the Islamic conquest, the name reverted to Beth Shean (in Arabic, Bisan).

Today Beth Shean offers visitors impressive sites to visit. The first is the 262-foot-high tell of Old Testament Beth Shean.

Archaeologists have discovered twenty strata or occupation levels here, including the remains of a Byzantine temple and two synagogues dating from the fifth and sixth centuries CE. The second notable site is the remains of the Roman city located at the foot of the tell, including the best preserved Roman theater in Israel; it dates to 200 CE and could have accomodated 5,000 spectators.

7: Beth Shean: The Tell

8: Beth Shean: Roman Theater

Beth Shemesh

Biblical References: Joshua 15:10; 21:16; Judges 1:33; 1 Samuel 6–7:2; 2 Kings 14:8-14; 2 Chronicles 25:21; 28:18.

Beth Shemesh is located about 12 miles (20 km) west-south-west of Jerusalem in the northern fringe of the Shephelah, in the Sorek Valley. The name Beth Shemesh means "House of the Sun (or of the sun-god, Shemesh)." The city is best remembered for its relationship to the Ark of the Covenant. The Philistines returned the Ark to the Israelites here after they had captured it during the battle of Aphek (see 1 Samuel 4:1-11; 6:12, 19-20). From Beth Shemesh the Ark was taken to Kiriath-jearim (Abu Ghosh). During this period, Beth Shemesh was a fortified outpost between Judah and Philistia.

During the reigns of kings Amaziah of Judah (800–783 BCE) and Jehoash of Israel (801–786 BCE) a major battle between the two kingdoms was fought here, in which Jehoash defeated and captured Amaziah. From here the army of Israel moved on to destroy and plunder Jerusalem (2 Kings 14:8-14).

117

Throughout the Old Testament period Beth Shemesh was well-known as a wine and olive producing center. The Philistines seem to have taken it from Judah during the reign of Ahaz; it was destroyed in the sixth century BCE, probably by Nebuchadnezzar, and never regained its former status.

Caesarea Maritima

Biblical References: Acts 8:40; 9:30; 10:1-9, 23-48; 12:18-19; 21:8; 23:23, 31-33; 25:1-12; and other references in Acts.

The impressive ruins of Caesarea Maritima are found on the Mediterranean coast about halfway between Tel Aviv and Haifa. In the New Testament period the port city was known as Caesarea Maritima (Caesarea by the Sea) to distinguish it from Caesarea Philippi. Today it is known simply as Caesarea. The city was built by Herod the Great and was one of his greatest accomplishments.

The first city located on this site was known as Strato's Tower. It was established during the fourth century BCE and named for the Phoenician king Strato. Josephus reports that the site was given to Herod the Great by Caesar Augustus after the deaths of Mark Antony and Cleopatra (*Antiquities* 15:213-217). Herod began a massive building program to enlarge the city and to construct a deep water port. He also renamed the city Caesarea in order to flatter Emperor Augustus. The construction began in 22 BCE and was completed in 10 BCE.

During the reign of Herod the Great, Caesarea was one of the largest ports in the known world. The plan of the city was well-conceived. One of its more interesting features was an elaborate underground sewer system, which was designed in such a way as to allow it to be flushed clean each day by the rising and falling tides.

After the death of Herod, the city was given to his son Archelaus. However, when Archelaus proved to be a poor administrator he was replaced with a Roman administrator (a prefect or governor). At this time Caesarea became the seat of the Roman government in Judea/Palestine, which it remained for over six hundred years. One of these Roman governors was Pontius Pilate. During the excavations of Caesarea a stone tablet was discovered with the following inscription: "Pontius Pilate, the Prefect of Judea, has dedicated to the people of Caesarea a temple in honor of Tiberius."[14] This is the only inscription ever found specifically naming Pilate, who lived here between 26 and 36 CE.

9: Caesarea: The Pilate Inscription

From the time of Herod through the First Jewish Revolt (66 CE) Caesarea's population was mixed between Jews and Gentiles. Josephus reports that there was great tension between these two groups in the city. Eventually the First Revolt began when a group of Gentiles desecrated a synagogue in Caesarea (*Jewish War* 2:284-308).

Several important biblical events took place in Caesarea. Philip preached here (Acts 8:40); Peter baptized Cornelius here (Acts 10:1ff., 24ff.); Herod Agrippa died in Caesarea (Acts 12:19-23); and Paul visited the city on several occasions (Acts 9:30; 18:22; 21:8; 23:23). Paul was also tried here by Festus (Acts 25:13) and departed from Caesarea to Rome, where he would be martyred (Acts 27:1-2).

Like most other historical sites in the Holy Land, several historical periods are represented in Caesarea. When visiting the site today one finds Hellenistic, Herodian, Roman, Byzantine, and Crusader ruins. The Crusaders conquered the city at least four times, and the remains of the Crusader city, built after Caesarea was taken by Louis IX of France in 1251, dominate the ruins even now. The Crusaders lost the city for the last time to the Mamelukes in 1261, after which Caesarea was more or less abandoned.

10: Caesarea: Crusader City Wall and Moat

To the north of the city are the remains of three aqueducts, which brought fresh water to Caesarea from springs near Mount Carmel. Two of these aqueducts adjoin each other; the first, or eastward one, dates to the Herodian city, and the other dates to the time of Hadrian, about 150 years later. A third, covered aqueduct lies about 100 yards to the east and dates to the third century CE.

Three other outstanding features of Caesarea are visible today. The first is the port of Sebastos, named for Augustus (the

11: Caesarea: Aqueducts

120

name Sebastos is Greek for Augustus). Sebastos was the first man-made port in antiquity, in which Herod had two breakwaters built out into the sea, roughly 150 feet (45 meters) out. The port was so large that it could accommodate up to 150 ships in its inner and outer harbors.

LEGEND:
1 *Harbor entrance*
2 *Towers*
3 *Main Herodian Break-*
   water
4 *Secondary Breakwater*
5 *Harbor Basin*
6 *Crusader Harbor*
7 *Crusader City*
8 *South Breakwater*

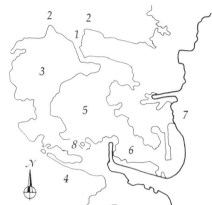

12: Caesarea: The Port of
Sebastos

The second is a large Roman theater. At the end of the First Jewish Revolt, the Romans had many Jews executed in this theatre. The third is the remains of the Hippodrome to the east of the city (marked by a modern arch), which was used for chariot races. The center obelisk around which the horses raced was brought by sea from Aswan in southern Egypt. It is now in ruins in the center of the field.

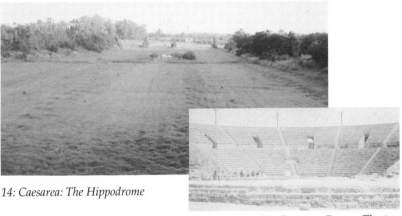

14: Caesarea: The Hippodrome

13: Caesarea: Roman Theater

Cana (Kana)

Biblical References: John 2:1-11; 4:46-54; 21:2.

Unfortunately, the Cana visited by many tourists, pilgrims, and students today is not the New Testament site. This village, modern Cana, is found about 4 miles (7 km) to the northeast of Nazareth. The second and more likely site of the biblical city is located about 8 miles (13 km) north of Nazareth.

Cana is mentioned three times in the Gospel of John in relation to the ministry of Jesus. First, it was the site of Jesus' first reported miracle, changing water into wine during a wedding feast (2:1-11). Second, Jesus was staying at Cana when he was asked to heal the son of a prominent Capernaum official (4:46-54). Finally, Cana is said to be the hometown of Jesus' disciple Nathaniel (John 21:2).

In modern Cana there are two churches that commemorate the miracle of Jesus' changing water into wine. There is not much to see at the more authentic site, however, and for this reason people rarely go there.

Capernaum

Biblical References: Matthew 4:12-16; 8:5; Mark 1:21; 2:1; Luke 4:23, 31-41; 7:1; 10:13-15; John 4:46; 6:17, 24, 59; and many other references in the Gospels.

During the New Testament Period, Capernaum was known as Kfar Nahum, which means the "Village of Nahum." No one knows who this Nahum was, but he must have been a prominent resident at an earlier time. Capernaum is located on the northern shore of the Sea of Galilee, near the mouth of the Jordan River.

Capernaum served as Jesus' home and headquarters during his Galilean ministry. The Gospels tell us that Jesus moved here after he was forced to leave his home in Nazareth (Matthew 4:13; Mark 2:1). He did not move here because Capernaum was a prosperous and influential city, as Tiberius and Magdala were wealthier and more cosmopolitan. He probably settled here because his early converts and disciples—Andrew, Peter, James, and John—lived in the area (Matthew 4:18-22).

In recent years an insula[15] has been excavated at the site traditionally known as St. Peter's House, revealing the remains of fourth- and fifth-century CE churches that had been built over a first-century CE house. One room seems to have been used as a place of prayer or worship in all three buildings over four centuries, leading to speculation that it might have been the room where Jesus lived or where he taught his disciples, and that the fourth- and fifth-century CE churches preserved the memory of the first-century house/church. While there is no hard evidence to support the idea that Jesus or any of his disciples actually lived at this specific site, the excavation does reveal the details of the kind of house complex that was common in the area at that time.

Several biblical events are set in Capernaum. Jesus healed a demon-possessed man in the synagogue of Capernaum (Mark 1:21-28); he also healed Peter's mother-in-law (Mark 1:29-31), a centurion's son (Matthew 8:5-13), and the servant of a centurion who had built the village synagogue (Luke 7:1-10). Jesus taught and healed many people in Peter's home (Mark 2:1ff.). Jesus later condemned Capernaum for its lack of faith and repentance, along with Chorazin and Bethsaida:

Then he began to reproach the cities in which most of his deeds of power had been done, because they did not repent.

> "Woe to you, Chorazin! Woe to you, Bethsaida! For if the deeds of power done in you had been done in Tyre and Sidon, they would have repented long ago in sackcloth and ashes. . . . And you, Capernaum, will you be exalted to heaven?
> No, you will be brought down to Hades. For if the deeds of power done in you had been seen in Sodom, it would have remained until this day."
>
> (Matthew 11:20-23; see also Luke 10:13-15)

Capernaum was also the seat of the Upper Galilee customs office.[16] The disciple Matthew had been a tax/customs official here. He was working in this capacity when he was called by Jesus to become a disciple. In Capernaum a modern visitor can see, along with the excavation of St. Peter's House, a restored synagogue that dates to the late fourth century CE. This synagogue was built on the foundation of a basalt synagogue from the time of Jesus. The fourth-century synagogue consisted of four separate areas: the main hall, used for prayer and worship; a small side room in the northwestern corner; a large courtyard; and a southern porch. The main prayer/worship

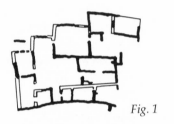

Fig. 1

16: Capernaum: Insula
Plan of St. Peter's House

Fig. 1 - First c. CE small houses for extended family, grouped around courtyards. Walls were covered with plaster. Had light roofs.

Fig. 2

Fig. 2 - 4th c. More solid construction and the addition of more rooms. This is the house which Egeria, the 4th c. pilgrim, no doubt saw.

Fig. 3 - A 5th c. octagonal church was constructed over earlier housing. An apse and a baptistry can be seen.

15: Capernaum:
St. Peter's House

Fig. 3

room contains two rows of columns. There are benches along the eastern and western walls. The front of the building faces Jerusalem, meaning that when people prayed they would face Jerusalem.

17: Capernaum: Synagogue—exterior

18: Capernaum: Synagogue—interior

Most of the major excavation work at Capernaum since 1968 has been directed by Father Virgil Corbo. While excavating and restoring the village Father Corbo discovered a large number of grinding stones and mortars, many incomplete. This suggests that Capernaum may have been one of the villages that manufactured these items for trade. Until this time it was thought that Capernaum's only industries were fishing and agriculture.

Chorazin

Biblical References: Matthew 11:21; Luke 10:13.

Chorazin is located in the hills just north of Capernaum. It is mentioned only twice in the Gospels. However, from these passages it seems likely that Jesus must have spent considerable time here teaching in the synagogue and performing miracles. Chorazin was condemned along with Capernaum and Bethsaida for the people's lack of faith and failure to repent.

Excavations have revealed that it was a city of some wealth and importance. A Roman road was found here, connecting the city with an important trade route to the north to Damascus. The ruins of a large synagogue, one of the earliest in the area, were also found here.

Today Chorazin is part of the National Parks system in Israel and is open for visitors. One of the striking features of the ruins is that all of the buildings were constructed out of dark basalt stone. The stone is common in the area and was produced from volcanic activity from a much earlier period.

Dan (Tell Dan)

Biblical References: Judges 18:1; 20:1; 2 Samuel 3:10; 17:11; 2 Chronicles 16:4.

Tell Dan is located some 25 miles (40 km) north of the Sea of Galilee near the modern Israel-Lebanon-Syrian border. It is one of Israel's most impressive sites and is rich with history.

The earliest occupation of the site dates to the middle of the third millennium BCE. According to Joshua 19:40-48, the tribe of Dan was given territory near the Mediterranean Coast, in the area of the Coastal Plain between Joppa and the Hill Country of Judea. The Danites were unable successfully to subdue the land here and were forced to move their people to a new location. In Joshua 19:47 this place is called Leshem; in Judges 18:7 it is called Laish.

Dan was one of the two worship centers established by Jeroboam I for the Northern Kingdom of Israel. The other cultic center was located at Bethel (1 Kings 12:29). Dan was destroyed by the Syrians during the reign of King Asa of Judea (913–873 BCE), and was rebuilt during the reigns of Omri (876–869 BCE) and Ahab (869–850 BCE).

The excavations, which began in 1966 under the directions of Avraham Biran of Hebrew Union College, have yielded several important findings. The high place of the temple built by Jeroboam, which consists of a three-tiered structure, has been restored. It is possible that the lowest tier was a place for women's offerings, the middle tier was for men and lower priests, and the upper tier was the location of a special chamber that functioned like the Holy of Holies at the Temple in Jerusalem. The golden calf built by Jeroboam would have been here on the upper tier. Behind the upper tier were rooms used as living quarters for priests or for storage.

19: Dan: Temple Complex

20: Dan: Middle Bronze Gate

At another location on the tell a Middle Bronze gate dating to the nineteenth/eighteenth century BCE has been uncovered. This is the oldest extant mud-brick gate of its kind found in the Middle East. If the Abraham stories found in Genesis are historically accurate, he would have passed through this gate on his journey from Haran to Canaan.

The remains of an Iron Age gate are also found here. One of the interesting features of this Iron Age gate is the place for the "Seat of the King." This was the place where the king and the elders of a city (his advisors) would sit to hear cases and render decisions.[17]

In the center of the tell is a central city square in which two levels have been exposed. The first, or highest, dates to the time of Jeroboam I, while the second, or lower, square dates to the pre-Dan city of Laish.

21: Dan: Iron Age Gate

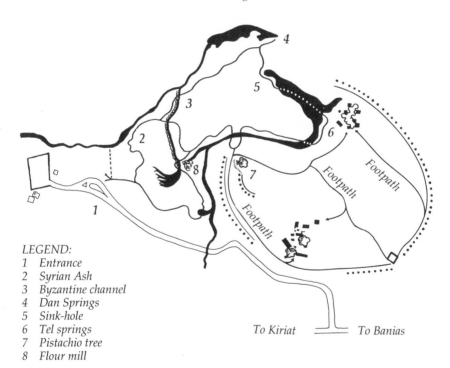

LEGEND:
1   Entrance
2   Syrian Ash
3   Byzantine channel
4   Dan Springs
5   Sink-hole
6   Tel springs
7   Pistachio tree
8   Flour mill

22: Dan: Diagram of Tell

129

As in the case of Beersheva, Dan was used symbolically to define Israel's geographical limits, representing Israel's northernmost boundary (1 Samuel 3:20, etc.). The site was occupied through the Hellenistic and Roman periods, and coins have been found dating to the time of Constantine.

The Dead Sea

Biblical References: Genesis 14:3; Deuteronomy 3:17; 4:49; Joshua 3:16; 12:3; 15:2, 5.

The Dead Sea, one of the geographical wonders of the world, is the lowest point on earth; its surface level is approximately 1,300 feet (390 m) below sea level. It is roughly 50 miles (80 km) long, 10 miles (16 km) wide, and has a depth of 1,300 feet in places in the north. The water level of the Dead Sea has been reduced in recent years due to a lack of rainfall and to the practice of drawing irrigation water from the Jordan and Yarmuk Rivers, its major tributaries.

Referred to in the Bible as the "Salt Sea," the "Sea of the Arabah," and the "Eastern Sea," the Dead Sea is best known for its wealth of minerals and chemicals, which include salt, bromine, sulfer, calcium, chloride, iodine, magnesium, and potash. Due to constant evaporation, the salt concentration of the Dead Sea is 30-33 percent (as compared with the 2-4 percent that is typical for the earth's other oceans and seas), making it incapable of supporting normal marine life (hence its name). The minerals of the Dead Sea were first used commercially by the Nabateans, beginning about 300 BCE.

Dothan

Biblical References: Genesis 37:17-24.

Dothan, located about 15 miles (24 km) north of Shechem, was, according to Genesis 37, the place where Joseph was sold into slavery by his brothers. This is the only biblical event reported to have taken place here.

Elah Valley

Biblical References: 1 Samuel 17:2, 19; 21:9.

Wadi Elah, or the Elah Valley, is the traditional site for the battle between the armies of Israel and the Philistines, which ended when David killed Goliath in single combat. The Elah Valley is found in the Shephelah of the Judean Hill Country between Jerusalem and the southwest coastal plain. It is a natural passageway connecting the areas of the Judean hills and the land of the Philistines.

En Gedi

Biblical References: 1 Samuel 23:29; 24:1-22; Song of Solomon 1:14; Ezekiel 47:10.

En Gedi, which means "Spring of the Kid" (or "young goat"), is located on the western shore of the Dead Sea between Qumran and Masada. The area was first settled during the Chalcolithic Period, roughly 3000 BCE. Remains of an ancient temple dating from this early period have been found in an area near the waterfall in the mountains above the costal area. This temple may have been used as a centralized place of worship by area tribes during this earlier period.

According to 1 Samuel 24, David sought refuge from Saul by hiding in a cave at (or near) En Gedi. At one point Saul entered the cave where David was hiding to relieve himself, not knowing that David was there, and David quietly cut off the fringe of Saul's garment (probably *a talit*). Later David showed Saul that he could have killed Saul if he had chosen to do so, but that he had spared Saul's life. Saul then repented, at least for the time being, and left David at En Gedi.

The first Israelite settlement at En Gedi dates to the seventh century BCE. Later, En Gedi served as a Hasmonean administrative and commercial center. The center was destroyed by the Romans during the First Revolt.

Today En Gedi is a popular tourist haven where people come to swim in the waters of the Dead Sea. Adjacent to the modern kibbutz, which was founded in 1955, are the remains of a sec-ond-century CE Roman bath complex and a fourth-century CE synagogue. The presence of these remains indicates that En Gedi must have returned to some prominence in the first years following the Bar Kochba Revolt (132–135 CE).

Ezion-Geber (Elat)

Biblical References: Numbers 33:35; Deuteronomy 2:8; 1 Kings 9:26-28; 10:11, 22 (implied); 22:47ff.; 2 Chronicles 8:17; 20:35-37.

Ezion-geber was Solomon's city on the Red Sea in the south-ern part of Israel, at the location of the modern city of Eilat. Solomon established this city to have direct access to the ship-ping lanes through the Red Sea to eastern Egypt, Africa, and India. The Queen of Sheba might have entered Israel through Elat when she visited Solomon (1 Kings 10:1ff.).

The Judean king Jehoshaphat (873–849 BCE) and the Israelite king Ahaziah (850–849 BCE) tried to work together to reestablish Ezion-geber as a port city, but their fleet was destroyed (2 Chronicles 20:35-37). The city was lost to the Edomites in about 733 BCE; there is evidence of its occupation during the Babylon-ian and Persian periods, but it was abandoned in the early fifth century BCE.

Today, Eilat is Israel's most popular resort and vacation cen-ter due to its beautiful beaches, warm climate, clear waters, and coral reef, which are excellent for snorkeling and scuba diving.

Gamla

Biblical References: None.

Gamla, which means "camel's hump," is known in Israel as the "Masada of the North." It was one of the first cities to fall during the First Jewish Revolt. Josephus was the first military commander for the rebels in the Galilee region, and given his privileged position his firsthand report has been essential in understanding what happened here. He was responsible for building fortification walls around Gamla in anticipation of a Roman attack (*Jewish War* 4:9-10). He describes the initial victory over the Romans by the Jews here, which gave them a false sense of invulnerability. Later the Romans returned in greater force and routed the Jews. Josephus reports that the Romans killed 4,000 people in the battle, and that 5,000 people "threw their children, their wives, and themselves also, down the precipices, into the valley beneath, which, near the citadel, had been dug hollow to a vast depth" (*Jewish War* 4:79).

Today, the authenticity of the site is in dispute. The arguments against locating the Gamla of the First Jewish Revolt at the contemporary site of the same name are twofold. First, the modern site does not conform to Josephus's description of Gamla. At the modern site the citadel is located to the west of the "camel's hump." Josephus states that the citadel of Gamla was south of the hump (*Jewish War* 4:8). Second, no material remains have been recovered that would suggest that the city was located here or that the mass suicide described by Josephus took place at this site. These discrepancies have led some to speculate that the Gamla of Josephus might be located elsewhere.

23: Gamla: The "Camel's Hump"

Gezer

Biblical References: 1 Kings 9:15-16.

Gezer is located about five miles (8 km) southeast of Ramala, just off the main highway between Jerusalem and Tel Aviv. Although it is not mentioned often or prominently in the Bible, Gezer was an important city in the ancient world. It is mentioned in early texts from Egypt and Mesopotamia. By the time of the United Monarchy, it was one of the major cities of Israel. The reason for its importance is its strategic location on the Via Maris.[18] By the Middle Bronze Period (roughly 1650 BCE) a fortified city had been built here. This city was later destroyed by the Egyptian Thutmose III in 1468 BCE. Details of this battle are found on the temple walls in the Valley of the Kings in Upper Egypt, at Karnak. Gezer is also mentioned frequently in the el-Amarna letters.

The city was given to Solomon by a pharaoh of Egypt (perhaps Shishak) as a dowry for Solomon's marriage to his daughter. Solomon rebuilt the city and fortified its walls, and at this time it rivaled Jerusalem, Hazor, and Megiddo in its wealth and splendor.

In the early 1900s, R. A. S. Macalister discovered the famous Gezer Calendar here. The Gezer Calender is a small (handsize) limestone tablet written in ancient Hebrew that contains information about agricultural procedures from the Israelite Iron Age. It has been a valuable aid in helping to date other ancient Hebrew documents in regard to style, script, and grammar, because it is one of the earliest examples of Hebrew writing ever discovered.

Gibeah

*Biblical References: Joshua 18:26; Judges 19-20; 1 Samuel 10:10, 26;
11:4; 13:2; 15:34; Hosea 5:8; 9:9; 10:9.*

Gibeah ("hill") is best remembered as the hometown or village of Saul and the location of his capital during his reign as king (1 Samuel 10:26). It is located about 5 miles (8 km) north-northeast of Jerusalem.

There is an earlier, uglier historical significance to Gibeah (Judges 19–20). Eleven of the tribes of Israel went to war against Benjamin over an act of sexual misconduct and murder. One of the results of this war was the destruction of Gibeah.

Gibeon

Biblical References: Joshua 9:1-17; 10; 2 Samuel 2:12-17; 21:1-9;
1 Kings 3:4-15.

Gibeon, located about 5 miles (8 km) northwest of Jerusalem, was an important village from the Israelite Conquest Period up to the time of David. According to Joshua 9, the Gibeonites, in order to be spared an attack by the invading Israelite army, tricked Joshua into making a treaty with them. For Joshua, this treaty violated instructions from God (Exodus 23:32; 34:12; Deuteronomy 7:2). Joshua 9:14 suggests that God should have been consulted before Joshua made this treaty with Gibeon. Even so, because of the treaty Israel gained control over a large area in the northern Judean hills. Later, as told in Joshua 10, God made the sun stand still over Gibeon during Israel's battle against the Canaanite kings, led by Adoni-zedek, the king of Jerusalem.

According to the biblical account, Saul broke a treaty with the Gibeonites and attacked them; this even led to a famine during David's reign, and prompted David to hand over seven descendants of Saul for ritual execution by the Gibeonites, possibly at the high place of Gibeon (2 Samuel 21:1-7). After Saul's death, Gibeon served as a neutral meeting place for Abner and Joab, who met here to discuss the kingships of David and Ishbosheth (2 Samuel 2:12-17). They met at a pool where a brief battle, won by Joab's men, ensued. The pool of Gibeon (actually a 36-foot deep shaft with an interior stairwell, which leads to a tunnel opening into a room the floor of which is below water level) is still visible for visitors today. At the beginning of his reign,

Solomon "went to Gibeon to sacrifice there, for that was the principal high place" (1 Kings 3:4). Presumably the building of the Temple in Jerusalem led to a decline in Gibeon's importance as a center of Israelite worship.

Gilgal

Biblical References: Joshua 4:19-24; 5:10-15; 9:6; 10:6ff.; 14:6; 1 Samuel 7:16; 10:8; 11:14-15; 13:8-10; 15:2ff.

Although the exact site of biblical Gilgal remains unknown, it was located somewhere to the northeast of Jericho, between Jericho and the Jordan River in the Rift Valley. The Israelite army camped at Gilgal once they had crossed over the Jordan River at the beginning of the entry into the land, and here Joshua built an altar of twelve standing stones. The Gibeonites came to meet Joshua in Gilgal when they made their treaty with Israel. The conquest campaigns were launched from Gilgal (Joshua 5:13ff.).

Saul was anointed king of Israel here (1 Samuel 11:14-15) and also rejected as king here (1 Samuel 15:12ff.). Gilgal was also known as a cultic center for Israelite sacrificial worship (1 Samuel 10:8).

Hammat Gader

Biblical References: None.

Hammat Gader is located about 5 miles (8 km) southeast of the Sea of Galilee, some 12 1/2 miles (20 km) from Tiberias, in the Yarmuk River Valley on the Israel-Jordan border. The site was inhabited between the years 3100 and 2350 BCE, and is best known for its mineral baths. The Romans built an elaborate bath complex here. Excavations have also revealed that it was popular as a pagan worship center. The hottest pool was known as Ma'ayan HaGehinom, or Hell's Pool; the temperature of this natural mineral pool is 124 degrees F (51 degrees C).

In New Testament times, people flocked to these pools (as well as those of Hammat Tiberias) for their medicinal purposes. People came to the Sea of Galilee looking for a miracle cure for their physical ailments. Today, it is still a popular spa not only for people from Israel but also for tourists.

Hammat Tiberias

Biblical References: None.

Hammat Tiberias is located just south of the modern city of Tiberias on the shore of the Sea of Galilee. During the Roman period the site was very popular, like Hammat Gader, for its mineral springs, which were known for their healing powers.

Hazor

Biblical References: Joshua 11:11-13; Judges 4:2; 1 Kings 9:15; 2 Kings 15:29.

Hazor is an ancient city found in the region of Galilee in Northern Israel, about 4 miles southwest of Lake Huleh and 10 miles north of the Sea of Galilee. It is mentioned as early as the Mari documents in the eighteenth century BCE and later in the el-Amarna letters in the mid-fifteenth century BCE. It is also mentioned in the Egyptian kings' lists of Thutmose (1504–1450 BCE), Amenophis II (1450–1425 BCE), and Seti I (1318–1304 BCE).

The city's first contact with the Israelites came during Joshua's northern campaign during the Conquest. Hazor was the only Canaanite city built on a hill that was destroyed by the invading Israelite army (Joshua 11:11-13). During the Period of the Judges, Israel was oppressed by Jabin, the king of Hazor (Judges 4). The Israelites later defeated the army of Hazor in a battle near Mount Tabor. During the reign of Solomon the upper city was refortified, and under Omri it was expanded. Hazor was destroyed by the Assyrians in 733/732 BCE and never regained its former prominence.

Archaeologists have discovered twenty-one layers of strata at Hazor from the Early Bronze Age to the Hellenistic Period. Several Middle Bronze temples have been found in the lower city, and these discoveries have led to a better understanding of Canaanite worship during the Middle Bronze Period. Archaeological work there has also revealed that the city was more of a fortress during the time of Ahab than it was an administrative center, as previously believed. As in Megiddo, Ahab built an elaborate underground water system to ensure that the city would have an adequate water supply in time of siege. Under Hazor there was a large pool that was connected to a deep shaft of some 60 feet (18 meters). A wide staircase was cut into the shaft leading to a tunnel, which led to the water, making it easy to retrieve the water for the people in the city. Large storehouses were also found here to ensure adequate food supply in times of war.

Hebron

Biblical References: Genesis 23:1-26; 49:29-32; 50:7-9, 12-14; Numbers 13:22; Joshua 14:14; Judges 1:20; 2 Samuel 3:2, 5, 32; 15:10; 1 Kings 2:11; 1 Chronicles 29:27.

Hebron is located about 19 miles (30 km) south of Jerusalem and twelve miles (19 km) south of Bethlehem. The biblical city was built on Jebel el-Remeida, the highest hill in the region (elevation over 3,000 feet), overlooking the caves of Machpelah. Habitation dates at least to 2000 BCE. The immediate area has an abundant supply of water, in wells and springs, and was well-known in antiquity for grape and olive cultivation.

The Arabic name for Hebron is el-Khalil, which means "the friend of God"; it is so called because of its ancient association with Abraham, who is known as the friend of God (2 Chronicles 20:7). It was here that Abraham received God's promise that he would father a great nation (Genesis 13:14-18). Abraham also bought a cave here for a burial site for his family (Genesis 23).

Many other biblical events and people are associated with the city of Hebron. During the Exodus, spies were sent to this area by Moses. They brought pomegranates and figs back to show the wandering Hebrews that the land was fertile (Numbers 13:22). David reigned in Hebron for seven years before moving the capital of the United Kingdom to Jerusalem (1 Kings 2:11; 1 Chronicles 29:27). It was also in Hebron that Absalom was declared king and launched his rebellion against his father (2 Samuel 15:10). The city was among those fortified by Rehoboam (2 Chronicles 11:5); it was taken by the Edomites after the Exile, and was recovered by Judas Maccabeus in 164 BCE.

The building surrounding and covering the caves at Machpelah has a fascinating history. At one time or another the building has served as a synagogue, a church, and a mosque. It is sacred for both Jews and Moslems. Inside the building are cenotaphs[19] representing the tombs of the Patriarchs. The actual burial sites are in the caves beneath the building. Since the middle part of the century the caves have been sealed. They are so sacred to both Jews and Moslems that it is now forbidden for anyone to enter the caves.

24: Hebron: The Machpelah

139

The Herodium

Biblical References: None.

The Herodium,[20] while not mentioned in the Bible, is a site related to the biblical period, and is mentioned in the writings of Josephus (in both the *Antiquities* and *The Jewish War*). It is located approximately 7 miles (11 km) south of Jerusalem and 3 miles (5 km) southeast of Bethlehem.

The Herodium was constructed during the massive building campaign of Herod the Great, from whom it takes its name. There are several reasons for Herod's construction of this fortress. It served as a desert retreat for Herod and his family; the climate here is very agreeable, and especially during the hot summers Herod would visit here. The Herodium also served as a district administrative center and as part of a series of fortresses built by Herod to help protect his kingdom. The site also commemorates a battle between Herod and his enemies that took place near here, in which Herod and his army were victorious.

There has been speculation that Herod built the fortress as a possible burial site. Josephus reports that Herod was buried here after his death in Jericho. "The body was carried two hundred furlongs to Herodium, where he [Herod] had given order to be buried" (*Jewish War* 1:673; see also *Antiquities* 17:199). His servants kept the location of Herod's grave secret to prevent its desecration by the people who hated him so deeply. During the First Jewish Revolt (66–70 CE), Jewish Zealots took the fortress. The Romans won it back in a small battle in 72 CE under the leadership of Lucilius Bassus. During the Second Jewish Revolt, also known as the Bar Kochba Revolt (132–135 CE), the Herodium was used by the Jewish rebels as a military and administrative center. There has even been speculation that Bar Kochba may have had his headquarters here. By the end of the revolt, the Herodium was abandoned.

During the Byzantine Period monks came here and established a church and monastery. The monastery remained until the Islamic invasions.

25: *The Herodium—exterior*

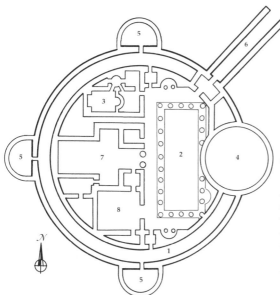

26: *The Herodium—interior*

27: *The Herodium—diagram*

1 *The Cylinder*
2 *The Inner Building*
3 *The Roman Bathhouse*
4 *The Eastern Round Tower*
5 *Three Semi-Circular Towers*
6 *The Main Stairway*
7 *Living Quarters*
8 *Reception Room*
  (Later Synagogue)

Hippos (Susita)

Biblical References: None.

Hippos, which is Greek, and its Aramaic counterpart, Susita, both mean "horse." The ruins of ancient Hippos are found on a mountain to the east of Kibbutz En Gev, overlooking the eastern shore of the Sea of Galilee. No one is quite sure why it was named "horse." The site was first occupied by the Seleucids during the Hellenistic Period. Later, during the Hasmonean Period, it became a Jewish city. The area was taken by Rome, and during the campaign of Pompey (63 BCE), and it became a part of the Decapolis. In 30 BCE the city was given to Herod the Great by Augustus. After Herod's death it was given to the Roman province of Syria.

Hippos is not mentioned in the Bible, and there is little reason to suspect that biblical events occurred there, even though it was a prosperous city, strategically located on the trade route that connected Damascus with Beth Shean (Scythopolis).

Jericho

Biblical References: Joshua 2:1; 3:5-7, 16; 6:26; 18:21; 2 Samuel 10:5; 1 Kings 16:34; 2 Kings 2:4, 18-22; 1 Chronicles 19:5; 2 Chronicles 28:15; Jeremiah 39:5; Matthew 4:1; 20:29-34; Mark 10:46-52; Luke 10:25-27; 18:35-43; 19:1-27.

With habitation dating to the eighth millennium BCE, Jericho is one of the oldest cities on earth. It is located just north of the Dead Sea, some four miles from the Jordan River. During biblical times the city was located on two or more different sites. Old Testament Jericho lies about one mile northwest of the modern village of Jericho, at Tell es-Sultan. Herod's Jericho palace and New Testament Jericho were located to the southwest of modern Jericho near the entrance to the Wadi Qelt.

Old Testament Jericho is best remembered for its association with the invading Israelite army during the Conquest. There continues to be considerable discussion concerning the biblical report of Jericho's destruction. Is Tell es-Sultan the city conquered by Joshua and his army? John Garstang, a well-known biblical archaeologist who worked here between 1930 and 1936, concluded that the walls he found were destroyed by an earthquake and fire at the time of the Israelite invasion, and he dated this destruction to 1380 BCE.[21] Kathleen Kenyon, a celebrated pioneer in Middle Eastern archaeology, came to different conclusions. Using the stratigraphic method that she developed, she argued that the walls discovered by Garstang dated to the Early Bronze Period (3200–2300 BCE). Kenyon found no evidence that the city was occupied during the time of the Israelite conquest, and concluded that Joshua and his army could not have conquered Jericho during the Late Bronze Period because no city existed on the site at that time.[22] Others have speculated that the walls might have been made of dried-mud brick at the time of the Israelite invasion, in which case they would have washed away over the centuries. In the final analysis, no one knows for sure one way or the other.

Even though there may not have been a fortified city here in Joshua's time, Jericho may well have been occupied during the Late Bronze Period. The presence of the powerful "Spring of Elisha" (Ein es-Sultan) would have guaranteed an ongoing settlement or habitation at the site. The presence of the spring and the proximity of the Jordan River have contributed to the fertility of the land around Jericho. Because agricultural productivity has been so rich and predictable, the city has been known as the "City of a Thousand Palms."

Whether Tell es-Sultan is the city taken by Joshua, it is clearly the site of Old Testament Jericho. Archaeologists have discovered twenty-two layers of strata here. Due to the poor techniques used in the early days of its excavation, some of the tell has been destroyed. Today there is very little to see at the site; although some of Garstang's and Kenyon's work is still visible, most evidence of Israelite occupation has eroded. The most impressive remaining feature, however, is very significant: a Neolithic tower dating to approximately 8000 BCE, which some consider to be the oldest human structure extant anywhere in the world.

28: Jericho: Neolithic Tower

29: Jericho: Herod's Palace

New Testament Jericho, or Tulul Abu el-Alaiq in Arabic, is found to the southwest of modern Jericho. After the deaths of Cleopatra and Mark Antony, Jericho was given to Herod the Great by Octavian. Herod built for himself a magnificent palace complex at the eastern end of the Wadi Qelt, where the wadi meets the Jordan Plain west of the Jordan River. During this period Jericho was a prosperous city; signs of wealth were everywhere, and the best example of its opulence was Herod's palace complex.

The combination of fear and fascination that Herod seems to have inspired in many people is reflected by Josephus.[23] Josephus also reports that Herod became depressed when he discovered that people would be happy when he died. To avoid this, he ordered that influential and prominent Jewish leaders from throughout the country be arrested and held in the Hippodrome in Jericho, and he gave the following instructions to his sister Salome and her husband, Alexas:

I know well enough that the Jews will keep a festival upon my death; however, it is in my power to be mourned for on other accounts, and to have a splendid funeral, if you will but be subservient to my commands. Do you but take care to send soldiers to encompass these men that are now in custody, and slay them immediately upon my death, and then all Judea, and every family of them, will weep at it whether they will or no. (*Jewish War* 1:660)

However, upon Herod's death, Salome informed the soldiers who were to carry out the mass execution that Herod had rescinded the order. The result was rejoicing in Israel by the people at Herod's death and not mourning. Following Herod's death, his body was taken to the Herodium, where he was buried in a secret place.

Jesus was in and around Jericho on several occasions. He would have passed through Jericho whenever he visited Jerusalem. Like Capernaum, Jericho was a place for collecting taxes, particularly the frontier tax paid by those entering the country from abroad (Luke 19:1-10). Jesus is also said to have performed miracles of healing here (Matthew 20:29-34; Mark 10:46-52). The Gospels and Christian tradition report that Jesus was baptized near here. Christian tradition also identifies the wilderness to the west of Jericho as being the place where Jesus experienced forty days of fasting, meditation, and temptation.

There are three other sites surrounding Jericho that should be mentioned. First is the Monastery of Qarantal, found on what is commonly known as the "Mount of Temptation." The monastery sits affixed to the side of the mountain, which overlooks Tell es-Sultan. Qarantal means "forty." This monastery was built in the twelfth century CE on the site of an earlier church. The original church had been built over a cave where early Christian tradition believed Jesus slept during his forty-day period in the wilderness. Today two Greek Orthodox monks reside here.

30: The Mount of Temptation

Second, the Monastery of St. Jerasimos is a fifth-century CE Greek Orthodox monastery located between modern Jericho and the Jordan River, to the southeast of Jericho. The monastery was built to commemorate Jesus' baptism near here. The traditional site of the baptism can no longer be visited because it lies in a closed military zone. Today there is only one monk stationed here. He keeps the monastery open and maintains the monastery's candle-making business. The candles are made from beeswax that is produced from bee hives on the monastery grounds.

Finally, in modern Jericho is the Church of Zacchaeus. This Greek Orthodox Church and monastery is dedicated to Jesus' encounter with Zacchaeus in Jericho. In the courtyard of the church is a sycamore tree that the monks claim dates to the time of Jesus.

146

Kursi

Biblical References: Matthew 8:28-34; Mark 5:1-20; Luke 8:26-39.

Kursi is located on the eastern shore of the Sea of Galilee just north of Kibbutz En Gev. In Jesus' day this area was known as the land of the Gadarenes (Matthew 8:28) or the Gerasenes (Mark 5:1; Luke 8:26). It was located on "the other side,"[24] meaning the Gentile side of the lake. The Gospels suggest that Jesus spent time here teaching, performing miracles, and getting away from the large crowds that followed him. He may also have traveled here to keep away from Herod Antipas, who was seeking him. Today the ruins of a fifth-century CE Byzantine monastery and church are found on the site.

Lachish

Biblical References: Joshua 10:32; 12:11; 15:39; 2 Kings 14:19; 18:14, 17; 19:18; 2 Chronicles 11:9; 25:27; 32:9; Nehemiah 11:30; Isaiah 36:2; Jeremiah 34:7; Micah 1:13.

Lachish is located approximately 30 miles (48 km) southwest of Jerusalem and some 15 miles (24 km) west of Hebron. It was one of the more important cities of Judah during the time of the divided kingdom. However, its history is much older than the Iron Age; archaeologists have dated habitation at the site as early as 8000 BCE. The tell is a large one, measuring some 30 acres in area at the base and 18 acres at the summit. Archaeologists have identified at least six strata at the site, though they disagree about their precise dating.

In the Bible, Lachish is first identified as one of the cities conquered by Joshua and his army during the southern campaign of the Conquest (Joshua 10:1-32). The Bible reports that this battle lasted two days. If this account is accurate, it is unlikely that Lachish was a heavily fortified city at the time of Joshua's campaign; had the city been fortified, it could probably not have been taken in two days. This seems possible, since there is no archaeological evidence indicating that the city was, in fact, fortified at the time.

Following its conquest by Joshua, the city lay in ruins for over two centuries. Later, during the reigns of David and Solomon, Lachish was renovated, and it was among the cities fortified by Rehoboam (2 Chronicles 11:5). Along with Azekah and Beth Shemesh, Lachish was a fortified outpost and helped to guard Israel's southern border. That Lachish was then a strong, fortified city is confirmed by Amaziah's flight there to escape from his enemies during a revolt against his rule (2 Kings 14:19) in 783 BCE.

In 701/700 BCE, Sennacherib, the king of Assyria, besieged and finally conquered the city. He then used Lachish as his headquarters during his campaign against other cities of Judah (2 Kings 18:13–19:37; 2 Chronicles 32). Sennacherib's campaign is also recorded on a carved relief found during the excavations of Ninevah in 1849–50, depicting the walls of Lachish. The city was conquered again in approximately 587 BCE by Nebuchadnezzer. Jeremiah reports that Lachish, Azekah, and Jerusalem were the last of Judah's fortified cities to fall before the Babylonian Exile.

Archaeologists excavating here in 1935 found in one of the guardrooms of the city's outer gate a collection of eighteen *ostraca* (storage jar fragments) inscribed in black ink; three more were discovered nearby in 1938. These "Lachish Letters" date to the time of Nebuchadnezzar's invasion of the city. The language of the letters is classical Hebrew, similar to that used by the prophet Jeremiah. Most of the letters were addressed to a city official named Ya'osh by a military commander named Hoshaiah. One of the letters contains the earliest extant use of the Hebrew word *nabi* or *nabhi*, which means "prophet." Letter four contains the following passage: "And let [my lord] know that we are watching for the signals of Lachish, according to all indications which my lord hath given, for we cannot see Azekah."[25] This passage implies that Azekah had been destroyed by this time and Nebuchadnezzar and his army were advancing on Lachish. After this destruction Lachish was never again a prominent city.

Latrun (Emmaus)

Biblical References: Luke 24:13-35; (Mark 16:12-13?).

Latrun is located about halfway between Jerusalem and Tel Aviv at the base of a Trappest Monastery. It is a traditional site for the location of New Testament Emmaus. This location, however, presents at least two problems. One, there is no archaeological evidence to support the tradition. Second, the distance seems to be a bit too far from Jerusalem. In New Testament times a healthy person could travel approximately twenty miles per day on foot. This would put Latrun on the fringe of this distance. Even if this is not the location of Emmaus, Jesus' encounter with two disciples on the road to Emmaus is remembered by the monastery here.

Masada

Biblical References: None.

While Masada is not mentioned in the Bible, and even though no biblical figure is reported to have been here, it is one of the most popular and significant archaeological sites in Israel. All that we know about Masada comes to us through the writings of Josephus and through archaeological research.

The site was first fortified by Alexander Jannaeus (103–76 BCE) to serve as a military post to guard his southern border. The fortress was taken by Herod the Great after the murder of his father, Antipater, in 43 BCE. When Herod visited Rome in 40 BCE, he left his family here because he knew they would be well protected on the mountain from his political and military enemies. After Herod consolidated his power in Judea he rebuilt Masada into an almost inpenetrable fortress/palace complex.

Josephus writes that Herod was motivated by two great fears: "Herod thus prepared this fortress [Masada] on his own account, as a refuge against two kinds of danger: the one for fear of the multitude of Jews, lest they should depose him and restore their former kings to the government; the other danger was greater and more terrible, which arose from Cleopatra, queen of Egypt, who did not conceal her intentions, but spoke often to Anthony, and desired him to cut off Herod, and entreated him to bestow the kingdom of Judah upon her" (*Jewish War* 7:300-301). To ensure that he could survive a long siege, should it be necessary, Herod built many storehouses for food. It is difficult to estimate just how much food could have been stored here, although it was enough to sustain some 967 persons for three years (70–73 CE) at the end of the First Jewish Revolt.

31: Masada: Aerial View

32: Masada: Storerooms

Herod also had cisterns dug out of solid rock at Masada that could hold up to one and one-half million cubic feet of water. Yigael Yadin, director of the Masada excavations and restoration, made these comments about this water system:

> How did Herod and his engineers think of filling these cisterns, when there was not then—nor is there today—any spring near Masada, and the rainfall is so rare and meagre? The solution reflected sheer genius, and like so many ingenious solutions, the concept was simple but the execution very difficult. They based their plan on the existence of two small wadis which pass to the north and the south of Masada. They constructed dams in two places, and from these dams they laid open channels to the two sets of excavated cisterns, one from the southern wadi to the top row, and the second aqueduct from the northern wadi to the bottom row. It was their assumption that with the rains, the water would be held up by the dams and by gravity flow would stream along the aqueducts and fill up the cisterns one after another.[26]

This plan supplied water to the lower cisterns. In order to bring water to the cisterns on top of the mountain, slaves and servants carried water on their backs.

It is assumed that Herod the Great never visited Masada; at least there are no reports that he did. Masada's principal inhabitants were a group of 967 Jewish men, women, and children who fled to Masada after the Romans had destroyed Jerusalem in 70 CE. After the Jewish Revolt had been quelled everywhere else, the Romans turned their attention to these refugees, and advanced on Masada with 15,000 men under the command of Flavius Silva. The earlier Roman attempts to take the stronghold failed due to the location of the fortress; the only pathway to the top of Masada, known as the Snake Path Trail, was too narrow and too easily defended for their forces to advance.[27] They were finally able to take the fortress by building a siege ramp up the western side of the mountain.

Rather than surrendering to the Romans, the Zealots defending Masada chose to die by their own hands. Eleazar, the leader of the Zealots occupying Masada, delivered a powerful address

151

33: Masada: Snake Path Trail

to his fellow Jews the night before the Romans would break through the western walls.[28] That night 960 Jewish Zealots—men, women, and children—died. The only persons to escape were two women and five children. Josephus reports that "there was an ancient woman, and another who was kin to Eleazar, and superior to most women in prudence and learning, with five children, who had concealed themselves in caverns under ground" (*Jewish War* 7:399). When the Romans finally broke through the walls the following morning they found that the Zealots had destroyed all their possessions. The only thing that was not destroyed was food. Eleazar had wanted the Romans to know that they had not taken their lives for lack of food, but rather the love of freedom.

For Jewish people everywhere Masada has become a symbol for standing against opposition. In Israel today, certain divisions of the Israel Defense Force take their military oath at Masada, swearing, symbolically, that "Masada will not fall again." After the fall of Masada in 73 CE the site was reoccupied only once; during the Byzantine Period, Orthodox monks established a monastery there, which was later abandoned.

The excavation of Masada was itself a remarkable achievement worthy of the memory of its defenders. The primary work began in 1963 under the direction of Yigael Yadin. Yadin estimated that the work would take at least ten years. However, there was great excitement from all over the world when it was announced that the excavation and restoration would begin. Yadin received thousands of requests from volunteers to join the project. The result of this overwhelming response was that the entire project was completed in two excavation seasons (October 1963–April 1964 and December 1964–March 1965). Yadin and his colleagues discovered physical evidence of occupation from several distinct historical periods, dating from the Chalcolithic Period and ending with the Byzantine Period. The two periods that were most apparent were from the time of Herod the Great and the Zealot occupation in 70 CE.

The Masada of Herod dominates the ruins. He had constructed for himself a magnificent Northern Palace complex built in three tiers. The Upper Terrace, which is about 900 feet above the Dead Sea, was probably built as Herod's private quarters. Yadin notes that "in the entire residential area on this terrace, there were no more than four original dwelling rooms and several corridors. It was quite clear that this northern palace, whose construction had demanded such formidable efforts and resources, was not intended to house a large number of people. It had been built for Herod alone."[29] The Middle Terrace, located about sixty feet below the Upper Terrace, was probably a place for relaxation much like a den or family room in modern American homes. The Lower Terrace, about 110 feet below the Upper Terrace, contained an eave or protective covering that would provide shelter in the time of strong winds, excessive sunshine, or periodic rainfall. Below the Lower Terrace there is a small bath complex. During the excavations, skeletal remains of a family (man, woman, and child) were found here along with personal items.

The bath complex conforms to the typical baths of this period. There are four very specific rooms here. The first is the *apodyterium*, or changing room. Second, we find a *frigidarium*, or cold room. Third, there is a *tepidarium*, or warm room. Finally, there is the *caldarium*, or hot room. The rooms of the bath complex were adorned with beautiful frescoes on the walls and ceilings and with beautiful tile floors.

34: Masada: Roman Bath House

The Western Palace is the largest building complex found on Masada, containing roughly 36,000 square feet of space. Yadin describes it as follows:

> The southeastern wing held the dwelling quarters, and consisted of large rooms and small service rooms built around a central court. The second wing, adjoining the north, also comprised a series of rooms around a central court, but this was solely a service wing. . . . The third wing forms the western section of the building and adjoins the two other wings. It originally housed the storerooms and administrative quarters.[30]

Thus it seems clear that the Western Palace was used for dwelling quarters (probably intended for Herod's family), an administrative center, storage, and a place where official guests were received.

The fortress was surrounded by a casemate wall (see Glossary) about 4,200 feet in length. Within the wall, archaeologists found remains of Zealot living quarters such as remains of pottery, clothing, tools, and the like. At one part of the wall a parchment was found upon which was written a copy of Psalm 150.

Considering his hostility to various Jewish factions, it may appear surprising that Herod built a synagogue at Masada. Herod was not opposed to religion. There are remains of synagogues found at his other major building projects as well. Herod was aware that some of his servants and soldiers practiced their religious faith. He sought to accommodate them by building a place for worship.

35: Masada: The Synagogue

Yadin also reports that the synagogue, originally built by Herod, was later remodeled by the Zealots when they arrived at Masada in 70 CE. The Zealots added a small room in the rear of the building, which was used for the storage of scrolls. They also added benches around the inside of the walls. In the storage room volunteers found fragments of fourteen scrolls, including biblical, apocryphal, and community scrolls. The scrolls contain five chapters of the Psalms, a fragment of the "Songs of the Sabbath Sacrifice" (which supplements the fragments of the same text found at Qumran), the Book of Jubilees, and fragments of Genesis, Leviticus, and Ezekiel.

36: Masada: Site Plan

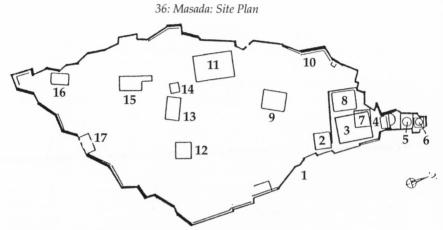

LEGEND
1. *Entrance/Snake Path Gate*, 2. *Building No. VIII*, 3. *Storerooms*, 4. *Northern Palace—Upper Terrace*, 5. *Northern Palace—Middle Terrace*, 6. *Northern Palace— Lower Terrace*, 7. *Bathhouse*, 8. *Building No. VII—Administration*, 9. *Building No. IX Officers Quarters*, 10. *Synagogue*, 11. *Western Palace*, 12. *Building No. XII— Residence of the Royal Family*, 13. *Building No. XI*, 14. *Swimming Pool*, 15. *Building No. XIII*, 16. *Great Pool*, 17. *Southern Wall*

Megiddo

Biblical References: Judges 1:27; 5:19; 1 Kings 9:15; 2 Chronicles 35:22; Zechariah 12:12; Revelation 16:16.

Megiddo, located about 16 miles (26 km) southeast of Haifa and 6 miles (10 km) southwest of Afula, has come to be associated with the end times. The book of Revelation says that the final battle between the forces of good and evil will take place at Armageddon (Revelation 16:16). In Hebrew, Har Megiddo means "mountain (or hill) of Megiddo." This association is a logical one: more people have been killed in battles for control of Megiddo, ranging in time from antiquity to World War I, than at any other place in the region.

Megiddo is located at the place where two very important ancient trade routes meet. The Via Maris, the north-south trade route connecting Europe and Asia with Africa, passed by Megiddo. There was also an important trade route through the Jezreel Valley connecting Jerusalem with the Phoenician cities.

This location made Megiddo strategically important: any power who could control the city would control the trade routes, guaranteeing economic prosperity, which would ensure a stronger army which, in turn, guaranteed more power and stability.

Megiddo was continuously occupied between the years of 4000 and 400 BCE. Archaeologists have found twenty strata here. The city is first mentioned in Egyptian hieroglyphics on the walls of the temple in Luxor, in Upper Egypt, which records the battle won by Thutmose III at Megiddo in 1468 BCE. Later, the invading Israelite army was unable to take the city during the conquest.[31] It did not become an Israelite city until the reign of King David. Under Solomon the city was refortified, and it became one of the kingdom's most powerful and influential cities (1 Kings 9:15). In 923 BCE, the city was destroyed by Shishak, and it was rebuilt by Omri and/or Ahab in the middle of the ninth century BCE. In 609 BCE, Josiah was killed here in a needless battle with Pharaoh Neco (2 Chronicles 35:22). Megiddo gradually declined in importance, and by 400 BCE the city was abandoned.

Some of the more interesting findings at Megiddo include city gates from different periods; Egyptian, Canaanite, Philistine, and Israelite pottery; an ancient Canaanite altar; a large complex of stables or storerooms; an elaborate water system featuring a deep shaft and underground tunnel (similar to the one at Hazor); and a tablet upon which was written a portion of the Gilgamesh Epic.[32]

The Monastery of St. George (The Wadi Qelt)

Biblical References: Matthew 4:1-11; Mark 1:12-13; Luke 4:1-13.

Although this monastery is not from the biblical period, it has played a role in subsequent Christian history and dominates the landscape in the Wadi Qelt, which is found between Jerusalem and Jericho. The Synoptic Gospels report that Jesus spent a forty-day period in the wilderness in prayer and fasting. Early church tradition holds that this time of searching and fasting took place in the area of the Wadi Qelt. The memory of this event led, indirectly, to the establishment of the Monastery of St. George.

St. George's was built in the late fifth century CE. Prior to this construction the area was a popular place for hermits, who came here to fast, pray, and seek God's direction, just as Jesus had done. Many of these monks stayed permanently to live out their lives in solitude. These hermit-monks lived in caves, hundreds of which can be found throughout the area. It is assumed that these early hermits formed a community for self-protection against the elements and bandits. The first organized monastic community here dates to 420 CE and included a community of five residents.

The first monastery was destroyed during the Persian invasions in 614 CE. It was not rebuilt until 1179. In 1483, Felix Fabri,[33] a Christian pilgrim visiting the holy shrines of the church, wrote in his journal that he visited the site of the monastery, where he found only ruins. No one knows when the monastery was destroyed the second time. In 1878 a reconstruction of the monastery was begun, and the project was completed in 1901.

Today only a few monks live and work here. Some hermits still live in caves near the monastery in the Wadi Qelt. From the monastery there is a pleasant hike to Jericho, which ends at Herod's Jericho palace complex, Tulul Abu el-Alaiq.

37: Wadi Qelt: The Monastery of St. George

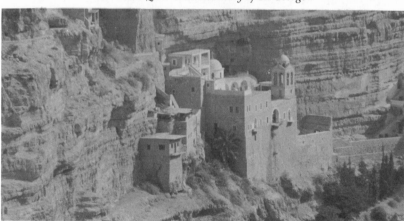

Mount Carmel (Mukhraqa)

Biblical References: 1 Kings 18:17-46; 2 Kings 2:25; 4:25; Isaiah 33:9; 35:2; Jeremiah 46:18; Amos 1:2; Song of Solomon 7:5.

Mount Carmel, located just to the northwest of Megiddo and southeast of Haifa, was considered a holy mountain as early as the fifteenth century BCE. In Egyptian texts it is referred to as a holy place. It has been revered as sacred by Canaanites, Israelites, and Greeks. Throughout the Old Testament period it was a symbol of beauty, majesty, and strength.

Mount Carmel is best remembered as the place where Elijah, as the champion of Yahweh, engaged 450 prophets of Baal in a contest (1 Kings 18:17-46). If one assumes the historicity of that event, there are compelling reasons to believe that it may have taken place at Mukhraqa, at the southeastern end of Mount Carmel. First, there are terraced areas at Mukhraqa, dating back to at least the early Iron Age, where there would have been ample room for all of the contestants.

Second, the biblical account reports that Elijah poured water over the sacrifice he had prepared. Bir el-Mukhraqa, a spring (now dried up), and the brook Kishon were both in the general area and accessible (1 Kings 18:33-40). Third, there is the name Mukhraqa itself, which means "sacrifice."

In 1826 the Carmelite Monastery was established at this place, and the monks here maintain that the first members of their order to come here did so in the late thirteenth century CE. From the top of the monastery there is a beautiful view of the Jezreel Valley and, on a clear day, the Mediteranean Sea and Caesarea Maritima.

38: Mt. Carmel: Elijah Statue

159

Mount Gerizim

Biblical References: Deuteronomy 11:29; 27:12; Joshua 8:33; Judges 9:7; John 4:19-21.

Mount Gerizim is located just to the southwest of Nablus (Shechem). It is the sacred mountain of the Samaritans. During the Passover the Samaritans participate in a special service here, lasting forty days, in which sheep are offered as a sacrifice. The meat from the sacrifices is eaten by the Samaritans, then the remaining bones, hides, hooves, and so on, are gathered and burned also as a sacrifice to God. This ceremony is carried out in accordance with provisions found in Exodus 12.

The ancient Samaritan temple was built here, probably in the fourth century BCE. For this reason Mount Gerizim came to be the most sacred religious center for the Samaritans. Jesus is said to have had an encounter with a Samaritan woman at Jacob's well, which is near here in the modern city of Nablus (John 4).

Mount Gilboa

Biblical References: Judges 7:1ff.; 1 Samuel 28:4, 31; 2 Samuel 1:6; 21:12; 1 Chronicles 10:1.

Mount Gilboa is visible from the tell at Megiddo, to the east-southeast, across the Jezreel Valley. The Bible reports two important events happening here. First, it was in the valley below Mount Gilboa that Gideon and his army surprised the Midianites and caused them to retreat (Judges 7); later the Midianites were defeated by the Israelite army. Second, Saul and Jonathan were killed here in a battle with the Philistines (1 Samuel 31); following their deaths, the Philistines took their bodies to Beth Shean, where they were hung on the city walls for display.

Mount Moreh

Biblical References: 1 Samuel 28:7; 2 Kings 4:8-37; Luke 7:11-17.

Mount Moreh is located across the Jezreel Valley to the east of Megiddo and to the south of Nazareth, Afula, and Mount Tabor. The Bible reports that there are three sites in the general proximity of Mount Moreh where biblical events occurred. First, Saul consulted a witch at the village of Endor (1 Samuel 28:7). The witch was able to call forth the spirit of the prophet Samuel, who told Saul of his and Israel's impending doom at the hands of the Philistines. Second, the village of Shunem is located to the southern side of Mount Moreh. Here the prophet Elisha regularly visited the home of a widow and her son. Elisha also performed the miracle of raising the widow's dead son to life (2 Kings 4:8ff.). Third, the village of Nain is found at the northern base of Mount Moreh, and here Jesus, like Elisha, is said to have raised to life the dead son of a widow (Luke 7:11-17).

Mount Tabor

Biblical References: Judges 4–5; Matthew 17:1-13; Mark 9:2-8; Luke 9:28-36.

Mount Tabor is found between Mount Moreh and Nazareth, in the eastern part of the Jezreel Valley. According to a tradition that dates to the Byzantine Period, it is the site of the Transfiguration of Jesus, which today is commemorated by a church at the top of the mount. However, Matthew implies that the Transfiguration happened near Caesarea Philippi (Matthew 17); Caesarea Philippi is located at the base of Mount Hermon, making it the more likely site.

Mount Tabor was the location of pagan worship centers in the Old Testament Period. During the Period of the Judges, Deborah and Barak led the Israelite army to victory here against the king of Hazor (Judges 4–5). Two other major battles occurred here: one during the war between the Seleucids and Ptolemies in 218 BCE; the second during the First Jewish Revolt in 67 CE.

Nazareth

Biblical References: Matthew 2:23; Luke 1:26; 2:39, 51; 4:16; 28–30; John 1:46; 2:45-46.

Christian tradition holds that the announcement of the birth of Christ was made to Mary in Nazareth. This was also Jesus' home village, the place where he grew from childhood to adulthood and announced the beginning of his ministry (Luke 4:16ff.) Today there are two beautiful churches to visit here. One is the Basilica of the Annunciation, which was completed in 1968. The Basilica is built over the site of three earlier churches. The first church, dating to the Byzantine Period, was destroyed during the Persian invasions in the early seventh century CE. A second church was built here during the Crusader occupation, and a third church was built by the Franciscans in the early eighteenth century CE. This church was torn down in the 1950s to make room for the Basilica.

39: Nazareth: The Basilica of the Annunciation

The second church associated with the life of Jesus is the Church of St. Joseph, built in 1914 over a set of caves that local tradition believes were part of Joseph's workshop and home.

Nazareth was a very small, even insignificant, village at the time of Jesus; the population could not have been more than one or two dozen families. Nazareth was not mentioned in the Talmud's record of the sixty-three prominent villages, towns, and cities of Galilee. This helps explain Nathaniel's reaction to Philip's announcement in John 1:45 (and 1:46).

Qumran

Biblical References: None.

Qumran is best known for its association with the dramatic discovery of the Dead Sea Scrolls. It is located on the northwestern shore of the Dead Sea, just a few miles south of Jericho and approximately 25 miles (40 km) east-southeast of Jerusalem.

The site was settled at least as early as the eighth century BCE, when Judah maintained a small military outpost here. About 150 BCE, during the reign of the Hasmoneans, a man known as the "Teacher of Righteousness" led a small group of religious ascetics into the wilderness and established the community. Their story is contained in the Damascus Document, several copies of which were found in caves 4, 5, and 6.[34] Other copies of this document, dating from the Middle Ages, were found in the nineteenth century CE in the storeroom of a medieval synagogue in Cairo, and they have come to be known as the Cairo manuscripts of the Damascus Document.

The Damascus Document reports that God "raised up a teacher of righteousness to lead them in the way of his heart."[35] The members of this sect, believed to be Essenes, were opposed to the Hasmonean kings, who had assumed the role of the priesthood in Jerusalem; they rejected the Hasmoneans as both kings and priests, because this contradicted their understanding of the Torah and the religious traditions of the faithful. Since they regarded the sacrificial worship in Jerusalem as having been defiled by the Hasmoneans, the Essenes established a new religious order away from the "heretics" in Jerusalem.

The site was destroyed by an earthquake in 31 BCE, after which most of the community's members moved to Jerusalem. Herod the Great apparently gave the Essenes a place to locate their community in Jerusalem's upper city, in an area once inhabited by the Hasmoneans.[36] Recently, the remains of what is believed to be an Essene Gate have been found near modern-day Mount Zion just outside the walls of the Old City in Jerusalem, confirming that an Essene settlement may have been located here during the Roman Period. The Essenes seem to have stayed in Jerusalem until the death of Herod the Great; sometime between 4 and 1 BCE they returned to Qumran and rebuilt the settlement there. The community continued to flourish until 68 CE, when it was destroyed by the Romans. As the Roman forces approached, the Essenes hid their precious religious scrolls in the caves near Qumran, where they were discovered beginning in 1947.

40: Qumran: Cave 4

No one can be certain how many people lived in and around Qumran at its zenith. Some scholars estimate that a maximum of fifty people could actually have lived within Qumran proper at any given time. Most of the members of the community lived in caves that surrounded the settlement. The settlement could provide services for up to five hundred people at one time. According to one estimate there were perhaps as many as 4,000 Essenes living throughout the country during the first century CE.[37]

Qumran is best known today as the site of the discovery in 1947 (and following years) of the Dead Sea Scrolls. For the most part, these date from between the mid-third century B.C.E. to the second half of the first century C.E. These scrolls have greatly enlarged our understanding of Judaism and Christianity in the first century CE. Until their discovery, the oldest text of the Hebrew Bible was from 900 CE, but among the scrolls we find copies or fragments of every book of the Hebrew Scriptures except Esther, thus affording scholars a text nearly a millenium older than was available earlier. The scrolls were hidden in eleven different caves near Qumran when the Roman army advanced before destroying Jerusalem in 70 CE. Cave No. 4, which can be seen near the ruins of the settlement, produced the largest number of scrolls. Many of the scrolls are preserved in the Shrine of the Book, which is part of the Israel Museum.

Other discoveries made at Qumran during its excavation and restoration are as follows. First, the Essenes had constructed an excellent water system. The closest source of fresh water for the community was the oasis of Ein Feshke, located about 3 km south of Qumran.[38] For this reason, an ingenious water collection system was built inside the settlement to collect scarce rainfall and to store it in reservoirs found throughout the community. The reservoirs were fed through a system of sloping channels (see the diagram of the site). This water was used not only for agriculture and sanitation, but also for ritual purification.

Second, archaeologists located the remains of the community scriptorium and library. The scriptorium was the place where some of the Dead Sea Scrolls were copied. The discoveries in the scriptorium included evidence of sharpened reeds (used as pens), pottery ink wells, and dried sheepskins (which were used to make scrolls). Also found nearby was a pit where charcoal was melted down to produce ink. Rooms adjacent to the scriptorium also contained ink wells and tables for writing. It is possible that these extra rooms were also used for copying scrolls.

41: Qumran: The Scriptorium

Third, a large dining room was found with an adjacent storage room. The size of the dining room indicates that it may also have been used for community meetings. In the storage rooms archaeologists found large numbers of drinking vessels, plates, beakers, and food bowls stacked in piles of twelve.

Fourth, miqvah baths, used for a religious ceremony of purification, were found in the complex. Due to the religious principles of the group, members were frequently involved with purification and ritual bathing. The ritually defiled persons would enter a miqvah by one set of steps, immerse themselves in the water, then exit by a separate set of steps once they had been ritually cleansed.

Fifth, a special council chamber was found next to the scriptorium. This chamber is small and must have been used only by the leaders of the community. The council chamber has an opening which allowed food and drink to be sent into the room, suggesting that possibly those involved in such a meeting may not have been allowed to leave until the council had reached a decision.

Sixth, a watchtower was uncovered in the northern wall of the

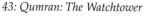

42: Qumran: Miqvah Bath

43: Qumran: The Watchtower

complex. This was a natural location for a watchtower, since the northern side was the only side without natural protection.

Seventh, a pottery workshop, complete with kilns, was found on the eastern side of the site. It is almost certain that the pots that contained the Dead Sea Scrolls were made here.

Finally, the excavators discovered the community cemetery, containing approximately 1,200 graves, just outside the city to the east, beyond the pottery workshop.

44: Qumran: Site Plan

1	*Tower*
2	*Scriptorium*
3	*Kitchen*
4	*Assembly/Dining Room*
5	*Potter's Workshop*
6	*Water Cisterns*
7	*Aqueduct*
8	*Stable*

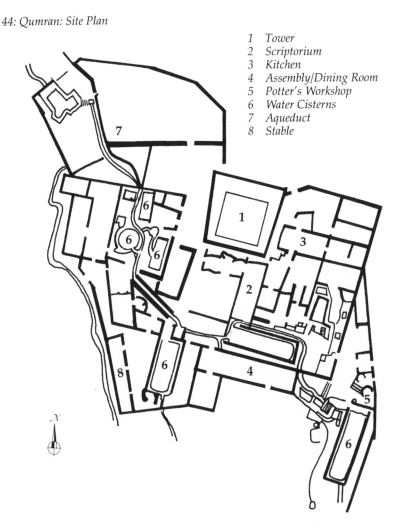

Samaria (Sebaste)

Biblical References: 1 Kings 16:24, 29; 20:1; 2 Kings 3:1; 6:24; 13:1, 6, 9-13; 17:6, 24; 18:10, 34; Isaiah 36:19; Micah 1:6; Amos 3:15; 6:4 (reference to Samaria); John 4:4, 9; Acts 8:4-5, 14.

Samaria was the capital of the Northern Kingdom of Israel. The city was established and built by Omri (876–869 BCE) and was later enlarged by Ahab (869–850 BCE) and Jeroboam II (786–749 BCE). During the reign of Jeroboam II, a wealthy upper class lived in Samaria, and the city was known for its houses and furniture of ivory. The preaching of the prophet Amos was directed at these people; he condemned the wealthy for their failure to show kindness and fairness to the poor.

Samaria was conquered by Sargon II of Assyria in 722/721 BCE. The Assyrians deported thousands from Samaria and replaced them with people from other conquered lands (2 Kings 17:24). The long-term effect of this plan was the rise of a new people in the land who would come to be known as Samaritans. The Samaritans were perceived by their Jewish cousins in Judah as an ethnically impure people who practiced a syncretistic, false religion.

During the Assyrian and Persian periods, Samaria was the capital city of a province of the same name. During the Hellenistic period it was rebuilt as a Greek city, and remained such until it was destroyed again by John Hyrcanus in 108 BCE. In 30 BCE the city was given by Emperor Octavian to Herod the Great, who rebuilt the city in magnificent fashion and changed its name to Sebaste (the Greek form of Augustus) in honor of the Emperor Augustus.

Sea of Galilee

Biblical References: Numbers 34:11; Joshua 12:3; 13:27; Matthew 4:18-22; 8:23; 15:29; Mark 4:35-41; 5:1; Luke 5:1-11; John 21:1-23.

The Sea of Galilee has been called by many different names over the centuries. In the Old Testament it is usually referred to as the "Sea of Chinnereth" or "Kinnereth." The word *kinnereth* is a corruption of the Hebrew word *kinnor*, which means "harp," because the lake or sea is harp-shaped.

The New Testament writers use different names for this body of water. Matthew and Mark usually refer to it as the Sea of Galilee; Luke calls it the Lake of Gennesaret; John calls it the Sea of Tiberias. The sea is approximately 12 miles (21 km) long and 8 miles (12 km) wide—the dimensions vary when the water level rises or falls—and is 680 feet (210 meters) below sea level.

There has been, as long as history recalls, a thriving fishing industry around the sea, mostly in small coves. Mendel Nun reports that "fishing methods on the lake did not change from the time of the Second Temple up to modern times, that is, up to 1955, when techniques used on the lake were revolutionized."[39] Because of this lack of change in techniques over the centuries, we can better understand fishing as it was practiced during the time of Jesus, which helps us to understand some of his parables more clearly.

For example, consider Jesus' parable in Matthew 13:47-48: "The kingdom of heaven is like a net that was thrown into the sea and caught fish of every kind; when it was full, they drew it ashore, sat down, and put the good into baskets but threw out the bad." An analysis of traditional fishing techniques makes it clear that the kind of net to which Jesus referred was a seine. The "bad" fish were the kinds not allowed by Jewish dietary law—fish without scales. The species of fish found in the Sea of Galilee that best fits this description is the catfish (*clarias lazera*).

The report of Jesus' calming the storm on the Sea of Galilee (Mark 4:35-41) makes sense in the light of the fact that sudden, violent storms are not uncommon on the sea here. Remember that the water surface is 680 feet below sea level. Across the sea from Capernaum, above the eastern shore, lie the Golan Heights, which is a very high plateau. Cool winds blow down off the Golan Heights and collide with warm air rising from the Sea of Galilee. When these two meet, there are sudden, unpredictable, and often violent storms. This phenomenon is not usually found on inland lakes.

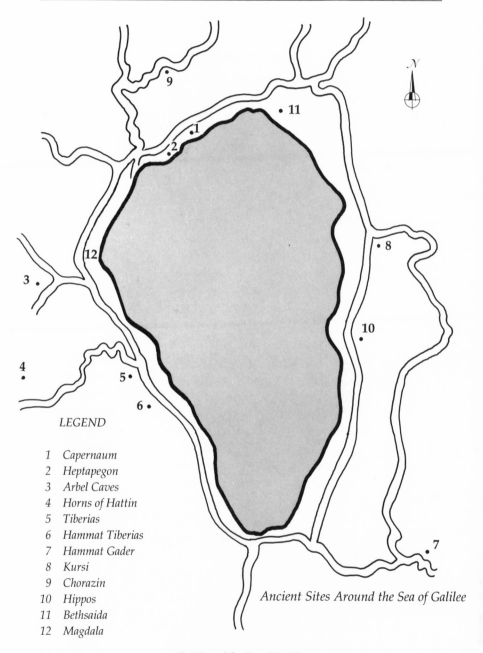

LEGEND

1   Capernaum
2   Heptapegon
3   Arbel Caves
4   Horns of Hattin
5   Tiberias
6   Hammat Tiberias
7   Hammat Gader
8   Kursi
9   Chorazin
10 Hippos
11 Bethsaida
12 Magdala

Ancient Sites Around the Sea of Galilee

45: Map of the Sea of Galilee

Sepphoris

Biblical References: None

Sepphoris is located in lower Galilee, about three miles northwest of Nazareth. It became the administrative center of Galilee during the Hasmonean Period. Sepphoris was destroyed after the death of Herod the Great; it was rebuilt by Herod Antipas, who lived there before making Tiberias his capital. After the fall of Jerusalem in 70 CE, the Sanhedrin relocated to Sepphoris before moving on to Tiberias.

Shechem (Tell Balata)

Biblical References: Genesis 12:6; 37:12-14; Joshua 17:2, 7; 20:7; 23:32; 24:1-28; Judges 8:22-23; 9:45; 1 Kings 12:1, 25.

Shechem (Tell Balata) is located about forty miles north of Jerusalem at a key mountain pass between Mount Ebal and Mount Gerizim, about one and one-half miles east of Nablus. The city has several associations with the Patriarchs. Abraham is said to have passed through the city on his way to Canaan (Genesis 12:6). It was the scene of the rape of Dinah and the revenge of her brothers on the inhabitants of the city (Genesis 34), and Jacob's sons are said to have pastured their flocks nearby (Genesis 37:12-14). At the time of the Exodus, the Israelites brought Joseph's body with them from Egypt and buried it near Shechem (Joshua 23:32), which became their first major religious center in the land.

It was at Shechem that Joshua conducted the great covenant ceremony between the tribes and Yahweh, recorded in Joshua 24, which established the Israelite tribal confederation:

> "Choose this day whom you will serve, whether the gods your ancestors served in the region beyond the River or the gods of the Amorites in whose land you are living; but as for me and my house, we will serve the LORD [Yahweh]." (Joshua 24:15)

This probably took place at the fortress-temple at Shechem,

which dates back to the seventeenth century BCE and is referred to as "the stronghold of the temple of El-berith" in Judges 9:46.

Shechem was also the site of the brief reign of Abimelech, whose story is told in Judges 9. He had himself declared king, violating the ethos of the tribal confederation. Shechem shortly turned against Abimelech, and in reprisal he destroyed the city and sowed its fields with salt. His triumph was short-lived, however, as he was killed soon after at Thebez, and the rule of the judges was restored. Its ancient Canaanite royal tradition no doubt helped Shechem to survive; Rehoboam went there to be crowned king in 924 BCE (1 Kings 12:1). After the revolt of the northern kings, Jeroboam I rebuilt the city and for a time made it his capital (1 Kings 12:25).

The Assyrians took Shechem in 722 BCE; over four feet of debris from their destruction of the city covered the walls. The city was rebuilt once more in about 350 BCE, and it became the principal religious center of the Samaritans, who had their temple nearby on Mount Gerizim. Its final destruction came at the hands of John Hyrcanus in 107 BCE; the city was razed to the ground and was never rebuilt.

Shiloh

Biblical References: Joshua 18:1; 21:2; 22:12; Judges 21:19; 1 Samuel 1:3-28; 2:12–4:18.

Located some ten miles north of Bethel and east of the Jerusalem-Nablus road, Shiloh is identified with modern Khirbet Seilun. Shiloh served as the major religious and administrative center for the Israelite tribes during the time of the Judges, and it became the seat of the priesthood until the Ark of the Covenant was captured by the Philistines during the Battle of Aphek (1 Samuel 4:1-11). Members of all the tribes came to Shiloh for sacrificial worship annually, and seven of the tribes cast lots here to determine their land boundaries.[40] First Samuel 1–4 reports the circumstances of Samuel's birth and how he came to live here in his early life. The city was probably destroyed by the Philistines

172

after the Battle of Aphek, though some archaeologists believe that it survived until the conquests of Sargon or Nebuchadnezzar. There are indications of continued habitation through the Persian and Babylonian periods, as well as clear evidence of later occupation in the Hellenistic, Roman, and Byzantine periods, but the city never regained its former status.

Tabgha (Heptapegon)

Biblical References: Matthew 5–7; 14:13-21; Mark 6:30-44; Luke 9:10-17; John 6:1-14; 21.

Tabgha is located on the western shore of the Sea of Galilee, roughly 2 kilometers south of Capernaum and some 7 miles (12 km) north of the modern city of Tiberias. Christian traditions associate at least three major events from the life and ministry of Jesus with this area.

First, this is the traditional location for Jesus' Sermon on the Mount. The actual site of the sermon is unknown; indeed, it is generally accepted that this "sermon" is actually an edited collection of Jesus' teachings from a "sayings source."[41] Today the modern Chapel of the Beatitudes (also known as the Church of the Sermon on the Mount and the Church of the Mount of the Beatitudes) sits on the hill overlooking Tabgha. This chapel was built in 1937/38, but a fourth-century CE church built lower on the hillside also commemorated the Sermon on the Mount. The modern chapel offers a beautiful panoramic view of the Sea of Galilee.

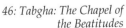
46: Tabgha: The Chapel of the Beatitudes

Second, the church at Tabgha marks the traditional site of Jesus' miracle of multiplication of the loaves and fishes (the feeding of the 5,000). This tradition dates at least to the visit of Egeria in 384 CE. She wrote that she visited a place with seven springs where Jesus fed the multitude, and she also mentions a stone altar where Jesus blessed the food. The modern church is built over the remains of a fifth-century church containing a stone altar. The remains of a fourth-century church can also be seen here. Mosaics from the fifth-century church make up part of the floor of the modern church, and the floors of the fourth-century church can be seen through special glass panels in the floors near the modern altar.

Third, Tabgha is the location of the Church of the Primacy of St. Peter. This church is built over a large flat rock, which ancient tradition holds to be the table where Jesus prepared breakfast for his disciples as reported in John 21. Many New Testament scholars doubt that John 21 was written by the same author of the rest of the Gospel.[42] It is probable that this addendum was placed here for theological and not historical reasons, and there is no way of knowing whether the account may be based on an earlier, historically reliable source.

47: Tabgha: The Primacy of St. Peter

The church was built in 1933 out of basalt stones from the surrounding area. The modern church, like many others, is built over a fourth-century church. Outside the church, near (or in) the Sea of Galilee, are six heart-shaped stones. These are the remains of what was once a twelve-column configuration, first mentioned in 808 CE, believed to have been built in honor of the twelve disciples. They were known as the "Twelve Thrones," and commemorated the twelve judgment seats of the disciples when they serve as judges for the twelve tribes of Israel (Luke 22:30).

Tiberias

Biblical References: None.

Tiberias, on the western shore of the Sea of Galilee, was built by Herod Antipas beginning in 20 CE to replace Sepphoris as the capital of Galilee. Herod wanted to build a city that would rival those built by his father, Herod the Great. Tiberias proved to be such a city, and it was named after Antipas's principal benefactor, Tiberias Caesar. It was the first Jewish *polis*—that is, independent city-state. Sovereign in internal and external matters, it was entitled to date its records from its foundation and to issue coinage.

Josephus led the forces that captured Tiberias in 66 CE, during the First Jewish Revolt, and surrendered the city to Vespasian's legions in 67 CE. This surrender probably averted the destruction of the city, which remained under Jewish rule until about 100 CE. By the second century CE, Tiberias was recognized as one of four major Jewish sacred sites (along with Jerusalem, Hebron, and Sepphoris); it remained a center of Jewish culture and learning through the fifth century CE, and the Palestinian Talmud was completed here just before the Tiberian Academy was closed.

JERUSALEM

The City of David (The Ophel)

Biblical References: 2 Samuel 5:6-10; 11:2; 1 Kings 8:1; 1 Chronicles 11:4-9; 2 Chronicles 5:2; 32:4.

The City of David, located on the Ophel hill in the southeast part of modern Jerusalem, is the oldest part of the city of Jerusalem; there is evidence of habitation dating back to the third millennium BCE. A small Jebusite city was located here before David made it the capital of the United Monarchy. There is no indication in the biblical record that Joshua attempted to capture the city during the period of the Conquest, or that the city was ever given to any of the Israelite tribes.

David showed himself to be a master politician in locating the capital of his kingdom in this neutral city, which did not belong to the territory of any of the tribes; this act promoted unity among the twelve tribes and helped to form them into a nation. David also recognized that the Gihon Spring provided an excellent source of fresh water for the city. The location of the spring, adjacent to the Ophel hill, also explains why the city was built on this lower mountain found between the Tyropean and Kidron Valleys. Cities in the ancient world were usually built on the highest hilltop in the area for defensive purposes. The

Ophel, however, is lower than the other hills or mountains around Jerusalem.[1]

Four other biblical sites are located here in the area of the City of David. These are the Gihon Spring, Warren's Shaft, Hezekiah's Tunnel, and the Pool of Siloam.

The Gihon Spring was Jerusalem's principal water source for most of its history. The word *Gihon* means "gushing." At periodic intervals during the day the spring erupts with considerable force, causing the water level in the tunnel to rise. The water from the Gihon Spring could support up to 2,500 people.

The Gihon Spring is located in a cave on the eastern side of the City of David. This cave provides a natural camouflage for the spring. To provide access to the water during time of siege, shafts were hewn through the rocky hillside of David's City (known as the Ophel) from inside the city's walls. Warren's Shaft is such a shaft. The tunnel, discovered by Charles Warren in 1867, was hewn during the time of the Jebusites. During a siege against the city, people would climb down the shaft and draw water from the spring in jars or buckets. Joab might have entered the city through this shaft when David took the city from the Jebusites (2 Samuel 5:8; 1 Chronicles 11:6).

During the reign of King Hezekiah (715–687 BCE) a new tunnel was hewn to bring water into the city during the siege of the Assyrians, led by Sennacherib in 701 BCE. Of this threat of attack the Bible reports, "Why should the Assyrian kings come and find water in abundance?" (2 Chronicles 32:4). Today this tunnel is known as Hezekiah's Tunnel, and it is a marvel of Iron Age engineering. To dig the tunnel, work crews began digging at opposite ends, through solid rock, until they reached the middle. The tunnel winds in a snake-like manner under the Ophel, beginning at the Gihon Spring and emptying into the Pool of Siloam. It is approximately 1,750 feet (525 m) in length.

In 1880 a young boy discovered an inscription near the Pool of Siloam which tells of how the tunneling and the meeting of the crews took place:

> While [the workmen raised] the pick each toward his fellow and while there [remained] 3 cubits to be tunneled [through, there

was heard] the voice of a man calling to his fellow, for there was a split in the rock on the right hand and on [the left hand]. And on the day of the tunneling through the workmen struck, each in the direction of his fellow, pick against pick. And the water started flowing from the source to the pool, twelve hundred cubits. And the height of the rock above the head of the workmen was a hundred cubits.[2]

Finally, there is the Pool of Siloam, dug as a repository for the waters of the Gihon Springs, flowing through Hezekiah's Tunnel.

The pool has been remodeled over the centuries by different rulers and for different purposes. John 9 reports that Jesus healed a blind man and told him to wash his eyes in the Pool of Siloam.

48: The Pool of Siloam

The Garden of Gethsemane

Biblical References: Matthew 26:36-56; Mark 14:32-50; Luke 22:39-53; John 18:1-14.

According to the Gospel accounts, the Garden of Gethsemane, located on the western slope of the Mount of Olives, is the site where Jesus was betrayed by Judas Iscariot and arrested by the soldiers of the High Priest, Caiaphas, following the Last Supper with the disciples. It is a place where Jesus probably came from time to time for solitude and prayer (Luke 22:39). Judas evidently knew that Jesus would be here, and was able to bring the soldiers to find him.

The name *Gethsemane* means "olive press." The remains of olive presses dating to the New Testament period have been found here, and olive trees are still abundant in the area. The road connecting Jerusalem to Jericho (and all points east) passed through or near to the Garden of Gethsemane. Old rock-hewn steps dating to biblical times are found near the Russian Church of Mary Magdalene near the Garden of Gethsemane.

Today there are two points of interest for visitors to Gethsemane. One is the garden itself. Priests who are assigned to the church tend the garden, and it is a well-kept place for quiet reflection. The garden contains some very old olive trees, which could conceivably date to the time of Jesus.

Second, the garden contains the beautiful Basilica of Agony. The church was built to commemorate Jesus' praying in agony before his arrest. The modern church, built in 1924, is located on the site of two earlier churches (Byzantine and Crusader). The Byzantine church was built in 379 CE and was destroyed by an earthquake in 745. The Crusader church was built in 1170. All three churches were built over a large rock that has traditionally been identified as the place where Jesus prayed:

> "Father, if you are willing, remove this cup from me; yet, not my will but yours be done." Then an angel from heaven appeared to him and gave him strength. In his anguish he prayed more earnestly, and his sweat became like great drops of blood falling down on the ground. (Luke 22:42-44)

The Basilica of Agony is better known as the Church of All Nations. Before the construction of the church began in 1924, an appeal was made to Christians throughout the world for financial assistance. The response was great. Since funding for the

49: The Garden of Gethsemane

church from churches and Christians from many different countries, the church came to be known, colloquially, as the Church of All Nations.

50: The Church of All Nations

The Mount of Olives

Biblical References: 2 Samuel 15:30; Matthew 21:1ff.; 26:30; Mark 11:1ff.; 13:3; 14:26; Luke 19:29, 37, 41-44; 21:37; John 8:1; Acts 1:6-12.

The Mount of Olives is located to the east of the Old City of Jerusalem, across the Kidron Valley. It is the tallest of the mountains and hills around Jerusalem, approximately 2,900 feet above sea level.

The Mount of Olives is best known for its association with the Judean ministry of Jesus. Bethany and Bethphage are villages on the eastern slope of the Mount of Olives. Three other sites on the Mount of Olives are associated with Jesus' ministry: the Church of Pater Noster (or Eleona Church), the Church of Dominus Flevit, and the Mosque of the Ascension.

Within the courtyard of the Church of Pater Noster is a cave. According to an early Christian tradition, now generally discounted, Jesus taught his disciples secretly in this cave. The

181

apocryphal Acts of John[3] claim that Jesus did teach his disciples in a cave located somewhere on the Mount of Olives; this could be the source of the early Christian tradition. Both the Bordeaux Pilgrim (333 CE) and Egeria (381–384 CE) report in their journals that they visited this cave.

Queen Helena, mother of Constantine, ordered the building of the Church of Eleona in the mid-fourth century CE. The name Eleona is a corruption of the Greek word *elaion*, which means "olives." This church was destroyed during the Persian invasion of 614 CE. In 1102, after Jerusalem had been taken by the Crusaders, two marble slabs were found, upon which were written the Lord's Prayer in Hebrew and Greek. It was assumed that this must have been the place where Jesus taught his disciples the Lord's Prayer. Today, around the walls of the church and courtyard, the Lord's Prayer is presented in approximately sixty-two languages. The church is known colloquially as the "Chapel of the Lord's Prayer" or "Pater Noster" (Our Father).[4]

The Church of Dominus Flevit ("the Lord wept") is located just above and east of the Garden of Gethsemane about halfway down the Mount of Olives. The church commemorates Jesus' weeping over the city of Jerusalem:

> As he came near and saw the city, he wept over it, saying, "If you, even you, had only recognized on this day the things that make for peace! But now they are hidden from your eyes. Indeed, the days will come upon you, when your enemies will set up ramparts around you and surround you, and hem you in on every side. They will crush you to the ground, you and your children within you, and they will not leave within you one stone upon another; because you did not recognize the time of your visitation from God." (Luke 19:41-44)

The church, built in 1954–55, is supposedly shaped in the form of a tear, though it takes some imagination to discern this. On each of the four corners of the church there is a tear vase to represent Jesus' weeping over the city. In ancient times it was considered appropriate for mourners to collect tears in such receptacles.

At the southern end of the church's courtyard is an ancient cemetery, which was discovered during the construction of the modern church. The cemetery dates to the sixteenth century BCE. The construction workers also found the remains of a fifth-century CE Byzantine monastery.

The Mosque of the Ascension marks the traditional site of Jesus' Ascension as reported in Acts 1:12. Although this site has been venerated by Christians throughout the history of the church, it also demonstrates how people's faith can be exploited. Inside the mosque

51: The Church of Dominus Flevit

is the impression of a footprint. The young guides who care for the mosque and sell tickets for admission to the site will tell unsuspecting visitors that this is the exact place from which Jesus ascended into heaven.

During the period between the fall of Jerusalem (in 70 CE) and the legalization of Christianity (under Constantine the Great, 275–337 CE), the Ascension of Jesus was remembered in a cave on the Mount of Olives. It is likely that the cave at the Church of the Pater Noster was venerated as the location of Jesus' Ascension. By the time of Egeria's visit (381–384 CE), the Ascension was remembered in an open area where the mosque is now located. By the Crusader Period a church had been built here. After the Crusaders were driven out of Jerusalem by the great Muslim leader Saladin, the site returned to Muslim control. The church was converted into a mosque and has remained a mosque since that time.

The Gospels are vague concerning the location of Jesus' Ascension. Matthew and John locate Jesus in Galilee prior to his Ascension. Luke states that the Ascension occurred on the Mount of Olives (Acts 1:6-12). Mark is silent on the matter.

Mount Zion

Biblical References: 2 Kings 2:10; Matthew 26:17-35; Mark 14:12-25; Luke 22:7-38; John 13–17.

Today Mount Zion is located near the Zion Gate, just to the north of the Hinnom Valley. In biblical times Mount Zion was associated with two other sites, the Ophel and Mount Moriah (2 Samuel 5:2). During the time of Jesus the area around the present-day Mount Zion was enclosed within the city walls of Jerusalem.

There are two biblical sites associated with this area. The first is the Tomb of King David. It has become a sacred place for Jewish people, but the site is not authentic. In the Bible we are told that David was buried in the City of David, on the Ophel (2 Kings 2:10). The location of David's tomb at this site cannot be dated before the Crusader Period. The Crusaders mistook this Mount Zion as the location of the City of David, and so the identification of David's tomb with this site is incorrect. With the discovery of the actual City of David more recently, it is now clear that David could not have been buried here. The site became a pilgrim site for Jewish people while they were not allowed to visit the Western Wall (before 1967). Today, even though Jewish people may visit the Western Wall, the Tomb of David on Mount Zion remains a holy shrine.

The second biblical site associated with Mount Zion is the Upper Room, where Jesus ate his last meal with his disciples (Matthew 26:26-29 and parallels). The building that is identified with the Upper Room today is not authentic, and the identification cannot be dated before the tenth century CE.

Another Christian tradition associates the coming of the Holy Spirit on the Day of Pentecost with this area. The Bible, however, reports only that "they were all together in one place" (Acts 2:1b). Other traditions suggest that Peter's Pentecost sermon was delivered on the Rabbi's Teaching Stairway at the southern end of the Temple Mount.

One other site on Mount Zion that deserves mention is the Dormition Abbey, a Benedictine monastery established in 1906.

Its official name, in Latin, is Dormition Sanctae Mariae, which means the "Sleep of Saint Mary." The church and monastery were remodeled in 1948 and 1967. According to one Christian tradition, the Dormition Abbey is built over the site of the Virgin Mary's tomb. The church here is one of the most beautiful in Jerusalem and is famous for its beautiful mosaic floor and acoustical quality.

St. Peter in Gallicantu

Biblical References: Matthew 26:57–27:5; Mark 14:53–15:1; Luke 22:54-71; John 18:12-27.

Located just below (south of) Mount Zion is St. Peter's Church, officially named St. Peter in Gallicantu, which means "St. Peter at the crowing of the cock." According to one Christian tradition, the church is built over the site of the house of Caiaphas, the High Priest during the time of Jesus. The Gospel writers locate Peter's denial of Jesus in a courtyard just outside the house.

Even though this is an ancient tradition, there is doubt about its authenticity. There are compelling arguments that dispute its authenticity. First, there is no specific and direct evidence to support this tradition. Second, Egeria mentions that the site of Caiaphas's house was at a different location during her visit to the city. Third, it would be unlikely for a palace of this type to have been built on a hillside because this position would not be secure or protected from an attack from above.

Yet, there are also arguments that support locating Caiaphas's house here. First, this site would have been in the Upper City of Herodian Jerusalem, a place where we could expect to find wealthy palaces. Second, in the basements of the church we find the remains of rooms that might have been used as jail cells during the Herodian Period. The presence of these cell-like rooms alone does not make a case for locating the house of Caiaphas here, but it does suggest that this was a place where a privy-council or a sanhedrin could have met. One of the places where such a privy-council might have met would have been the home/office of the High Priest.[5] Third, other discoveries (rooms, cisterns, cellars, etc.) dating to the Herodian Period indicate that the owner of this house was a wealthy and, perhaps, prominent person.

In the final analysis, no one knows for certain whether this site marks the location of the house of Caiaphas.

52: St. Peter's Church in Gallicantu

The Old City

There are seven gates leading into and out of the Old City of Jerusalem today. These are, beginning in the southeastern corner and moving clockwise, the Dung Gate, Zion Gate, Jaffa Gate, New Gate, Damascus Gate, Herod Gate, and Lion's Gate (or St. Stephen's Gate). The two busiest gates today are the Damascus and Jaffa Gates.

53: The Jaffa Gate

54: The Damascus Gate

The present walls of the Old City were built by the Ottoman ruler Suleiman the Magnificent, between 1537–1542 CE. Since that time there have been renovations, but the walls have remained essentially the same. The walls of the Old City today do not conform to the location of the walls of the Herodian Period; they are farther to the north than those from the time of Jesus (see the diagram of the Old City).

55: The Walls of the Old City

56: Diagram of the Old City

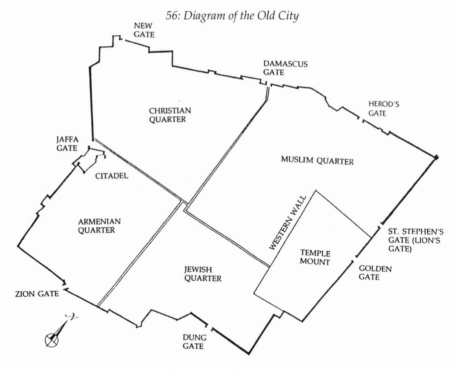

The Jewish Quarter

The dominant feature of the Jewish Quarter is the Western Wall, which is sometimes referred to as the Wailing Wall.[6] This is the holiest site or shrine in Judaism. The Western Wall is all that remains of the grand Herodian Temple, which was destroyed by the Romans in 70 CE. Recent excavations at the southern end of the Haram es-Sharif (the Temple Mount) have exposed more of the wall. However, Jewish pilgrims usually do not visit this area for prayer. A visitor to the wall may be startled to see thousands of pieces of paper placed in the nooks and cracks of the Western Wall. An old Jewish legend associated with the Western Wall holds that an angel comes from heaven each night and collects the prayers that have been written on the paper and carries the prayers to God.

57: The Western Wall

There are three other significant biblical or historical sites in or around the Jewish Quarter. The excavations outside of the southern and southwestern walls of the Temple Mount, carried out under the direction of Benjamin Mazar between 1968 and 1977, resulted in several important findings. First, a major street was discovered running north and south along the Western Wall, that had been built by Herod the Great during his renovation program here. Second, Mazar discovered that the southwestern gate into the Temple Court (Court of the Gentiles) had not been connected to a bridge that crossed the Tyropean Valley, as suggested by Edward Robinson in 1838. The arch found here has come to be known as Robinson's Arch. Mazar found evidence that suggests that the Gate at Robinson's Arch was connected to a large stairway from the street below into the Court of the Gentiles. Third, a double and triple gate were found in the southern wall. The Double Gate (or Western Huldah Gate[7]) is found directly north of the Rabbi's Teaching Stairway. This teaching stairway connects the southern end of the Temple Mount with the Ophel. The Triple Gate (Eastern Huldah Gate) is found near the southwestern corner of the Temple Mount. Both of these gates are now sealed. Fourth, a stone bearing the inscription "To the place of trumpeting,"[8] was found in the debris below the southwestern corner of the Temple Mount. According to Josephus, this trumpeting took place on the southwestern pinnacle of the Temple (*Jewish War* 4:582; see also Matthew 4:5 and Luke 4:9). Fifth, near the southwestern corner of one of the large stones of the Western Wall of the Temple Mount is the carved inscription of a passage from Isaiah 66:14:

> You shall see, and your heart shall rejoice;
> your bodies shall flourish like the grass.

The inscription was possibly placed here by Julian the Apostate (361–363 CE). Sixth, there are many remains dating to the Byzantine and Ummayad periods (661–750 CE).

A second significant historical site found in the Jewish Quarter is the restored Roman Cardo. The Cardo was the main north/south street of the Roman city Aelia Capitolina.[9] It was the most important street in Jerusalem after the Bar Kochba Revolt (132–135 CE). The third significant historical site is the Burnt House, which consists of the remains of a dwelling destroyed by the Romans during the First Jewish Revolt (66–70 CE).

Today the Jewish Quarter is bustling with life. Some of the city's most expensive apartments are found here. In the heart of the Jewish Quarter is an open courtyard area. In the spring and summer months this area teems with music, artists, families, and friends gathering for conversation or entertainment.

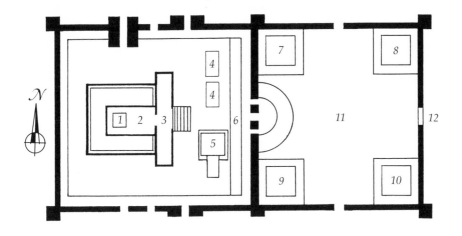

58: *Sketch of the Second Temple*
LEGEND: *1. Holy of Holies, 2. Sanctuary, 3. Porch, 4. Slaughter House, 5. Altar, 6.*
Court of the Israelites, 7. Chamber of Lepers, 8. Chamber of Wood, 9. Chamber of Oils,
10. Chamber of Nazirites, 11. Women's Court, 12. The Beautiful Gate

The Armenian Quarter

The Armenian presence in Jerusalem dates to the fourth century CE. Armenia is believed to have been the first country officially to accept the Christian faith in about 300 CE. As a result of their faith, Armenian Christians established a presence in Jerusalem, through churches, monasteries, and schools, at an early date.

The history of Armenia is both rich and tragic. Unfortunately, Westerners know very little of this history. Many visitors to Jerusalem have their first experience of the Armenians and their history, faith, and culture. It may be helpful to offer a brief historical overview of the Armenians and their community in Jerusalem.

The land of Armenia was located in what is now Eastern Turkey and the southwestern part of the former USSR. By the time of the Romans, it had become a vassal state; later it was controlled by the Byzantines, Arabs, and Turks. In the early six-teenth century CE, Armenia became a part of the Ottoman Empire. It remained in Turkish control until World War I, when the Treaty of Sevres gave Armenia its independence. In 1920, the country was invaded by both Turkey and Russia; the Turks claimed the western half of Armenia, and the Russians took the eastern half. Today, what is left of Armenia is a small republic in the former USSR.

One of the great tragedies of the past century is the sys-tematic campaign of genocide by the Turks against the Arme-nians, beginning in the late 1890s. By World War I between 1,800,000 and 2,000,000 Armenians had been killed. Thou-sands of others escaped to Jerusalem, which came to be something of a capital of Armenia in exile. Since that time, there has been a strong Armenian presence in the city, cen-tered in the Armenian Quarter of the Old City. Today, the Armenian Quarter is inhabited by refugees who escaped the holocaust in Turkey and the descendants of those refugees. Since World War I the Armenians have made a positive con-tribution to the Christian community in Jerusalem. Recently, however, hardships in Israel have forced many young Arme-nians to leave the country for the West. By the end of the 1980s the Armenian population in Jerusalem had been greatly reduced.

The two major biblical/historical sites found in the Armen-ian Quarter are the Cathedral of St. James and the Chapel of St. Mark. The Cathedral of St. James dates to the twelfth century CE when the site was given to the Armenian Orthodox Church by the Crusaders. The church is built over the traditional site of the execution of James, the brother of Jesus and the leader of the Christian movement in Jerusalem until his death (about 62 CE).[10]

During the Ottoman Period the Turks would not allow the ringing of church bells. Outside the main entrance of the church is a hanging plank, which was used as a substitute for a church bell. Priests would strike the plank with a ham-mer to call the people to worship and/or prayer. Even today this tradition continues. The rapping sound of the plank being struck can be heard throughout the Armenian Quarter.

The Chapel of St. Mark is a Syrian Orthodox Church. The members of this church believe that it is built over the site of the home of St. Mark. Their tradition also affirms that Peter came to this house (of St. Mark) when he was released from jail by an angel (Acts 12:6-17). Inside the church is a beautiful painting of the Virgin Mary with the Christ child. Members of the church believe that this painting was done by the evangelist Luke. Two other traditions are associated with the church here: that the Virgin Mary was baptized here, and that the Lord's Supper took place in an Upper Room in the house of St. Mark.

The Christian Quarter

The holiest shrine in Christendom is located in the Christian Quarter of the Old City. This is the Church of the Holy Sepulchre, built over the place where, according to Christian tradition, Jesus was executed, buried, and resurrected. During the Roman Period, under the governorship of Pontius Pilate, this site may have been used as a place for executions. It was located near the road that connected Jerusalem with Caesarea Maritima, a busy highway where executions would have served as a warning to all travelers not to cause trouble. During this period, a rock quarry was located here, just outside the city walls of Jerusalem. Excavations have revealed a part of this rock quarry at the church's lowest levels. Archaeologists have also found first-century tombs in the church. One of these tombs, found near a Coptic chapel behind the Holy Sepulchre, has been called the tomb of Nicodemus, although there is no proof that the Nicodemus mentioned in John's Gospel was buried here.

One of the more interesting of the recent discoveries in the church of the Holy Sepulchre is found in two small chambers

59: The Church of the Holy Sepulchre (photo)

60: The Church of the Holy Sepulchre (diagram)
LEGEND: 1. The Entrance—12th Century, 2. Steep stairs just inside the entry, leading up to Calvary, 3. Downstairs—Chapel of Adam; one can see the rock through a glass plate, 4. The stone of unction where Jesus was prepared for burial, 5. The tomb monument of Jesus's burial, 6. The Crusade church, now Greek Orthodox, 7. The Crypt of St. Helena, mother of Constantine, 8. Grotto of the Cross, 9. Chapel of Longin, 10. Chapel of the Garments, 11. Chapel of Derision, 12. Chapel

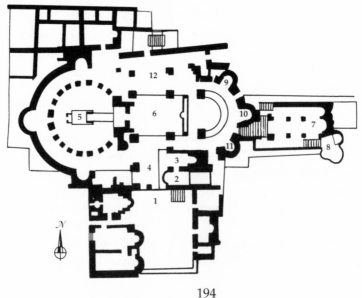

behind the Chapel of St. Helena. The following were found here: (1) the exterior wall from the Byzantine Church; (2) a large drain pipe that led from the Byzantine Church; (3) a pool was found at the lowest levels, which may have been used as an early Judeo-Christian ritual bath or baptism pool; (4) pottery pieces, some dating to the first century CE; (5) the wall of a very early room, which may have been from a chapel or a synagogue-church; and finally (6) on this early wall is an early drawing of a small boat—the kind of boat common to Mediterranean culture from the early centuries of the Common Era. Beneath the drawing is an inscription in Latin, which translates: "O Lord, we arrived."[11] Much of this evidence indicates that from a very early date, followers of Jesus came to this place to remember his execution, burial, and resurrection.

Outside the walls of the Old City along Nablus Road, which runs northwest from the Damascus Gate, one can find the Garden Tomb. In 1883 the British general Charles Gordon believed that a stone outcropping reminded him of what he believed Calvary should look like, and nearby he discovered a tomb. He surmised that this may have been the location of the crucifixion and burial of Jesus, but the authenticity of the site is highly doubtful. The tomb itself dates from many years before the first century CE, and Jesus was said to have been buried in a new tomb. Furthermore, the site of the Church of the Holy Sepulchre was venerated as that of Jesus' death already in the second century CE, whereas "Gordon's Calvary," as the Garden Tomb is popularly known, was not suggested until the nineteenth century CE, with no earlier claims to veneration by the faithful. Yet the well-kept gardens and the serenity of the site make it an ideal place for pilgrims to pause and reflect upon the events of Holy Week and Easter.

The Church of the Holy Sepulchre has an interesting history. It was built under orders from Constantine, the first Christian emperor of the Roman Empire. The work began in 326 CE and was completed in 335 CE, the year of the church's dedication.

61: The Garden Tomb

Additional work was carried on until 348. Constantine's mother, Helena, played a major role in having this church built. After she had visited the sites in the land in the early fourth century, she encouraged her son to build churches commemorating the great events in the life of Jesus.

The church was destroyed by Fatamin Caliph Hakim in 1009, when he took the city, and later it was rebuilt during the Crusades. For the most part the church today is as it was during the Crusader occupation of Jerusalem. The building was damaged, however, on two other occasions: in 1808 a serious fire destroyed the church's rotunda, and in 1927 an earthquake seriously damaged the building. Since the six Christian groups that dispute ownership of the Church of the Holy Sepulchre could not agree among themselves about who would pay for the repair work, none was undertaken until 1959.[12] Even now visitors to the church can see the ongoing repair work inside the church building.

One other aspect of the church should be mentioned. Very

few visitors know about the monastery of the Ethiopian Orthodox Church located on the roof of the church. This is one of the
oldest religious orders in the Holy Land. The Ethiopians trace
their spiritual history to King Solomon, and they claim that
their ancestors converted to Judaism after the visit to Solomon
by the Queen of Sheba. Then, after the coming of Jesus, they
recognized him as the Messiah of their faith, whose coming had
been foretold by the prophets of Israel. Their Christian faith,
according to the monks who live here, is a logical extension of
the Judaism practiced by their ancestors in Ethiopia. The monks
are devout, friendly, and always happy to have visitors. They
are willing to sit and talk about their history and theology with
anyone who takes the time to ask. The Ethiopians have two
small chapels inside the church building, beneath their living
quarters, which contain beautiful mosaics depicting the history
of their movement.

The Muslim Quarter

The Muslim Quarter is the largest of the four quarters that
comprise the Old City. The two principle features of the Muslim Quarter are the Via Dolorosa and the Temple Mount (the
Haram esh-Sharif), which is discussed separately below.

The Via Dolorosa, known in English as the "Way of Sorrows"
or the "Way of the Cross," is the traditional route of Jesus' walk
to Calvary from Pilate's headquarters at the Antonia Fortress (to
the Church of the Holy Sepulchre in the Christian Quarter). It is
likely that Jesus followed at least a portion of this path on his
walk to Calvary. It is important to note, however, that the
ground level of the contemporary street is at a much higher level
than the street in Jesus' time, due to the process of destruction
and rebuilding that has occurred since the Second Temple
Period.

Along the Via Dolorosa are the traditional "Stations of the
Cross," which Christians from all over the world venerate as
they retrace the steps of Jesus. Some of the Stations commemo-
ate events found in the Gospels, while others are supported

only by church tradition. Since many Christians are unable to make the journey to Jerusalem to venerate these places, the Stations have been included in most Roman Catholic churches since the twelfth century. Each Friday a group of Franciscan priests leads a procession on the Via Dolorosa to commemorate Jesus' walk to Calvary.

Today there is really only one place along the Via Dolorosa where pilgrims can walk on pavement (stones) where Jesus might have walked. This place is found outside the front gate of the Armenian Catholic Church where the Via Dolorosa meets El Wad Street. Here paving stones from the time of Jesus are exposed in the contemporary street.

Another prominent site found in the Muslim Quarter is the Sisters of Zion Convent. At the lower level of the convent one finds what may have been the courtyard of the Antonia Fortress, the Roman military headquarters of Jerusalem during the Herodian Period.[13] Here visitors can see traces of a game board carved by Roman soldiers on the surface of some of the stones; this pavement is known as the Lithostratos.

The Antonia Fortress was built by Herod the Great in 37–35 BCE and named for his close friend Mark Anthony. When the Roman governor, or prefect, was in Jerusalem, the Antonia Fortress may have served as his headquarters, as it may have for Pilate. The Antonia Fortress was heavily damaged in the sack of Jerusalem during the First Jewish Revolt (70 CE). The pavement known today as the Lithostratos, with its carving, almost certainly comes from the time of Hadrian, but the "King's Game," of which it preserves evidence, was known in the time of Jesus and Herod the Great.

The "King's Game" apparently helped to boost the morale of soldiers posted in Judea, which was considered the worst assignment in the Roman army. By throwing dice, the soldiers would choose a burlesque "king"; following additional throws of the dice, the "king" would be mocked and abused both verbally and physically. The resemblance between this game and the mockery of Jesus by the soldiers reported in the Gospel (Matthew 27:27-31; Mark 15:16-20) is striking.

62: Lithostratos— The Pavement

To the eastern end of the courtyard area are the remains of a Roman street. There are grooves in the street that would have helped to keep horses from slipping or falling on the slick paving stones.

There are three other sites in the Muslim Quarter that should be mentioned. The first is St. Anne's Church. Although it has no biblical significance, this church is located in an area that has traditionally been identified as the home of the Virgin Mary during her childhood. The church was built in 1140 CE by the Crusaders and was named for Mary's mother, Anne. It was lost when the Muslims retook the city in 1187. In 1192, it was converted into an Islamic theological academy by Saladin. During the Crimean War (1853–1856) the French helped the Turks drive the Russian army out of Turkey. As a reward for their assistance, the church was given to the French. The building was restored to resemble the Crusader church. Today the church is best known as an example of Crusader architecture and also for its excellent acoustical quality, which makes it a popular place for concerts.

63: St. Anne's Church

The second site, adjacent to St. Anne's Church, is the Pool (or Pools) of Bethesda. The Gospel of John reports that Jesus healed a paralyzed man here (5:2ff.). During the Roman Period a temple dedicated to the god Serapis was located on this site.[14]

The third site is actually an area: the bazaar (street markets) of the Old City. A stop in this area is always a must for visitors to Jerusalem, because the bazaar can give them at least a small taste of what life in the city might have been like in biblical times.

64: Bethesda Pools

65: The Old City Bazaar

The Temple Mount (Haram esh-Sharif)

The Temple Mount, known in Arabic as the Haram esh-Sharif ("Noble Sanctuary"), is located atop Mount Moriah, across the Kidron Valley from the Mount of Olives. It continues to be the most majestic and impressive site in Jerusalem (and probably the entire country). The site is sacred to Jews, Christians, and Muslims; according to the traditions of all three religions, this is the site where Abraham prepared his son for sacrifice (Genesis 22).[15] David bought the site and built an altar on it (2 Samuel 24:18ff.), and here Solomon built the First Temple (1 Kings 5–6). Solomon's Temple was destroyed by the Babylonians in 587/86 BCE. The construction of the Second Temple began in 520 BCE and was completed in about 516. It was extensively renovated and remodeled by Herod the Great in 20/19–18 BCE,[16] and destroyed by the Romans in 70 CE. Only the Western Wall survives from the Second Temple.

Jerusalem is the third holiest site of Islam, after Mecca and Medina: "The sacred nature of Jerusalem is confirmed for the Muslims above all by the Night Journey, in which the prophet Muhammed was brought by the angel Gabriel to the Dome of the Rock on the Temple Mount. From here they ascended together into the heavens (Koran 17:1)."[17] The Vision of the Night Journey was given to Muhammed, who related it to his followers, and it became one of the bases upon which later Muslims laid claim to the Dome of the Rock. The story was embellished through time, but basically it is said that Muhammed mounted a winged horse in Mecca and flew to Jerusalem, accompanied by the archangel Gabriel. From the top of the rock they ascended to heaven on a ladder of golden light to receive instructions from Allah, after which they returned to the rock. Following a conversation with Old Testament prophets, Muhammed returned to Mecca on his winged horse. Many tourists are misled into believing that Muhammed's ascent from the Dome of the Rock was a surrogate for death, reminiscent of Elijah. This is not the case.

The Second Temple

Josephus writes that the Second Temple was larger and more magnificent than the Temple of Solomon:

> And now Herod, in the eighteenth year of his reign, and after the acts mentioned, undertook a very great work, that is, to build of himself the temple of God, and make it larger in compass, and to raise it to a most glorious of all his actions, as it really was, to bring it to perfection, and that this would be sufficient for an everlasting memorial to him. (*Antiquities* 15:380)

The dimensions of the Temple were as follows: "The south wall, 929 feet; the west wall, 1,595 feet; the north wall, 1,041 feet; and the east wall, 1,556 feet—a total of about thirty-five acres."[18] This was an enormous structure.

Around the walls, on the inside, were colonnades that were called the Temple's porticoes. Josephus reports that "the works that were above those foundations, these were not unworthy of such foundations; for all the cloisters were double, and the pillars to them, and that stone was white marble" (*Jewish War* 5:190). The colonnade on the eastern side of the platform, overlooking the Kidron Valley and the Mount of Olives, was known as the portico of Solomon. The Gospel of John reports that Jesus taught here (John 10:22-39). Other rabbis used the colonnades surrounding the platform area for teaching as well.

Several important courts were located in the Temple area at the time of the Second Temple. The largest of these courts was the Court of the Gentiles, which covered the large area surrounding the Temple itself. Important commercial activity took place in the Court of the Gentiles. Persons coming to Jerusalem could purchase animals here to use for sacrifice. It was in the Court of the Gentiles that Jesus is reported by the Gospels to have attacked those engaged in such practices.

Upon entering the Temple area through the Beautiful Gate (Acts 3:2), one would enter the Court of the Women (of Israel). This court contained four chambers, one in each corner. These were the Chambers of Lepers, Wood, the Nazirites, and Oils. Women were not allowed beyond the Court of the Women.

66: Model of the Second Temple

Moving west from the Court of the Women, only males were allowed to pass through the Nicanor Gate. There were two remaining courts between the Nicanor Gate and the Temple. These were the Court of Israel and the Priests' Court. Only men in good standing—that is, in a state of ritual purity or cleanliness—could enter the Court of Israel. The Court of Priests contained the altar where sacrifices were offered to God. Beyond the Court of the Priests was the sanctuary, which was also divided into three parts: the porch or entrance, the nave or sanctuary, and finally, the Holy of Holies. The Holy of Holies could be entered only once a year, on the Day of Atonement, and only by the High Priest.

On the outside of the gate leading into the Temple area was a warning written in Greek and Latin. The inscription read: "No Gentile to enter the fence and barrier around the Temple. Anyone caught is answerable to himself for his ensuing death."[19] It is more than obvious that non-Jews were not allowed to enter the Temple or any of the inner courts around the Temple.

67: The Court of the Gentiles

203

The Dome of the Rock

When Jerusalem was conquered by Omar in 638 CE, he learned that the Christians had been using the Temple Mount as a garbage dump. He was so angered by this that he had the area cleaned and built the Dome of the Rock on the site. Construction on the mosque began in 688 and was completed in 691. There were probably two major reasons for the building of the Dome of the Rock. First, the mosque was built to commemorate Muhammed's journey to heaven from this site. Second, the Muslim leaders of the city wanted to build a mosque or shrine to compete in beauty and splendor with the churches of Jerusalem. A third possible reason was that tradition holds that this was the place where Abraham, in obedience to God, was prepared to sacrifice his son Isaac (Genesis 22).

The mosaics found within the Dome of the Rock date to the seventh century CE. Written around the inner circumference of

the dome is a plea in Arabic to Christians, urging them to abandon their heretical belief in three gods and to embrace the One True God, Allah. The inscription affirms that Jesus was a prophet of God, but not God himself. The exterior of the building was renovated in 1963.

Outside the Dome of the Rock, to the east, is a smaller building, called the Dome of the Chain.

68: The Dome of the Rock

There are two theories about its presence and purpose. One is that the building was constructed to serve as a model for the Dome of the Rock. There is a strong resemblance between the two. A second possibility is that this building once served as the treasury for the Haram esh-Sharif. No one knows for sure which, if either, of these theories is correct.

The Al Aksa Mosque is also rich in history and beauty, and it is a site that must be seen when visiting Jerusalem. The mosque was built between 705 and 715 CE. It was heavily damaged twice by earthquakes, in 715 CE and again in 775 CE. The last major restoration occurred between 1938 and 1942. The marble columns in the mosque were donated by Mussolini, and the interior painting was funded by King Farouk of Egypt.

In 1969, a fanatical Christian set fire to the building. He had hoped that the Jews would rebuild the Temple if the mosques were destroyed; he also believed that the Messiah would return once the Temple had been rebuilt, and that by destroying the mosques he would hasten the coming of the Messiah.

69: Al Aksa Mosque

The Valleys Around the Old City

The three valleys that almost surround the Old City are mentioned many times in the Bible. They are the Tyropean, Kidron, and Hinnom Valleys.

Josephus (*Jewish War* 5:140) calls the Tyropean Valley the "Valley of the Cheesemakers." This valley is located just to the west of the Ophel. It is difficult to see the Tyropean Valley today, because it is so small and some of it has been filled during construction and reconstruction projects in the Old City. The best view of the Tyropean Valley is from the ramparts above the Damascus Gate.

The Kidron Valley is located between the Mount of Olives and the Temple Mount (Haram esh-Sharif). The Arab village of Silwan is visible on the eastern edge of the Kidron Valley. Silwan is located on the possible site of the village of Bathsheba from the time of King David (see 2 Samuel 11:2ff.). All travelers coming to Jerusalem from the east passed through the Kidron Valley to enter Jerusalem. On the night of Jesus' arrest, according to the Gospel accounts, he and his disciples passed through the valley from the place of their Passover meal to his place of prayer in the Garden of Gethsemane. The most notable biblical sites associated with the Kidron Valley are the Garden of Gethsemane, the village of Silwan, the City of David, Hezekiah's Tunnel, and the traditional tombs of the prophets and Absalom.

The Hinnom Valley is located just south of the Old City, running east and west. In the Old Testament Period this valley was famous as a place for child sacrifice and idol worship (Jeremiah 7:31ff.). During the Herodian Period the city's garbage dump was located here; the garbage was burned, so there was often smoke and fire in the valley. Jesus made symbolic reference to the unfaithful being cast into "gehenna," thus using the Hinnom Valley as a symbol or example of a wasted or worthless life.

70: Sketch of the Valleys of Jerusalem

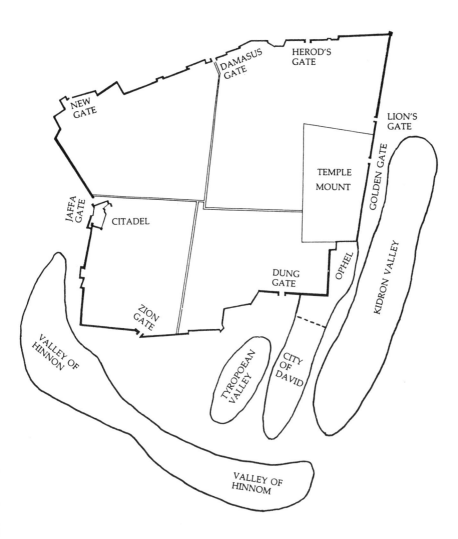

JORDAN

Amman (Ammon)

Biblical References: Genesis 19:38; Numbers 21:24; Deuteronomy 2:19, 37; 3:11; 23:4; Joshua 12:2; 13:10, 25; 15:60; 2 Samuel 11:1; 12:26-31; 1 Kings 11:7, 33; 1 Chronicles 19:1ff. 20:1; 2 Chronicles 20:1, 10, 22-23; 26:8; Isaiah 11:14; Jeremiah 9:26; 25:21; 49:2, 3, 6; Ezekiel 21:20; 25:5; Amos 1:14; and many other references.

Amman is the contemporary capital of the Hashemite Kingdom of Jordan. The biblical city was known as Rabbath-Ammon and also as Rabbath, the capital of the Ammonites, to which there are numerous references in the Bible.

The Bible reports that the founder (or "father") of the Ammonite kingdom was a descendant of Lot (Genesis 19:38). Later the Ammonites were condemned for not showing hospitality to the Hebrews during their wilderness sojourn (Deuteronomy 23:3-4). A portion of the Ammonite land was later given to the tribe of Gad (Joshua 13:25). During the reign of David, Amman was the site of the siege or battle where Uriah was killed (2 Samuel 11:1ff.). At this time Joab defeated the city and claimed it for David (2 Samuel 12:26-31).

After the death of Alexander the Great, Amman was given to the Ptolemies; under Ptolemy II the city was rebuilt and named Philadelphia. The city was captured by the Seleucids (Antiochus III) in about 218 BCE. After the invasion and conquest of

Pompey (63 BCE) the city became a part of the Roman Empire; Pompey included Philadelphia in the Decapolis.

Today some of the ruins of the Roman city are still evident, including a Roman theater that could seat up to 6,000 people; a Roman temple that was dedicated to Hercules; and a nymphaeum, a shrine to the Nymphs, which was used as a place for weddings and wedding receptions. There have also been many discoveries from other historical periods.

Dibon

Biblical References: Numbers 21:26-31; 32:3, 34; Joshua 13:8-9, 17; 2 Kings 3:4-6; Jeremiah 48:18, 22.

The ruins of ancient Dibon, the former capital of Moab, are located about 40 miles (64 km) south of Amman and some 12 miles (19 km) east of the Dead Sea. Dibon is best known as the site where the Moabite Stone, or Mesha Inscription, was discovered.

The Bible reports that Dibon was conquered by Sihon, the Amorite king (Numbers 21:26-31). Later, after the Israelite invasion, the city was given to the tribes of Gad and Reuben (Numbers 32:1-3). Gad rebuilt the city some time after this (Numbers 32:34).[1] After David united the Israelite tribes, Moab became subjugated to Israel (2 Samuel 8:2).

During the period of the divided monarchy, Moab was a vassal state of Israel. Omri forced the Moabites to pay a tribute of 100,000 sheep and the wool of 100,000 rams (2 Kings 3:4). This relationship continued during the reign of Ahab. After his death, however, Moab, under King Mesha, successfully revolted against Israel, and Moab's independence was established (2 Kings 3:4ff.).

The Moabite Stone, or Mesha Inscription, is a record of the successful military campaign of the Moabite King Mesha against Israel and its king, Jehoram. This stele was discovered in 1868 by the Reverend Frederick Klein, a German missionary. Subsequently there were two competing offers to purchase the Moabite Stone. As a result of these offers the stele was broken into small fragments, many of which were lost; fortunately, an impression of the stele had been made prior to its destruction, and the fragments that were lost have been replaced with reproductions made from the impression.² The original stele is now in the Louvre in Paris; a copy is on display in the British Museum in London.

Heshbon

Biblical References: Numbers 21:25ff.; 32:3, 37; Deuteronomy 1:4; 2:24ff.; 4:46; Joshua 21:34-40; 1 Chronicles 6:81; Isaiah 15:4; 16:8-9; Jeremiah 48:2ff.; 49:3.

Biblical Heshbon has been identified with the modern Tell Hesbân. The tell is located approximately 15 miles (24 km) southwest of Amman, 6 miles (10 km) north of Madaba, and some 40 miles (64 km) east of Jerusalem. Tell Hesbân is one of the largest tells in Jordan.

Heshbon was once the capital of the Amorites, whose king, Sihon, attacked the Israelites following a request for passage through Amorite land as the Hebrews were moving to invade Canaan (see Numbers 21:21-26). The Israelite army defeated the Amorites and settled in some of their cities, including Heshbon. When the land was divided among the twelve tribes, Heshbon was first given to Reuben (Numbers 32:3, 37). Later Heshbon is listed as one of the cities of Gad that were given to the Levites (Joshua 21:38-39).

Josephus reports that John Hyrcanus captured the cities of Madaba and Samega during his reign, in about 129 BCE (see *Antiquities* 13:255). Heshbon is not specifically mentioned here, but Josephus lists Heshbon as being one of the cities controlled by the Jews during the reign of Alexander Janneus (103–76 BCE) (*Antiquities* 13:395-397). Therefore, Heshbon was probably conquered along with Madaba and Samega. Later, Herod the Great built a fortress here (named Esbus) to provide a defense for his eastern border (*Antiquities* 15:294).

Excavations of the tell, which began in the late 1960s, have revealed occupational levels dating from the Iron Age into the Mameluke Period. So far, the remains of the Amorite city of Sihon have not been found. This suggests that the Heshbon of Sihon might be located elsewhere or that the biblical account in Numbers 21 might be anachronistic.

Jerash (Gerasa)

Biblical References: Matthew 8:28; Mark 5:1; Luke 8:26, 37.

Jerash, known in biblical times as Gerasa, is located approximately 24 miles (40 km) north of Amman (on the King's Highway), 37 miles (59 km) southeast of the Sea of Galilee, and some 20 miles (32 km) east of the Jordan River. The geographical area around Jerash (Gerasa) was known as the "country of the Garasenes" (Mark 5:1). (It was also known as the country of the Gergesenes or Gadarenes.)

Jerash's history can be traced at least as far back as the Early Bronze Age. Noted archaeologist Nelson Glueck located evidence of Early Bronze Age occupation in his work here in 1938. There is also evidence that the site was occupied in the Middle Bronze Period. However, Jerash is usually best remembered as a Hellenistic and Roman city.

After the Seleucids defeated the Ptolemies, they built a new city here, which included the earliest temple to Zeus. Josephus writes that the city and territory were conquered by Alexander Jannaeus (*Antiquities* 13:393-397). Pompey took the city for Rome during his invasion (63 BCE) and made it one of the cities of the Decapolis. During the First Revolt of the Jews against Rome, the city was taken by the Jewish rebels (Josephus, *Jewish Wars* 2:457-458). Jerash was reclaimed for Rome by Vespasian shortly after this (*Jewish Wars* 4:486-490). The city continued to prosper throughout the Roman Period, and by the fourth century CE it was a Christian city. Representatives from Jerash participated in many of the early church councils after 359 CE, and remains of many early churches are found in its ruins. In the 630s the city fell to the Arabs.

Excavations began here in 1925 under the direction of John Garstang and George Horsfield, with work continuing sporadically since then. Even today, parts of the city are being excavated and restored by groups from Europe and the United States, as well as the Jordanian Department of Antiquities.

The excavations have revealed much of Jerash's splendor. Some of the more outstanding remains include the following: First, the Arch of Hadrian is found near the southern gate of the city. This arch was erected in 129 CE to commemorate the visit of Hadrian to the city. Second, moving from the southern gate is the city's Forum, a large open area surrounded by Ionic columns. Third, the Temple of Zeus, built in 163 BCE, is located on a hill overlooking the Forum. Fourth, and adjacent to the Temple of Zeus, is the Southern Theatre. This theater was built during the first century CE and had a seating capacity of between four and five thousand. Fifth, the cardo, or Cardo Maximus, a street lined with some 260 Ionic and Corinthian columns, passes through the center of the ruins. Visitors to the city who walk on this street can still see impressions in the paving stones left by chariots in the first century. Sixth, near the first intersection of streets down the cardo are the remains of a fourth-century Christian cathedral, only one of at least a dozen churches found here. Seventh, the Temple of Artemis is found just to the northeast of the cathedral. Artemis was the patron goddess of the city, and a temple for her worship was built during the second century CE and is probably the most impressive of the extant ruins.

Finally, an early Christian tradition suggests that Paul might have spent time here after his flight from Damascus (Galatians 1:17-18). He reports that he spent three years in "Arabia," but does not say where in Arabia. Jerash, considered as being Arabia, would have been a safe place for Paul after his conversion.

71: Jerash: The Forum   *72: Jerash: Hadrian's Arch*

Kerak

Biblical References: 2 Kings 3:25; Isaiah 16:7, 11; Jeremiah 48:31, 36.

The ruins of Kerak are located on the King's Highway not far from the southern portion of the Dead Sea. In biblical times it was known as Kir-hareseth, Kir-haresh, or Kir-heres. The only biblical significance of the site relates to Mesha, the Moabite king. After the death of Ahab (of Israel) Mesha rebelled against his successor, Jehoram. Israel, Judah, and Edom attacked Mesha here at Kerak. After Mesha sacrificed his son by burning him on the city walls, the attacking armies withdrew (2 Kings 3:4-8, 25-27).

During the Crusades several impressive castles were built here and in the surrounding area. The last of the Crusaders to command the castle at Kerak was Renaud de Châtillon. In violation of an agreement allowing pilgrims access to the holy sites of the land, Renaud attacked Muslim pilgrims. This led to the battle between Renaud's army and that of Saladin at the Horns of Hattin in 1187 CE, where the Crusaders were defeated by the Arab army and Saladin executed Renaud.

Madaba

Biblical References: Numbers 21:30; Joshua 13:9, 16; 1 Chronicles 19:7; Isaiah 15:2; 1 Maccabees 9:35-42.

Madaba is located approximately 20 miles (32 km) south of Amman, on the King's Highway. The city was taken by the Israelites after they defeated the Amorites and King Sihon (Numbers 21:21-31). It was again conquered by Israel during the reign of David, when Joab and his army defeated the Syrians (Arameans) and the Ammonites here (see 1 Chronicles 19:7, 10-15). Madaba is also mentioned in the Moabite Stone, where Mesha claims that he was able to retake the city during his rebellion against Israel.

During the Maccabean Period, John, one of the sons of Mattathias, was killed at Madaba. His death was avenged by his brothers Jonathan and Simon (1 Maccabees 9:35-42). Josephus reports that Madaba was later taken by John Hyrcanus during the Hasmonean Period (*Antiquities* 13:254-255). However, during the reign of John Hyrcanus II (63–40 BCE), Madaba was given to the Nabateans as a reward along with other cities (*Antiquities* 14:14-18). During the early Byzantine Period, Madaba became a Christian city with its own bishop, but after the Islamic invasions it was abandoned.

The central feature of the city today is the famous Madaba

mosaic map of the Holy Land. This map, discovered in 1884, dates to the sixth century CE. Because it is the oldest extant map of the Holy Land, it has been a valuable aid for archaeologists and historians in the Bible lands. Sadly, much of the map was destroyed during the construction of St. George's Church, built over the site in 1896. The remainder of the map is incorporated in the floor of this church today.

73: The Madaba Map

Machaerus

Biblical References: Matthew 14:1-12; Mark 6:14-29; Luke 9:7-9.

The ruins of Machaerus are located just to the east of the Dead Sea, between Madaba and Kerak. Most of what we know about the site is provided by Josephus.

The site was first built and fortified by Alexander Jannaeus (103–76 BCE). Later Herod the Great built a palace/fortress complex here to guard his eastern frontier. After his death, Machaerus was given to Herod Antipas, who ruled Perea; he probably came here during the summers, since Tiberias is usually hot and uncomfortable during the summer months. Josephus informs us that John the Baptist was imprisoned and executed here by Herod Antipas (*Antiquities* 18:116-119).

Mount Nebo (Mount Pisgah)

Biblical References: Numbers 23:14; Deuteronomy 32:49; 34:1.

No one is certain as to the exact location of the biblical Mount Nebo. Today, church tradition locates Mount Nebo approximately 6 miles (10 km) northwest of Madaba. Pilgrims come to this site to commemorate Moses' looking over into the land of Canaan and the place where he died.

In the fourth century CE a small church was built here as a monument to Moses (and his tomb). This church has been renovated several times over the centuries, and in the 1930s the ruins of the earlier churches were acquired by the Franciscans. Excavations here, carried out under the supervision of the Franciscan Biblical Institute, revealed that a large Byzantine monastery had been located here, with beautiful and elaborate mosaic floors dating to the sixth and seventh centuries CE.

Pella

Biblical References: None.

Pella is located in the Jordan Valley about halfway between the Jabbok and Yarmuk Rivers, about 2 miles (3 km) east of the Jordan River. The tell that marks the site of ancient Pella is located near the spring Ain el-Jirm.

The ancient name of the city was Pihilu or, perhaps, Pelel. It was mentioned in the el-Amarna letters (fourteenth century BCE) and in other early Egyptian texts (fifteenth–thirteenth centuries BCE). During this period Pella was well-known commercially as a place for making parts used in the construction of Egyptian chariots. Since it is not mentioned in the Hebrew Bible, it must have declined some time after the Israelite conquest of Canaan.

The city regained influence when it was under the control of the Seleucids. Later, it was destroyed by Alexander Jannaeus in approximately 82 BCE. After Pompey conquered the land for Rome, Pella witnessed a period of renewed growth and prosperity.

Pella is best remembered for its association with the early Christian community at the time of the Jewish Revolt. Many Christians fled Jerusalem after the Romans destroyed the city and took refuge in Pella; Eusebius records this flight in his *Ecclesiastical History*.[3] Even though some Christians later returned to Jerusalem, many remained in Pella, establishing a strong Christian presence here. In 635 CE, the Arabs took the city during the Islamic invasion of the land. In 746/47 Pella was destroyed by an earthquake and was never rebuilt.

Petra (Sela)

Biblical References: Judges 1:36; 2 Kings 14:7; Isaiah 16:1; Jeremiah 49:16.[4]

Petra is one of the most magnificent sites found anywhere in the world. It has often been identified, perhaps incorrectly, as

the biblical city of Sela, since Petra and Sela both mean "rock." The ancient capital city of the Nabateans (discussed below) was located here. The city is isolated behind large sandstone mountains in southern Jordan. To reach the city one must travel through a narrow trail, or *siq*. At the end of the siq lies Petra, the city carved into the mountains that protect it.

74: Petra: The Siq

Although remains from both the Paleolithic and Neolithic periods have been found near here, the city's known history dates from 312 BCE when the Greeks tried unsuccessfully to take Petra by force. From this point the Nabateans evolved into one of the ancient Middle East's most successful commercial empires, and along with them their capital city prospered and grew.[5]

In 63 BCE, Pompey failed to take the city for Rome. Two later attempts to conquer the city also failed. Finally, Trajan defeated the Nabateans, took the city, and annexed Nabatean lands in 106 CE.

During the Byzantine Period, Petra was a smaller and less important town. The city witnessed a brief occupation at this time by small groups of Christians, and some of the larger tombs dating to the Nabatean occupation were used as church buildings. However, the site was gradually abandoned. By the time of the Arab conquest (seventh century CE) only a few monks, who lived in the area as hermits, remained.

Except for the brief occupation during the Crusades, Petra was lost until 1812, when it was rediscovered by J. L. Burckhardt. Some of the outstanding features found in its remains are the Khazneh Far'un, or "treasury" (thought to be the tomb of one of the Nabatean kings), the high place, various tombs, and a large theater.

The Nabateans

Biblical References: None.

The Nabateans were a pre-Islamic Arab tribe who first appeared in the sixth century BCE. They were a simple, nomadic desert tribe, very common to Arabia. As mentioned above, they successfully defended Petra against the Greeks in 312 BCE. Originally, the Nabateans were directly involved in trading. However, after they discovered how invulnerable Petra was to attack, the city became a caravan station. The Nabateans shifted their focus from being traders to maintaining the trade routes. They also became involved in providing safe passage for caravans through their lands. For these services they received handsome fees. They prospered in this endeavor and were a wealthy people from 312 BCE to 106 CE, when they were conquered by the Romans.

75: Petra: The Treasury

OTHER SITES

Goshen

Biblical References: Genesis 45:10; 46:28-34; 47:1-12.

According to the book of Genesis, the land of Goshen was the area in the northeastern section of the Nile Delta of Egypt that was settled by Joseph's family, including his brothers and his father, Jacob. This area contains some of the best grazing land in Egypt, and it is understandable why it would have been desirable for a family of shepherds (see Genesis 47:6).

The capital city of the Hyksos and of Ramses—known alternatively as Avaris, Tanis, or Per-Ramses (see the separate entry below) was located nearby. Exodus 12:37 reports that "the Israelites journeyed from Ramses to Succoth"; if, as some believe, this marks the beginning of the exodus from Egypt, it may have begun from the land of Goshen.

Kadesh-Barnea

Biblical References: Genesis 16:14; Numbers 13:1 (implied); 13:26; 20:1ff. (esp. 15-20); Deuteronomy 1:19; 32:51; Judges 11:16-17.

Kadesh-Barnea is located in the northeastern part of the Sinai Peninsula, just south of the present border between Israel and

Egypt. According to the biblical accounts, the Israelites seem to have camped here for most of their "wilderness" period, the time between their exodus from Egypt and their entry into the promised land. This seems plausible, since the area has both abundant grazing land and an adequate water supply, and it is much more hospitable than the nearby wilderness areas of Zin and Paran.

The Bible associates many events of the Exodus with Kadesh-Barnea. First, it was from here that God commanded Moses to send spies into the land of Canaan. When ten of these spies brought back reports that the land was filled with powerful inhabitants, the Israelites chose not to attempt to enter the land. This brought about the loss of the promise of the land to the first generation who had come out of Egypt, except for Joshua and Caleb, who had urged the Israelites to take the land as God had promised they should do (Numbers 13:30). Second, Miriam, the sister of Moses and Aaron, died at Kadesh-Barnea (Numbers 20:1). Third, Moses lost the promise of entering the promised land by failing to bring water to the people in the manner prescribed by God (Numbers 20:10-13). Fourth, while at Kadesh-Barnea, Moses sought permission from the king of Edom for the passage of the Israelites through his territory in order to reach Canaan; this permission was denied (Numbers 20:14-21). Finally, Aaron died nearby at Mount Hor, the precise location of which is unknown (Numbers 20:22ff.).

Per-Ramses (Avaris, Tanis)

Biblical References: Exodus 1:11; 12:37; Psalm 78:12, 43; Isaiah 19:11-13; Ezekiel 30:14 (13-19).

Per-Ramses (or simply Ramses) was located in the northeastern corner of Egypt near the edge of the Sinai Peninsula. The city has been known by different names throughout its history, and scholars still debate its exact location. During the period of the Hyksos occupation of Egypt it was known as

Avaris and served as their capital city. During the reign of the Pharaoh Ramses (1290–1224 BCE) the city, which had been called Tanis under Ahmose I, was renamed Per-Ramses and again was made Egypt's capital. Today it is known once more as Tanis.

Sinai (Horeb)

Biblical References: Exodus 3:1; 19:1ff.; 24:16; 31:18; 34:2, 4, 29, 32; Leviticus 7:38; 25:1; Numbers 1:1; 3:1; 28:6; 1 Kings 8:9, 19; 2 Chronicles 5:10; Psalm 68:8, 17.

Although today the entire peninsula separating Israel and Egypt bears the name Sinai, the Bible speaks of Sinai as a wilderness (Exodus 19:1) or as a mountain (Leviticus 7:38). By a tradition dating at least to the time of Justinian I (527–565 CE), Mount Sinai is identifed with the mountain known today as Jebel Musa ("the mountain of Moses") in the southern part of the peninsula. Justinian assisted the building of St. Catherine's Monastery (to the northwest of Jebul Musa) on a site where earlier hermits or monks had settled, believing that it was the place to which Moses brought the Israelites to camp near the holy mountain, and from which he went up into the mountain to receive the Ten Commandments (Exodus 19–20). Over the centuries this tradition has become institutionalized, and today Moses' encounter with God is remembered here.

There are a number of reasons for doubting the traditional association of Mount Sinai with Jebel Musa. First, it is not located on the main trade route between Midian and Egypt, which would probably have been familiar to Moses. Second, the area does not have an adequate water supply to support a large number of people with their flocks. Third, Jebel Musa is very high, and climbing it, as Moses is reported to have done, is very difficult even today. Therefore it appears there are some difficulties with associating Jebel Musa with Mt. Sinai.

It has been suggested that Har Karkom (see the entry below) is a more plausible contender for the biblical Mount Sinai than is Jebel Musa. Nevertheless, Jebel Musa is a majestic place, and St. Catherine's Monastery marks a site that has been a place of pilgrimage for over 1,500 years. Har Karkom lacks the support of antiquity and tradition.

Har Karkom

Biblical References: see Sinai.

There are several reasons for locating Mount Sinai at Har Karkom, an obscure mountain in the Negev, near Kadesh-Barnea, rather than at Jebel Musa (see the entry on Sinai above).

First, Har Karkom is closer to major trade routes than is Jebel Musa. Second, there is a plain near Har Karkom large enough to have provided space for a number of people and their animals, and there is an ample supply of water nearby, at the springs of Beer Karkom, En Avdat, and Kadesh-Barnea. Third, Har Karkom is a much smaller mountain than Jebel Musa, which is a difficult climb, and it better fits with the biblical account of Moses going up and down the mountain several times. Also, archaeologists have recently discovered the remains of an ancient high place and a cave on the top of Har Karkom.[1] These findings seem to indicate that Har Karkom may be considered as a possible site for Mount Sinai.

The Wilderness of Sin

Biblical References: Exodus 16:1; 17:1; Numbers 33:11-12.

The exact location of the Wilderness of Sin is unknown. Some scholars believe that it should be placed in the Sinai Peninsula. This location is based on the assumption that the biblical Rephidim is to be found in the Sinai, and that the Wilderness of Sin is near Rephidim (Exodus 17:1). Others believe that it should be placed in proximity to the Wilderness of Paran (Numbers 12:16), which is in the Negev. The wilderness area near the Makhtesh Ramon, in the Negev, is today known as the

Wilderness of Sin. In the final analysis, much of this debate depends on the location of Mount Sinai. Those locating Mount Sinai at Jebel Musa will place the Wilderness of Sin in the southern part of the Sinai Peninsula; those identifying Mount Sinai with Har Karkom will place the Wilderness of Sin in the Negev.

APPENDIXES

ARCHAEOLOGICAL METHOD

W hat do archaeologists do? The *Oxford American Dictionary* defines *archaeology* as "the scientific study of past human life and culture through material remains." The aim of the archaeologist is the elucidation of human cultural history through the recovery and reconstruction of physical artifacts. Two aspects of this objective are crucial: excavating particular sites with maximum care and control, and recording the results of the excavation in great detail for maximum information retrieval.

How do archaeologists do this? Before putting a spade into the ground, the archaeologist will first learn all that can be discovered about the site or *tell* (the Arabic word for "hill") to be excavated. Such information can be found in ancient records, folklore, the Bible, or other archaeological sites. It will give the archaeologist some idea of what to expect at the site—what its various strata may contain, and which archaeological periods may be present. Many sites appear as hills because the accumulation over the centuries of construction followed by destruction and then more construction over that have created a mound of ruins. Also, a town that has been deserted for centuries can become covered with layers of wind-blown soil and surface growth. Most ancient cities were built on elevated ground in the first place in order to enhance their defensive capabilities.

Once the surface growth has been cleared away, the archaeologist is ready to lay out a *square*. This is a 10 X 10 meter area, marked off with strings and made perfectly square (hence the name). Some archaeologists prefer 8 X 8 meter squares. Some thought is given to placing the square in relation to the overall excavation plan. It may be that an earlier *probe* will assist the archaeologist in determining the plan of attack. The string that marks the limit of the square will eventually mark the *baulk*, that is the vertical face or wall that is created as the soil is removed, creating a hole in the ground. The baulk also refers to a 1-meter wide walkway around the surface of the square.

After removing surface growth and laying out the square, it is necessary to "take elevations." Surveyors determine the exact distance of the square above sea level and create a *datum point* in or near the square, from which future elevations can be taken. In archaeology, unlike most other sciences, the evidence is destroyed as the work proceeds, and careful measurements must make it possible, at least in theory, to reconstruct what no longer exists. When the digging begins it is not done through-out the 10-meter square; smaller, temporary squares are marked off with strings within the larger area, so that one may begin with a small, 2 X 2 meter area. Before digging actually commences, one must establish a location for the *dump*—that is, a place to deposit the dirt that will be removed.

So the digging begins, usually with a small trowel, which is the archaeologist's basic tool. Other tools include a *patish*, or small hand-pick; a back-hoe (rather like an ordinary garden hoe); a dustpan to collect the dirt removed; a pick-axe; a broom; and, for fine work on skeletons or mosaics, brushes and dental picks. As one begins to scrape away the dirt into the dustpan, it is deposited into a *gufa*, or rubber pail. As the gufas fill, they in turn are emptied into a wheelbarrow, and the dirt is carried to the dump. One digs until there is a change in soil composition or some significant artifact or feature appears (wall, skeleton, packed earth, etc.). Each layer, or *locus*, is dug separately from all the other layers with maximum control. A locus designates an area or layer with its own unique characteristics—such as sandy soil, compact dirt, ashes, a wall, pile of rocks, and the like. Each locus is given its own number and pottery bucket. As one digs, the pottery is saved in the bucket having its locus number.

When one decides that the locus is changing characteristics, a new locus is opened, elevations are taken, a new number and pottery bucket are assigned, and a soil sample may be taken. Inasmuch as "recording for maximum information retrieval" is an objective of the enterprise, every dig has its field desk and a designated recorder who will make out a new page for each locus, recording in detail all the relevant information that pertains to each locus.

Modern archaeology follows a method that is referred to as *stratigraphy*. Experience has shown that ancient cities developed various *strata* (levels) through their history of culture and civilization, or of destruction or decomposition. The aim of stratigraphic digging is to separate the artifacts and pottery from each locus as cleanly as possible, as each locus is dated by the latest artifact within it. One or more loci make up a *phase*, a set of phases constitutes a *stratum*, and the various strata illuminate the history of the site. The dating of a stratum depends on the artifacts discovered within the various loci, the most common artifact being the remains of pottery, called sherds.

Ancient pottery exhibits features unique to the time and place of its creation. It was made from varying forms of clay, fired and finished differently, and shaped with varying styles of lip, body, base, and handles. Experts in pottery "reading" are often able to date pottery to within fifty years of its creation, using the feel of its texture or the firing of its skin or sometimes even its taste, as well as its shape. Occasionally one finds a *terra sigilata* ("signed sherd"), which contains the name or logo of the potter, in which case one has an exact dating. Each day on a dig the pottery is "read" by experts, and the date is recorded on the locus sheet. Needless to say, it is crucial that the pottery from one locus not be mixed in the bucket with that of another locus.

As the digging proceeds and new loci are opened, it soon becomes evident that one is going backward in time. The pottery over a period of several weeks will proceed backward through the archaeological periods until one arrives at the earliest stratum of civilization at the site. As one proceeds to remove more and more dirt, a large hole in the ground is created. Indeed, if the entire square is excavated the hole will measure 10 X 10 meters and may be as much as 4 or 5 meters deep. Thus artificial "walls" are created around the four sides of the hole in the ground. This is the baulk. Digging stratigraphically, it is usually possible to detect the various strata in the baulk, and they are labeled. Visitors to an active site will often see such tags along the side of the baulks, each one indicating a different locus or time period.

It is essential that baulks be kept as vertical as possible, for which reason someone will be assigned to "trim the baulk," making it conform to a plumb-bob string secured at the surface to ensure that the baulk, or "wall," is indeed straight up and down. Experts in stratigraphy can sometimes reconstruct the history of a site simply by "reading the baulk"—that is, pointing to a destruction layer of ash or to other strata depicting activities unique to a particular time period. The remains of Old Testament Jericho have some thirty strata in several baulks, pointing to that many layers of occupation of the city.

As one proceeds, records are kept of artifacts uncovered, either with the locus number or by assigning a new locus. Smaller artifacts may include coins, jewelry, bones (human or animal), pottery that has remained intact, metal objects, construction debris (carved stones or inscriptions), and lamps. If one suspects that a locus may contain smaller objects, the soil from that locus may be sifted in order to find coins, jewelry, or glass fragments.

A number of features that often appear in archaeological digs present special challenges. One is the robber trench, where part of the locus has been "robbed" for use in a later structure, leaving one with the impression that the locus is in fact earlier than it really is. For example, an archaeologist who might one day be digging up your twentieth-century home could find an antique you owned that dates from the fourteenth century and thereby conclude that you lived in the fourteenth century. Another problem is that dirt floors are difficult to detect as such. Yet another difficulty is intrusions, such as pits or wells or burials. A grave could be dug by someone in 400 CE, but in going down into the ground six feet, the actual burial may be at a 300 CE level, and that is where we would find it today, even though the deceased was from 400 CE.

Occasionally one comes across a *sealed locus,* which could be a hard-packed floor or a wall or pavement. Because the locus is hard, nothing that comes from a later date can penetrate it. This means that the latest dateable object one discovers under the seal will give a fairly accurate date for the locus. It's as though today someone were to dig up a concrete floor and discover a dated coin under the floor. It stands to reason that the concrete was not poured earlier than the date on the coin. In this way walls can be dated by reading the pottery found under the walls.

A fairly recent innovation in Palestinian field archaeology is the *top plan,* which is a stone-for-stone record of everything done in a square each day. It shows all the main features, the areas being excavated, locus numbers, elevations, and pottery buckets. Top plans are drawn to scale on grid paper. In this way one has a careful record, day by day, of the actual work of each square. Another way of preserving evidence is through photography. Many digs have their official photographer, but it is also useful for each square to have an instant camera handy for regular use before an object is removed or a significant change is made. Over the course of a dig there may be numerous volunteers and a change in supervisors, so it is impossible to rely on memory. The square supervisor also keeps a daily journal of field notes, which record, hour by hour, what is happening. These field notes are invaluable when months or even years later some questions arise relating to the dig.

Let us assume that you are visiting a dig somewhere in Israel during the summer months, when most digs are active. You will discover that most of the workers are volunteers who have come from many parts of the world and who have no special skills or experience in archaeology. As you approach the site, you will see someone sitting at the field desk keeping records, and this person may be the square supervisor. In the square itself there may be two people carefully scraping up dirt with their trowels, and occasionally tossing some pottery into a bucket. Two others may be taking elevations and soil samples upon opening a new locus. Another person will be sifting, while another is on the wheelbarrow detail, collecting gufas and emptying them at the dump. Perhaps one will be articulating a mosaic or a skeleton, while you hear the voice of another from beneath a circular opening that has proved to be an old well. Toward the end of the working day (which, because of the summer heat, often begins at 5:00 A.M. and ends by 1:00 P.M.), one will be assigned to draw the top plan. Later in the day the group will wash the pottery brought up that day and attend the readings of the pottery from the previous day.

Archaeology involves a lot of hard, hot, sometimes tedious work, and rarely provides any "Indiana Jones"-type thrills. Not every day at a dig is exciting, nor are dramatic finds frequent, but the general experience of being the first to come across an object or a culture that has been buried for many centuries, even millennia, is rewarding.

CHRONOLOGICAL CHARTS

CHRONOLOGICAL CHART 1: ARCHAEOLOGICAL AGES/HISTORICAL PERIODS

Paleolithic Period	before 14,000 BCE
Mesolithic Period	14,000–8000 BCE
Neolithic Period	8000–4000 BCE
Chalcolithic Period	4000–3200 BCE
Early Bronze Age	3200–2000 BCE
	EB I: 3200–3000
	EB II: 3000–2800
	EB III: 2800–2400
	EB IV: 2400–2000
Middle Bronze Age	2000–1550 BCE
	MB I: 2000–1800
	MB II: 1800–1650
	MB III: 1650–1550
Late Bronze Age	1550–1200 BCE
	LB I: 1550–1400
	LB II: 1400–1200
Iron Age	1200–332 BCE
	Iron I: 1200–900
	Iron II: 900–600
	Iron III: 600–332 (Persian Period)
Hellenistic Period	333–63 BCE
	Maccabean: 167–140

	Hasmonean: 140–37
Roman Period	63 BCE–324 CE
	Herodian: 37–4
Byzantine Period	324–638
Early Islamic Period	638–1095
	Umayyad: 661–750
	Abbasid: 750–969
	Fatimid: 969–1171
Crusader Period	1095–1291

CHRONOLOGICAL CHART 2: THE KINGS OF ISRAEL AND JUDAH

(All dates are BCE and approximate)

JUDAH		ISRAEL	
Davidic Dynasty:			
922–915	Rehoboam	922–901	Jeroboam I
915–913	Abijah		
913–873	Asa	901–900	Nedab
		900–877	Baasha
		877–876	Elah
		876	Zimri (7 days)
		Dynasty of Omri:	
873–849	Jehoshaphat	876–869	Omri
		869–850	Ahab
		850–849	Ahaziah
		849–843	Jehoram
849–842	Jehoram		
843–842	Ahaziah		
		Dynasty of Jehu:	
842–837	Athaliah	842–815	Jehu
837–800	Joash		
800–783	Amaziah	815–801	Jehoahaz
		801–786	Jehoash
783–742	Uzziah (Azariah)	786–749	Jeroboam II

236

JUDAH		ISRAEL	
750–742	Jotham as regent	746–745	Zechariah
		745	Shallum
742–735	Jotham as king	745–737	Menahem
		737–736	Pekahiah
735–715	Ahaz	736–732	Pekah
732–724	Hoshea	722/1	Fall of Samaria and the Northern Kingdom
715–687	Hezekiah		
687–642	Manasseh		
642–640	Amon		
640–609	Josiah		
621	Josiah's Reform		
609	Jehoahaz II		
609–598	Jehoiakim		
598/7	Jehoiachin (for 3 months)		
597	First deportation of the Jews to Babylon		
597–587	Zedekiah		
587/6	Babylonian Exile: Fall of Jerusalem and destruction of the First Temple		

CHRONOLOGICAL CHART 3: THE PROPHETS OF ISRAEL AND JUDAH

(All dates are BCE and approximate)

c. 850	Elijah (during the reign of Ahab)
849–820 (?)	Elisha (late Omri Dynasty–early Jehu Dynasty)
c. 750	Amos
c. 745	Hosea
742–700	Isaiah
722–701	Micah
628–622	Zephaniah
c. 626	Nahum
626–587	Jeremiah
c. 605	Habakkuk
c. 593	Ezekiel

c. 540	Second Isaiah
c. 530	Third Isaiah
520–515	Haggai
520–515	Zechariah
500–450	Malachi
c. 500	Obadiah
c. 400	Joel

CHRONOLOGICAL CHART 4: ROMAN EMPERORS

(All dates after Augustus are CE)

27 BCE–14 CE	Augustus
14–37	Tiberius
37–41	Caligula
41–54	Claudius
54–68	Nero
68–69	Galba/Otho/Vetillius
69–79	Vespasian
79–81	Titus
81–96	Domitian
97–105	Nerva
105–117	Trajan
117–138	Hadrian
138–161	Antoninus Pius
161–180	Marcus Aurelius
180–192	Commodus
193–211	Septimus Severus
211–217	Caracalla
218–222	Elagabalus
222–235	Alexandus Severus
235–284	26 different emperors
284–305	Diocletian
305–311	Contenders struggled for power
311–324	Constantine emperor in West
324–337	Constantine sole ruler

CHRONOLOGICAL CHART 5: HERODIAN KINGS/GOVERNORS OF JUDEA

37–4 BCE	Herod the Great
4 BCE–6 CE	Archelaus in Judea
4 BCE–39 CE	Antipas in Galilee/Perea
4 BCE–34 CE	Philip in Gaulanitus
37–44 CE	Agrippa I: in Gaulanitus
41–44 CE	Agrippa I: in Judea, Galilee, Perea
53–100 CE	Agrippa II

CHRONOLOGICAL CHART 6: ROMAN PROCURATORS OF JUDEA

(All dates are CE)

6–8	Coponius
8–12	Ambivius
15–26	Valerius Gratus
26–36	Pontius Pilate
37	Marullus
37–41	Herennius Capito
44–46	Cuspius Fadus
46–48	Tiberius Alexander
48–52	Ventidius Cumanus
52–60	Antonius Felix
60–62	Porcius Festus
62–64	Clodius Albinus
64–66	Gessius Florus

GLOSSARY

Acropolis—In ancient cities, the acropolis was the highest or elevated part of the city, usually found at the city's center. Temples and royal palaces were usually located on the acropolis. (From Greek: *acro* = "high," *polis* = "city").

Agora—An open square in Greek (or Hellenistic) cities where the market was located. The agora also served as a place for religious, political, or philosophical discussions or speeches.

Agrapha—Literally, "unwritten." The sayings of Jesus not found in the canonical Gospels but recorded elsewhere.

Amarna Letters—A set of tablets written in cuneiform discovered at Tell el-Amarna in Egypt. The Amarna Letters date to the reigns of Amenhotep III and IV (Akhenaton), to the fourteenth century BCE.

Amphitheater—An open air theater with seats surrounding the stage in a curving manner, used for entertainment. Whereas a theater was a half-circle with the stage as the focal point, an amphitheater was a completely enclosed circle of oblong tiered seats.

Apocrypha—Extracanonical books of the Old and New Testaments. The word *apocrypha* means "hidden" and was first used by Jerome, who included fourteen Old Testament Apocryphal books in the Vulgate.

Apse—The semi-circular end of a building, usually that of a church, where the altar is located and the clergy sit. It is usually the area forward of the Communion rail.

Ashlar Masonry—Stones of soft limestone cut into square, rectangular, or oblong pieces used in the construction of ancient buildings.

Arabah—The depression or valley which begins at the Sea of Galilee in the north and continues to Eilat on the Gulf of Aqabah. It is used especially for that extension of the valley from the southern end of the Dead Sea to Eilat.

Armageddon—A famous Old Testament battlefield site (2 Kings 9:27; 23:29) located in the Jezreel Valley. This Greek word comes from the Hebrew *Har Megiddo*, which means "hill" or "mountain of Megiddo." According to Revelation 16:16, the final battle between the forces of good and evil will be fought here.

Augustus Caesar—Roman emperor from 27 BCE to 14 CE.

Baal—The chief Canaanite god, the god of fertility.

Bar Kochba—The leader of the Second Jewish Revolt against Rome (132–135 CE). The name means "the son of the star."

Baulk—The vertical "wall" which is created by archeologists as they dig, often indicating various levels of habitation in various time periods.

Bema—A large platform, usually found in an agora, for public speaking.

Capital—The upper portion of a distinctive column or pillar found in Greco-Roman architecture.

Casemate Wall—A hollow double wall used as a storeroom in times of peace. It also has internal walls that divide the space between the two main walls. The hollow areas were filled during sieges to strengthen the walls.

Cenotaph—A marker or monument to a person whose body is buried in a different location. The tomb of David or Abraham (in Hebron) are examples of cenotaphs.

Codex—An earlier book form usually written on papyrus or parchment. A codex was made from separate sheets pasted together and bound into book form.

Cubit—An ancient measurement used in the Middle East. The cubit was measured from the tip of the middle finger to the elbow. The Hebrew cubit was approximately eighteen inches in length.

Cuneiform—The word means "wedge" from the Latin word *cuneus*. This ancient form of writing is so named because its characters resemble a wedge. Cuneiform was probably invented by the Sumerians and later adopted by other Middle Eastern cultures.

Cyclopean Masonry—A type of construction found in the Bronze Age. It consists of the use of larger, unhewn stones mixed with small stones to create city walls.

Dead Sea Scrolls—Scrolls and scroll fragments written in Aramaic, Greek, and Hebrew, discovered in 1947 and subsequent years in caves near Qumran, near the Dead Sea. They range in date from the mid-third century BCE to the second half of the first century CE.

Decalogue—A Greek word meaning "the ten words," designating the Ten Commandments.

Decapolis—Loose federation of ten Greek cities dating to Alexander the Great, all in Transjordan except Sythopolis (Beth Shean).

Diaspora—The dispersion, or scattering, of the Jewish people from their ancestral homeland in Israel (587/86 BCE and 135 CE).

Dolmen—A tomb covered with three larger stones, two standing vertically and one horizontally, fitting on the two upright stones.

El—In general, the Hebrew word for "god." More specifically, the name of the highest god in the Canaanite pantheon and one of the names of the God of Israel found in the Old Testament.

Elohim—A transliteration of the Hebrew word for "gods"; an ancient Hebrew name for God found in the Old Testament.

Epigraphy—The study of ancient inscriptions found on coins, monuments, statues, and buildings.

Essenes—A Jewish sect associated with the community at Qumran and generally thought to be the group who wrote the Dead Sea Scrolls.

Eucharist—Christian sacrament commemorating Jesus' Last Supper with his disciples, also known as Holy Communion, the Lord's Supper, or the Sacrament of the Altar. From the Greek word for "thanksgiving."

Faience—A greenish or blue-colored glazed earthenware pottery made of clay, iron, sand, and/or copper. It is used to make ornate pottery, jewlery, and figurines.

Fertile Crescent—The name of the crescent-shaped area stretching from Egypt to the Persian Gulf.

Forum—A central public square found in Roman cities. The forum was usually surrounded by shops, offices, or temples. It also served as the city's market and the place where officials conducted their business.

Gemara—A commentary, dating to the third century CE, on the Mishnah. The Gemara is Part II of the Talmud.

Gilead—One of the geographic regions of Transjordan, located between the Arnon and Yarmuk Rivers.

Gilgamesh Epic—Babylonian writing containing the flood epic, paralleling the biblical accounts of the flood.

Glacis—An incline or slope in front of a fortification wall to allow defenders to more easily repel their attackers. It is usually characterized by stones of some sort embedded in its surface.

Habiru—The name of a peasant, nomadic class of people (servants, slaves, outlaws, etc.) found in the ancient Middle East. The name Habiru has often been associated with the name Hebrews.

Halakah—Jewish religious law. *Halakah* means "follow" and refers to the following of rabbinical interpretation(s) of the Torah.

Hasidim—The "Pious Ones." The name refers to Jews who refused to renounce their faith during the persecutions of Antiochus Epiphanes IV (second century BCE). Today the name refers to an ultra-conservative Jewish sect rooted in eighteenth-century CE Eastern European Jewish culture.

Hasmoneans—The name of the dynasty founded by the Maccabees (167–63 BCE) and named for Hasmon, an ancestor of the Maccabees.

Hellenism—The influence of Greek culture, language, thought, etc., spread throughout the world beginning with Alexander the Great (late fourth century BCE).

Hellenists—Individuals (Jews or Gentiles) who favored the adoption of Greek culture.

Herodians—Jewish supporters of the Herodian dynasty.

Hexateuch—The first six books of the Old Testament.

Hieroglyphics—Ancient Egyptian writing that used pictures to convey meaning; this type of writing preceded the use of alphabetic scripts.

Hinnom Valley—A valley south of Jerusalem (the Old City) used as a garbage dump during the time of Jesus. The Hinnom Valley became a symbol of punishment for lost souls after death (Gehenna).

Hippodrome—An oval-shaped arena used primarily for horse and chariot racing.

Idumea—Home country of the family of Herod the Great, located to the south and east of Judea. The name is a corruption of "Edom."

In Situ—In archaeological terms, *in situ* refers to a part of a site that has been left "in place" during an excavation or restoration; that is, left exactly as the archaeologists found it.

Lintel—A horizonal beam or slab over a window or door.

Maccabees—The family of the priest Mattathias, who led the revolt of the Jewish people against Antiochus Epiphanes IV and the Seleucids in 167 BCE. The name Maccabee comes from a Hebrew word that means "hammer." Judas, son of Mattathias, was called Maccabee, because his guerrilla army would strike the Seleucids with hammer-like blows.

Mari Texts—A set of tablets found in Mari—a major city in Mesopotamia, located on the Euphrates River in the west—that provide information about the culture, including the religious practices, of eighteenth century BCE.

Massebah—A standing stone or stones as a memorial.

Mattathias—A priest who, along with his sons, started the Jewish revolt against the Seleucids.

Mesolithic Period—The Middle Stone Age (14,000–8,000 BCE).

Mesopotamia—The land between the Tigris and the Euphrates rivers. It means "between the rivers."

Midrash—A form of interpretation of the Hebrew Scriptures from rabbinic Judaism. The word *midrash* means to "search out."

Mishnah—A literary collection of Jewish (Pharisaic) oral law dating from about 200 CE. It is the first (oldest) part of the Talmud.

Moab—An area in Jordan found between the Arnon River and the Zered Brook, in central Jordan.

Molech—God of the Ammonites.

Negeb (or Negev)—Israel's southern desert, located between the Judean Wilderness and the Sinai Desert.

Neolithic Period—The New Stone Age (8,000–4,000 BCE).

Nero—Roman emporer from 54–68 CE. He was probably the emperor responsible for the executions of Peter and Paul.

Nuzi Documents—Tablets found at Nuzi in northwest Mesopotamia that provide insights into ancient Hurrian culture from the fifteenth century BCE. Some of the customs practiced by the Hurrians are similar to those reported in the Bible associated with the Patriarchs (see Genesis 15:2ff.; 25:31-34).

Obelisk—A standing stone with a pyramid-shaped top, often containing inscriptions.

Ophel—The low ridge projecting southeast from the Old City of today, which was the northern part of the City of David.

Oral Tradition—Traditions passed down orally from one generation to another, before being written down. Much of Israel's early history was passed down orally.

Ossuary—A box in which bones of deceased persons were buried.

Ostracon (ostraca, pl.)—Ancient potsherd(s) with writing on them.

Paleolithic Period—The Old Stone Age, before 14,000 BCE

Parousia—Literally, "arrival"; it refers to the second coming of Christ.

Passover (Pesach)—The annual Jewish celebration or commemoration of the Hebrew exodus from Egypt. The holiday is based on the remembrance of the angel of death passing over Hebrew homes the night when Egypt's firstborn (of both people and livestock) died. See Exodus 12:1-51.

Pella—A biblical city located in modern Jordan, near the Jordan River. Jewish Christians came to Pella and established a strong Christian presence after the destruction of Jerusalem in 70 CE.

Pentateuch—A Greek word referring to the first five books of the Old Testament, or Hebrew Bible.

Pentecost—Jewish festival (Feast of Weeks) fifty days after Passover. This is also the day the Holy Spirit came upon the disciples in Jerusalem; remembered as the birthday of the church.

Pharisees—Jewish religious sect at the time of Jesus. The name comes from the Hebrew word *parosh,* which means "to separate."

Philistines—A people who settled in Israel's southern Coastal Plain in the twelfth century BCE. They were the descendants of the "Sea Peoples," who originally came from the Aegean Islands.

Phoenicia—A country located on Israel's northwestern and Lebanon's southwestern coasts.

Pillar—A standing stone used to support a building or roof.

Plinth—A stone slab upon which a pillar or column sat.

Portico—An open structure with a roof supported by pillars or columns.

Procurator—A Roman administrative/military official (leader) of a province during the New Testament Period.

Pseudepigrapha—A collection of books or writings attributed to biblical figures, written between 200 BCE and 200 CE but not found in the biblical canon.

Ptolemies—The Greek dynasty founded by Ptolemy, one of the generals of Alexander the Great. They ruled in Egypt from 323–30 BCE and in Palestine until 198 BCE.

Ptolemy I—One of the generals of Alexander the Great. He ruled in Egypt from 323–285 BCE and founded the Ptolemaic Dynasty.

Ptolemy II—Son of Ptolemy I, ruled 285–246 BCE. Instituted a Ptolemaic ruler cult, built the Pharus lighthouse, a museum and a library, and a canal from the Nile to the Red Sea.

Ras Shamra Texts—Tablets found in Syria dating to 1365–1180 BCE, detailing the religious, political, social, and historical events in Canaan prior to the Hebrew invasion.

Sadducees—The conservative Jewish establishment party who controlled the Temple and the priesthood and who collaborated with the Romans during the New Testament Period.

Sanhedrin—Generic term referring to various Jewish religious and civil councils during the Hasmonean and Roman periods.

Scribes—Jewish legal scholars and experts in religious law.

Seleucids—Greek dynasty founded by Seleucus, a general of Alexander the Great, centered in Syria 312–64 BCE; the Seleucids controlled Palestine 198–167 BCE.

Seleucus—A general of Alexander the Great and founder of the Seleucid dynasty, who ruled 312–280 BCE.

Septuagint—The Greek translation of the Hebrew Scriptures, also designated as the LXX (the Roman numeral for seventy). According to tradition, the translation was made by seventy different scholars, each translating the entire Hebrew Scriptures, and at the conclusion of their work they found that all their translations were identical. The first books to be translated (Torah) were done in the 3rd century BCE, and the last were translated in the 1st century BCE.

Shephelah—A hilly region of valleys and foothills located between the mountains of Judea and Israel's southern Coastal Plain.

Sherd—A piece of broken pottery.

Stele—A carved or inscribed standing stone column or pillar sometimes used as a monument.

Stratigraphic Method—An excavation method that reveals the different levels or strata of occupation at an archaeological site.

Stratum (strata, pl.)—A horizonal layer or level usually found with other parallel layers arranged on top of one another at an excavation site.

Synoptic Gospels—The name given to the first three Gospels (Matthew, Mark, and Luke) due to the large quantity of common material; the term *synoptic* means "to see together."

Talmud—A collection of Jewish religious traditions consisting of the Mishnah and the Gemara.

Targum—An Aramaic translation of portions of the Hebrew Bible.

Tell (or Tel)—A mound or hill produced artificially from occupational debris on the site of ancient cities.

Tiberias—A city on the southwestern shore of the Sea of Galilee; built by Herod Antipas in 20 CE to be the capital of the Galilee region.

Tiberius—Roman emperor 14–37 CE.

Torah—The Jewish Law and first five books of the Hebrew Bible.

Vespasian—Roman emperor 69–79 CE. He was the commander of the Roman army during the First Jewish Revolt (66–70 CE).

Vulgate—The Latin translation of the Hebrew Bible, produced by Jerome in the fourth century CE.

Wadi—A dry river or creek bed (except during the rainy season).

Yahweh—The personal name of God found in the Old Testament and designated with the consonants *YHWH*.

Zealots—Nationalistic Jewish revolutionaries who sought to expel the Romans from Jewish lands during the New Testament Period.

Ziggurat—An ancient temple tower, shaped like a stepped pyramid, and associated with Mesopotamian kingdoms.

Zion—The name used to designate one of the three possible hills or mountains around Jerusalem in biblical times and today.

NOTES

Geographical Overview

1. Yohanan Aharoni, *The Land of the Bible: A Historical Geography* (Philadelphia: Westminster Press, 1979), 3.

2. The boundaries of Israel vary depending on where one starts and stops measuring. Some, for example, include the Golan Heights, while others do not. To say that Israel is 350 miles long and 70 miles wide includes land that is presently occupied by Israel and the ownership of which is in dispute.

3. James R. Beasley, et al., *An Introduction to the Bible* (Nashville: Abingdon Press, 1991), 69.

Historical Overview

1. Leon Wood, *A Survey of Israel's History* (Grand Rapids: Zondervan, 1970), 27ff.; Merrill F. Unger, *Archaeology and the Old Testament* (Grand Rapids: Zondervan, 1954), 105-7. First Kings 6:1 says that "in the four hundred eightieth year after the Israelites came out of the land of Egypt, in the fourth year of Solomon's reign over Israel, in the month of Ziv, which is the second month, he began to build the house of the LORD." Conservative biblical scholars use this verse for their chronological dating of Old Testament events. Since there is no dispute concerning the dates of Solomon's reign, these scholars arrive at the date of the Exodus by simple addition (480 + 957 = 1437 BCE). Then

by using additional calculations, involving the reported ages of the patriarchs, they arrive at the date of the Patriarchal Period.

2. James K. West, *Introduction to the Old Testament* (New York: MacMillan, 1981), 120-21.

3. J. Maxwell Miller and John H. Hayes, *A History of Ancient Israel and Judah* (Philadelphia: Westminster Press, 1986), 74-79.

4. West, *Introduction to the Old Testament*, 120-21.

5. During the Middle Bronze period, Ur was located on the Euphrates River. Later the course of the river shifted, and today the site of ancient Ur is several miles from the river.

6. Joseph may have served in the government of the Hyksos, who were alien rulers in Egypt from approximately 1720 BCE. The Hyksos were finally expelled by Ahmose I (1570–1545 BCE). Like the Hebrews, they were a mixed ethnic group. Many of the Hyksos were, no doubt, Semitic, so Joseph would have been accepted, since he too was an alien Semite.

7. Many scholars have made comparisons between the Hebrews and the Habiru (or 'Apiru). The Habiru were first mentioned approximately 2050 BCE. The term refers, generally, either to an ethnic group or, more likely, to a social class of disenfranchised people who lived as refugees or rebels outside the authority of the state. It is possible that the patriarchs were Habiru, as were many Hebrews in Egypt. However, not all Habiru were Hebrews.

8. The Bible presents several apparently contradictory accounts of the nature of the exodus. Exodus 12:33-36 hints that not only did the Egyptians want the Hebrews to leave, but that the Hebrews took with them much of the wealth of Egypt. Exodus 13:14-19 suggests that the Hebrews left victoriously as an army: . . . . Exodus 12:39 seems to claim that the Hebrews were driven out, but Exodus 14:5 implies that the Hebrews simply slipped away. In the final analysis we cannot be certain which, if any, of these accounts is the most reliable for historical reconstruction. Modern scholarship has tended to explain the discrepancies involved by appealing to the "Documentary Hypothesis" (see the helpful overview of this theory in Beasley, et al, *An Introduction to the Bible,* 39-40). For a lively and provocative discussion of these and similar issues, see Richard Elliot Friedman, *Who Wrote the Bible?* (New York: Harper & Row, 1987).

9. Most scholars today conclude that there was probably not one large single exodus but rather several smaller migrations from Egypt to Canaan. Some of these date from the expulsion of the Hyksos. The account found in the book of Exodus may relate more specifically to the

Joseph clan of Jacob's sons. Archaeological evidence shows that by the time this last group arrived Hebrews were already living in Canaan.

10. Modern biblical scholarship commonly refers to the biblical material from Deuteronomy through 2 Kings (excluding Ruth) as the "Deuteronomistic history." Opinions differ as to the date at which older historical material was edited into its present form, but there is a general consensus that the person(s) known as the "Deuteronomist" shaped a narrative of Israel's history that combined the old covenant theology from the J and E traditions, which saw Israel's destruction as the result of apostasy, with the promise given to David as a sign of hope for the future. See the discussion of this process in Friedman, *Who Wrote the Bible?* 101-49.

11. West, *Introduction to the Old Testament*, 231.

12. Some biblical historians—e.g., Unger (197ff.) and Wood (237ff.)—date the United Monarchy from the reign of Saul (1020 BCE) through that of Solomon (922 BCE). However, Saul appears more properly to belong to the later period of the judges rather than to the United Monarchy.

13. Ish-bosheth is also referred to as Ish-baal.

14. Jeroboam had rebelled against Solomon (1 Kings 11:26ff.). Solomon made efforts to have Jeroboam killed. Therefore, Jeroboam sought refuge in Egypt and stayed there until the death of Solomon.

15. Baal was an ancient fertility God whom the Israelites found— and whom some of them worshiped—when they entered the land of Canaan. The cult of Baal was widespread in the Syro-Palestinian world, and it had many local variations. Opposition to the cult of Baal became a characteristic of the Israelite religious tradition, as is reflected in the Elijah stories.

16. Bruce Vawter, *Introduction to the Prophetical Books* (Collegeville, Minn.: The Liturgical Press, 1965), 63.

17. Y. M. Grintz, "Jews," *Encyclopedia Judaica* (New York: Macmillan, 1971), 10:22.

18. Contemporary scholars continue to discuss the dating of these writers, with many placing Nehemiah at 445 BCE and Ezra at 398 BCE.

19. Ernst Ludwig Ehrlich, *A Concise History of Israel*, trans. James Barr (New York: Harper & Row, 1965), 80-81.

20. Frederick L. Moriarity, *Ezra and Nehemiah* (Collegeville, Minn.: Liturgical Press, 1966), 16.

21. The Greek name for Greece, transliterated into English, is *Hellas*. The period of Greek domination of the ancient world, from the rise of Alexander the Great to the emergence of the Roman Empire, is com-

monly known as the Hellenistic Period. Those who favored the adoption of the Greek language and of Greek customs and culture at the expense of local cultural and linguistic traditions were called Hellenists, and the process through which the influence of Greek civilization spread through the Mediterranean and the Near East is referred to as Hellenization.

22. The name *Hasidim* comes from the Hebrew *hasid*, "pious ones," and refers to a movement of conservative religious Jews who emerged around 200 BCE in to opposition to the Hellenization of Jewish cultural and religious traditions.

23. This Maccabean coin has often been found in archaeological sites in Israel and can be seen in the Israel Museum; it is in half-shekel or shekel pieces, bearing on one side the inscription "Jerusalem the Holy," and on the other the designated value.

24. Ehrlich, *A Concise History of Israel*, 110.

25. The term is Greek, and means a council of leaders. According to later Jewish tradition, the Sanhedrin in Jerusalem was the supreme council and highest court of justice in Judaism; it met at the Temple and was composed of seventy-one members, headed by the high priest. This tradition may not be entirely accurate, but it is very likely that a council of Jewish leaders bearing the name Sanhedrin did exist at this time in Jerusalem.

26. Josephus devotes an entire chapter to the description of Herod's Temple.

27. The Sicarii were extremist Jewish militants who carried a hidden knife or dagger (Latin: *sica*), which they were pledged to use against the Roman occupation forces.

28. Justin Martyr, *Dialogue with Trypho*, 78, in *The Ante-Nicene Fathers*, eds. A. Roberts and J. Donaldson, 10 vols. (original edition 1885–1896; rerinted Grand Rapids: William B. Eerdmans, 1979), 1:237.

29. The Lithostratos that is visible today almost certainly dates from the time of Hadrian (117–135 CE), not from the time of Herod and Jesus; see the discussion on page 198.

30. Meir Ben-Dov, *In the Shadow of the Temple* (Philadelphia: Harper & Row, 1982), 190.

31. The Bordeaux Pilgrim is the earliest known Christian pilgrim from Western Europe to visit the Holy Land. His account, the *Itinerarium Burdigalense*, is mostly a list of the places he visited, but it does contain brief descriptions of some sites in Israel. An English translation by A. Stewart was published by the Palestine Pilgrim's Text Society (London, 1887).

32. G. Frederick Owen, *From Abraham to the Middle East Crisis* (Grand Rapids: Wm. B. Eerdmans, 1957), 170.

33. See *Egeria: Diary of a Pilgrim*, trans. George E. Gingras, Volume 38 in *Ancient Christian Writers* (New York: Newman Press, 1970).

34. Steven Runciman, the eminent historian of the Crusades, writes that one of the chief reasons for the failure of the Second Crusade was "the difference in habits and outlook between the Franks resident in the East and their cousins from the West. It was a shock for the Crusaders to discover in Palestine a society whose members had in the course of a generation altered their way of life." Runciman, *A History of the Crusades*, 3 vols. (New York: Harper & Row, 1962–1965), 2:291. The first generation of Crusaders who had settled in the East did nothing to assist their "cousins" in the Second Crusade, who represented more of a threat than a hope of deliverance; indeed, they neither wanted nor needed "deliverance"!

35. Owen, *From Abraham to the Middle East Crisis*, 215.

36. Ibid., 224.

37. Henry Treece, *The Crusades* (New York: Mentor Books, 1962), 113, writes that "the crusades hastened many changes . . . smaller estates were broken up and made into larger units," in part because some crusaders failed to return home. "Often the fiefs passed into the hands of remaining daughters (because the sons were missing), and so by marriage passed to other families." Treece also suggests that a more "liberal frame of mind," in the sense of a greater toleration for new ideas, took over in the West as a result of the experiences of the Crusaders in the East.

Biblical Sites: Israel (Outside Jerusalem)

1. Aphek is discussed in detail under biblical sites.

2. Yohanan Aharoni, *The Archaeology of the Land of Israel* (Philadelphia: Westminster Press, 1982), 61.

3. Yohanan Aharoni, *Israel Exploration Journal* (1967):237.

4. An insula functioned like an ancient apartment complex or commune. These were common in both the Old and New Testament periods. Each insula would comprise several rooms for individual families, each family usually having one room each for their quarters. There were also community rooms shared by all the families living in the insula. These included a large open courtyard with benches around the walls where people could sit. There was also a community

kitchen and, at times, a community storage area.

5. A cubit was approximately 18 inches long. This would make the altar at Arad roughly 90 x 90 x 54 inches.

6. The Protestant traditions of Christianity do not include the Apocrypha among the canonical books, whereas the Roman Catholic Church accepts them as deutero-canonical. References to apocryphal texts are included here (and in other places) because these writings are of historical significance and chronological relevance.

7. See the section on Aphek above.

8. The Shephelah is one of the geographical subregions of Israel. It is discussed and defined more fully in the "Geographical Overview" section.

9. Tell Lachish was excavated by a team led by James Starkey between 1932 and 1938. In 1935, eighteen *ostraca* (pottery fragments containing written messages) were discovered in a room near the city gate. These letters were written in biblical Hebrew around the time of the invasion by the Babylonians. They have served as an aid to scholars involved in linguistic research in ancient biblical Hebrew. All of the letters were addressed to Ya'ush, a prominent city official of Lachish.

10. Keith N. Schoville, *Biblical Archaeology in Focus* (Grand Rapids: Baker Book House, 1978), 426.

11. Pixner made this suggestion in private conversation with Charles Page at Banyas in February 1992.

12. According to Nehemiah 11:32, the people of the tribe of Benjamin lived in the village of Ananiah. Beit Ananiah would mean "House of Ananiah," and could be remembered as Bethany.

13. In the *Protevangelium Jacobi* we find a detailed discussion of Mary's family history. See David R. Carrlidge and David L. Dungan, *Documents for the Study of the Gospels* (Philadelphia: Fortress Press, 1980), 107-17.

14. Robert J. Bull, "Caesarea Maritima: The Search for Herod's City," *Biblical Archaeology Review* 8, 3 (May/June 1982): 24-41.

15. See note 4 above.

16. The people of Jesus' day were the most heavily taxed people throughout the periods covered in the Bible. The Jewish people of Judea and Galilee were required to pay seven separate taxes. These were taxes on crops and income (*Antiquities* 14:303), a sales tax (*Antiquities* 17:205), a poll tax (Luke 2:1ff.), and a frontier or entrance tax when a person would enter the country from being outside, such as coming into Galilee from Gaulinitis (Matthew 17:24-25; Luke 19:1-10;

Romans 13:7). These were all civil taxes. There were also three religious taxes that were required. These were a poor tax (Luke 21:1-4; 1 Corinthians 16:1-30), a Temple tax of one-half shekel per person per year to maintain the Temple in Jerusalem, and the tithe, or money given to support the local synagogues.

17. There are many biblical references for the place of the king's seat in the city gate where the king would handle official business (see Judges 19:15; Ruth 4:2). The gate at Tell Dan is the best preserved gate from this period in the country. It is surrounded by a large open square (roughly 20 by 10 meters). In 2 Samuel 19:8; 2 Chronicles 32:6, Hezekiah meets his military commanders to discuss the impending invasion of Sennacherib).

18. For a discussion of the Via Maris, see the "Geographical Overview," above.

19. A cenotaph is a monument that has been erected to honor or remember a person or event. The cenotaphs of Machpelah honor the memory of the Patriarchs buried in the caves below the building.

20. This fortress is known both as the *Herodium* and as the *Herodion.* The material produced by the National Park Service in Israel today uses the latter term; the former is preferred here to distinguish the fortress (Herodium) from the historical period (Herodian).

21. See John Garstang, *The Story of Jericho* (London: Marshall, Morgan, and Scott, 1948); see also his *The Annals of Archaeology and Anthropology* 19 (1932): 3-22; 20 (1933): 3-42; and 21 (1935): 143-68.

22. Kathleen Kenyon, *Digging Up Jericho* (London: Ernest Benn, 1957); see also Kenyon, *Archaeology in the Holy Land* (Nashville: Thomas Nelson, 1979), 181ff.

23. Thus Josephus's graphic description of Herod's final illness:

The distemper seized upon his whole body, and greatly disordered all its parts with various symptoms; for there was a gentle fever upon him, and an intolerable itching over all the surface of his body, and continual pains in his colon, and dropsical tumors, about his feet and an inflamation of the abdomen, and a putrefication of his privy member, that produced worms. Beside which he had a difficulty of breathing upon him, and could not breath but when he sat upright, and had a convulsion of all his members. . . . Accordingly, he went over to Jordan, and made use of those hot baths at Callirrhoe, which run into the lake Asphaltitis. . . . And here the physicians thought proper to bathe his whole body in warm oil; whereupon his eyes failed him, and he came and went as if he was dying, and as a tumult was then made by his servants, at their voice he revived again (*Jewish War,* 1:656-657b).

24. There are many New Testament examples of Jesus' coming to the "other side," meaning the other side of the Sea of Galilee. Some of these are found in Matthew 8:18; 14:22; 16:5; Mark 5:1, 21; 6:45; and Luke 8:22. To people living in Capernaum and other Jewish towns around the sea, there was a tension between "our side" and "the other side." "Our side" was the good side, the kosher side. Their side, or "the other side," was the nonkosher side, the bad side, where pagan Gentiles lived. Understanding this tension helps us to understand better some of the New Testament stories locating Jesus on the "other side." Jesus probably refused to allow the man he healed (Mark 5:1ff.) to come with him because the man would not have been accepted in kosher Capernaum. The presence of this Gentile with Jesus and his disciples would have also created a credibility problem for them on "our side."

25. Schoville, *Biblical Archaeology in Focus,* 426.

26. Yigael Yadin, *Masada* (New York: Random House, 1966), 26.

27. The top could only be reached by climbing the Snake Path Trail, a single-file path. When the Romans tried to attack the fortress by sending soldiers on the Snake Path they were simply picked off by Zealot archers one at a time.

28. Eleazar's speech is given as follows by Josephus:

> Since we, long ago, my generous friends, resolved never to be servants of the Romans, nor any other than God himself, who alone is the true and just lord of mankind, the time is now come that obliges us to make that resolution true in practice. And let us not at this time bring a reproach upon ourselves for self-contradiction, while we formerly would not undergo slavery, though it were then without danger, but must now, together with slavery, choose such punishments also as are intolerable; I mean this, upon the supposition that the Romans once reduce us under their power while we are alive. We were the very first that revolted from them, and we are the last that fight against them; and I cannot but esteem it as a favor that God hath granted us, that it is still in our power to die bravely, and in the state of freedom, which hath not been the case of others, who were conquered unexpectedly. It is very plain that we shall be taken

within a day's time; but it is still an eligible thing to die after a glorious manner, together with our dearest friends. This is what our enemies themselves cannot by any means hinder, although they be very desirous to take us alive. Nor can we propose to ourselves anymore to fight them and beat them; it had been proper indeed for us to have conjectured at the purpose of God much sooner, at the very first, when we were so desirous of defending our liberty, and when we received such sore treatment from one another, and worse treatment from our enemies, and to have been sensible that the same God, who had of old taken the Jewish nation into his favor, had now condemned them to destruction; for had he either continued favorable, or been but in lesser degree displeased with us, he had not overlooked the destruction of so many men, or delivered his most holy city to be burnt and demolished by our enemies. To be sure, we weakly hoped to have preserved ourselves, and ourselves alone, still in a state of freedom, as if we had been guilty of no sins ourselves against God, nor been partners with those of others; we also taught other men to preserve their liberty. Wherefore, consider how God hath convinced us that our hopes were in vain, by bringing such distress upon us in the desperate state we are now in, and which is beyond all our expectations; for the nature of this fortress, which was itself unconquerable, hath not proved a means of our deliverance; and even while we have still a great abundance of food and a great quantity of arms, and other neccessities more than we want, we are openly deprived by God himself of all hopes of deliverance; for that fire which was driven upon our enemies did not, of its own accord, turn back upon the wall which we had built; this was the effect of God's anger against us for our manifold sins, which we have been guilty of in a most insolent and extravagant manner with regard to our own countrymen; the punishment of which let us not receive from the Romans, but from God himself, as executed by our own hands, for these will be more moderate than the other. Let our wives die before they are abused, and our children before they have tasted slavery; and after we have slain them, let us bestow that glorious benefit upon one another mutually and preserve ourselves in freedom, as an excellent funeral monument for us. But first let us destroy our money and the fortress by fire; for I am well assured that this will be a great relief to the Romans, that they shall not be able to seize upon our bodies, and shall fail to our wealth also: and let us spare nothing but our provisions; for they will be testimonial when we are dead that we are not subdued for want of neccessaries; but that, according to our original resolution, we have preferred death before slavery. (*Jewish Wars* 7:850)

29. Yadin, *Masada*, 62.

30. Ibid., 117-18.

31. According to Judges 1:27ff., the city was allotted to the tribe of Manasseh, but they were unable to take Megiddo and other cities found within their territorial boundaries.

32. The Gilgamesh Epic contains an ancient Babylonian flood story. It is one of the world's oldest narratives, dating to perhaps before 2000 BCE, and has parallels to the biblical account of the flood in Genesis 6–9.

33. Felix Fabri was a German priest of the Dominican order who made two trips to the Holy Land, one in 1480 and a second in 1483. Some of the provisions of Fabri's contract with the captain of the ship that brought him to the Holy Land and some of the guidelines for visitors to the holy shrines have been printed in J. Maxwell Miller, *Introducing the Holy Land: A Guidebook for First-Time Visitors* (Macon: Mercer University Press, 1982), 15-18; these make interesting reading for modern travelers to the Holy Land.

34. There is a total of eleven caves in the vicinity of Qumran where most of the scrolls and scroll fragments were found.

35. Michael A. Knibb, *The Qumran Community* (New York: Cambridge University Press, 1987), 18.

36. Herod disliked and distrusted the Hasmoneans even more than the Essenes. By giving the Essenes some of the Hasmonean property, Herod effectively removed a potential enemy and a threat to his physical presence.

37. See James Price, *The New Testament: Its History and Theology* (New York: Macmillian, 1987), 38.

38. Ein Feshka means "Spring of the Cliffs," or "Spring of the Hole in the Rock." It is one of the two sources for fresh water along the Dead Sea. The other is located at En Gedi.

39. Mendul Nun, *The Sea of Galilee and Its Fishermen* (Kibbutz En Gev: Kinnereth Co., 1989), 5.

40. Those tribes were Benjamin, Simeon, Zebulun, Issachar, Asher, Napthali, and Dan (Joshua 18:19).

41. For a helpful explanation of the sources of the Synoptic Gospels, refer to Beasley, et al., *An Introduction to the Bible*, 321-25, 348-52, 366-

69, or to Stephen L. Harris, *The New Testament: A Student's Introduction* (Mountain View: Mayfield, 1988), 98ff.

42. See, for example, Hayes, *Introduction to the Bible*, 445: "Chapter 21 of the Gospel appears to be an addendum added to the work after the original conclusion at John 20:30-31. Whether by the original author or someone else is difficult to tell."

Biblical Sites: Jerusalem

1. The higher mountains in Jerusalem are Mount Moriah and Mount Zion.

2. Miller, *Introducing the Holy Land*, 84.

3. The Acts of John are a part of the New Testament Apocrypha. Matthew 24:3ff. implies that Jesus taught his disciples privately on the Mount of Olives, particularly concerning the end times.

4. Locating the teaching of the Lord's Prayer at this site is problematic and does not accord with the biblical accounts of Jesus' life and ministry. Matthew locates the teaching of the Lord's Prayer in Galilee during the Sermon on the Mount (Matthew 6:9-13). Luke (11:1ff.) reports that Jesus may have been near the home of Mary and Martha (in Bethany) when he taught his disciples the Lord's Prayer.

5. The High Priest during this period has enormous power. Not only did he control the Temple and its cultic activity, but he also had the power to administer civil law on the behalf of the Roman government. On this issue Ellis Rivkin reports:

The Roman imperial framework, within which Jesus' life, preaching, trial, crucifixion, and attested resurrection took place, is clear enough. At the pinnacle of power and authority was the emperor, who exercised his authority over the Jews either through puppet kings, like Herod, or through procurators, like Coponius and Pontius Pilate. These imperial instruments, in turn, sought to carry out their responsibilities to the emperor by appointing high priests, who were selected for their pliancy rather than their piety. Their function was to serve as the eyes and ears of the puppet king or procurator, so as to head off demonstrative challenges to Roman rule. Of these high priests, only one—Caiaphas—had such piercing eyes and such keen ears that he was able to keep the confidence of the procurators he served as long as they remained in office.

But even Caiaphas could scarcely have done this job single-handedly. It is highly likely that he appointed a council, or sanhedrin, consisting of individuals who were well aware of the dire consequences that would follow any outbreak against Roman authority. (Ellis Rivkin, *What Crucified Jesus?* [Nashville: Abingdon Press, 1984], 31.)

6. Some people call this the Wailing Wall because of the sounds made by those who are praying here. Most Jewish persons prefer to call this holy place the Western Wall.

7. The Huldah Gates are named for the prophetess Huldah (2 Chronicles 34:22-28). Josiah sought her counsel after the discovery of the book of the law.

8. Josephus reports that the beginning of the Sabbath was signalled by the blowing of a trumpet from this pinnacle (*Jewish War* 4:580-82). A trumpet was also blown to signify the beginning of holidays and feast days. See Ben-Dov, *In the Shadow of the Temple,* 95; and Siegfried H. Horn, *Biblical Archaeology: A Generation of Discovery* (Washington: Biblical Archaeology Society, 1978), 59.

9. After the Jews were defeated by the Romans in the Second Revolt, or the Bar Kochba Revolt, the Roman Emperor Hadrian had Jerusalem rebuilt and renamed Aelia Capitolina. After this, Jews were not allowed to enter the city.

10. Josephus reports the execution of James as follows:

This younger Ananus . . . took the high priesthood, was a bold man in his temper, and very insolent; he was also of the sect of the Sadducees, who were very rigid in judging offenders, above all of the rest of the Jews, as we have already observed; when, therefore, Ananus was of this disposition, he thought he had now a proper opportunity (to exercise his authority). Festus was now dead, and Albinus was but upon the road; so he assembled the sanhedrin of judges, and brought before them the brother of Jesus, who was called Christ, whose name was James, and some others, (or, some of his companions); and when he had formed an accusation against them as breakers of the law, he delivered them to be stoned. (*Antiquities* 20:199-200).

11. There is some debate as to the dating of this drawing. Some archaeologists date this drawing to the fourth century CE. Others date it earlier. Much of the work in this area was directed by Bishop

Gereugh Kapikian of the St. Tarkmanchatz School, in the early 1980s. Additional archaeological investigations here at the Church of the Holy Sepulchre have been carried out by Professor Virgillio C. Carbo of the Biblicum Franciscanum in Jerusalem.

12. The churches who dispute the ownership of the Church of the Holy Sepulchre, and who have chapels inside the church, are Roman Catholic, Greek Orthodox, Armenian Orthodox, Syrian Orthodox, Ethiopian Orthodox, and Coptic Orthodox.

13. There is considerable debate as to the location of Jesus' trial before Pilate and the beginning of the walk to Calvary. In truth, no one knows where these events took place. Currently three places are mentioned in this discussion: (1) the Antonia Fortress, which was the Roman military headquarters in Jerusalem. It is possible that Pilate would have stayed here, particularly if we assume that Herod Antipas might have stayed in his father's old palace when he would come to Jerusalem for special occasions such as the Passover. (2) Herod's Palace might have been Pilate's Jerusalem quarters. Much of this depends on one's understanding of what the "praetorium" might have been (Matthew 27:27ff.; Mark 15:16ff.). The definition is broad. (3) Some biblical scholars in Israel (such as Bargil Pixner) have recently discussed the Hasmonean Palace as a possibility. As mentioned above, in the final analysis, no one knows where these events occurred.

14. In ancient Egyptian mythology, the god Serapis was the god of the dead, and he later came to be identified with healing. It is possible that he was a synthesis of the Egyptian gods Osiris and Apis. Ptolemy I, after he was given control of Egypt and Palestine following the death of Alexander the Great, became the patron of the Serapis cult. By the Roman Period, Serapis was worshiped as a god of healing. His temple in Jerusalem was located just outside the Antonia Fortress.

15. Jews and Christians believe that Abraham was going to offer his son Isaac as a sacrifice in obedience to God's command. Muslims believe that Abraham was going to sacrifice Ishmael.

16. Josephus offers a detailed description of the reconstruction or renovation of the Temple by Herod in *Antiquities* 15:380ff. and *Jewish War* 5:184ff.

17. Cyril Glasse, *The Concise Encyclopedia of Islam* (San Francisco: Harper & Row, 1989), 208.

18. W. Harold Mare, *The Archaeology of the Jerusalem Area* (Grand Rapids: Baker Book House, 1987), 141-42.

19. Jerome Murphy-O'Connor, *The Holy Land: An Archaeological*

Guide From Earliest Times to 1700 (New York: Oxford University Press, 1985), 57.

Biblical Sites: Jordan

1. Since Gad and Reuben were given land here (Numbers 32:1-5) and since Gad built Dibon (Numbers 32–34), it seems likely that Reuben was later absorbed into Gad. However, there is a second possibility. In *The Land of the Bible* (207-8), Aharoni suggests that the settlement of the land might have happened in waves (earlier and later):

> It is also worthy of note that Gad is the brother of Asher, both of them being sons of Zilpah the handmaiden of Leah. . . . Asher certainly belonged to an early wave and this is evidently expressed in the genealogical scheme. . . . By contrast, Reuben apparently belonged to a later wave which entered the region only in the thirtenth century. . . . Thus the Reubenites encountered serious difficulties in the process of their settlement, especially since other tribes had preceded them.

2. The Moabite Stone was broken by Bedouin tribesmen, who heated it, poured water on it, and then hammered it into small pieces, apparently in the belief that more money could be obtained by selling the fragments separately. Charles Clermont-Ganneau, a representative of the French government stationed in Jerusalem, is credited with making the impression that preserved the body of the text.

3. See the edition of C. F. Crusé, *The Ecclesiastical History of Eusebius Pamphilus* (London: George Bell and Sons, 1897), 74-75.

4. There is general disagreement as to whether Petra and the biblical city of Sela are the same. The biblical references given here relate to Sela, which might have been located farther to the north.

5. The Nabateans' commercial success was established through their control of the major trade routes connecting Egypt and Arabia with major trading centers in the north and east.

Other Sites

1. See Emmanuel Anati, *Mountain of God.*

SUGGESTIONS FOR FURTHER READING

General

Davies, Graham I. *Megiddo*. Grand Rapids: Eerdmans, 1986.

Davies, Philip R. *Qumran*. Grand Rapids: Eerdmans, 1982.

Eusebius. *The History of the Church*. Translated by G. A. Williamson. Minneapolis: Augsburg, 1975.

Gingras, George E. *Egeria: Diary of a Pilgrimage*. New York: Newman Press, 1970.

Grant, Michael. *History of Rome*. New York: Macmillan, 1978.

Hussey, J. M. *The Byzantine World*. New York: Harper and Bros., 1961.

Josephus. *The Works of Josephus Complete and Unabridged*. Translated by William Whiston. Peabody: Hendrickson, 1987.

Knibb, Michael A. *The Qumran Community*. Cambridge: Cambridge University Press, 1988.

Miller, J. Maxwell. *Introducing the Holy Land: A Guidebook for First-Time Visitors*. Macon, Ga.: Mercer University Press, 1982.

Murphy-O'Connor, Jerome. *The Holy Land: An Archaeological Guide from Earliest Times to 1700*. 3rd ed. New York: Oxford University Press. 1992.

Rivkin, Ellis. *A Hidden Revolution.* Nashville: Abingdon Press, 1978.

―――. *What Crucified Jesus?* Nashville: Abingdon Press. 1984.

Runciman, Steven. *Byzantine Civilization.* New York: Meridian Pub. Co., 1959.

―――. *A History of the Crusades.* 3 vols. New York: Harper and Bros., 1964.

Shanks, Hershel. *Ancient History.* Washington, D.C.: Biblical Archaeology Society, 1988.

Yadin, Yigael. *Masada.* Jerusalem: Steimatzky Ltd., 1984.

Bible History

Beasley, James R., et al. *An Introduction to the Bible.* Nashville: Abingdon Press, 1991.

Bright, John. *A History of Israel.* Philadelphia: Westminster Press, 1981.

Ehrlich, Ernst Ludwig. *A Concise History of Israel.* Translated by James Barr. New York: Harper & Row, 1965.

Ferguson, Everett. *Backgrounds of Early Christianity.* Grand Rapids: Eerdmans, 1989.

Friedman, Richard Elliott. *Who Wrote the Bible?* New York: Harper & Row, 1987.

Grant, Michael. *The History of Ancient Israel.* New York: Charles Scribner's Sons, 1984.

Hayes, John H., and Paul K. Hooker. *A New Chronology for the Kings of Israel and Judah and Its Implications for Biblical History and Literature.* Atlanta: John Knox Press, 1988.

Metzger, Bruce M., and Roland E. Murphy, eds. *The New Oxford Annotated Bible, with the Apocryphal/Deuterocanonical Books,* New Revised Standard Version. New York: Oxford University Press, 1991.

Miller, J. Maxwell, and John H. Hayes. *A History of Ancient Israel and Judah.* Philadelphia: Westminster Press, 1986.

Owen, G. Frederick. *From Abraham to the Middle East Crisis.* Grand Rapids: Eerdmans, 1957.

Price, James L. *The New Testament: Its History and Theology.* New York: Macmillan, 1987.

Treece, Henry. *The Crusades.* New York: Mentor Books, 1962.

Archaeology

Aharoni, Yohanan. *The Archaeology of the Land of Israel.* Translated by Anson F. Rainey. Philadelphia: Westminster Press, 1978.

Avi-Yonah, Michael. *The Holy Land: From the Persian to the Arab Conquest (536 BC–AD 640).* Grand Rapids: Baker Book House, 1977.

Ben-Dov, Meir. *In the Shadow of the Temple.* Jerusalem: Keter Publishing, 1982.

Kenyon, Kathleen. *Archaeology in the Holy Land.* Nashville: Thomas Nelson, 1979.

McRay, John. *Archaeology and the New Testament.* Grand Rapids: Baker Book House, 1991.

Mare, W. Harold. *The Archaeology of the Jerusalem Area.* Grand Rapids: Baker Book House, 1991.

Perdue, Leo. G., et al. *Archaeology and Biblical Interpretation.* Atlanta: John Knox Press, 1987.

Schoville, Kenneth N. *Biblical Archaeology in Focus.* Grand Rapids, Mich.: Baker Book House, 1978.

Shanks, Herschel. *The City of David: A Guide to Biblical Jerusalem.* Washington, D.C.: Biblical Archaeology Society, 1973.

Geography

Aharoni, Yohanan. *The Land of the Bible: A Historical Geography*. Philadelphia: Westminster Press, 1979.

Reference

Achtemeier, Paul J., gen. ed. *Harper's Bible Dictionary*. San Francisco: Harper & Row, 1985.

Aharoni, Yohanan, and Michael Avi-Yonah. *The Macmillan Bible Atlas*. New York: Macmillan, 1977.

Frank, Harry Thomas. *Discovering the Biblical World*. Maplewood: Hammond, 1988.

Mays, James L., gen. ed. *Harper's Bible Commentary*. San Francisco: Harper & Row, 1988.

Pritchard, James B. *The Harper Atlas of the Bible*. New York: Harper & Row, 1987.

INDEX